Register Now for to You

Your print purchase of *Counseling Gifted Students,* **includes online access to the contents of your book**—increasing accessibility, portability, and searchability!

Access today at:

http://connect.springerpub.com/content/book/978-0-8261-3655-8 or scan the QR code at the right with your smartphone and enter the access code below.

8ED3TBGD

Scan here for quick access.

CS

SPRINGER / PUBLISHING COMPANY

View all our products at springerpub.com

Advance Praise for *Counseling Gifted Students: A Guide for School Counselors*

Counseling Gifted Students: A Guide for School Counselors is a very well-organized text. There is an excellent balance between theory, research, and practical application. There is a consistent answer to the question of "What do we do with what we know?"

"This is a text that will be most useful to counselor educators, school counselors, and parents. It is always the right time for an important book. Wood and Peterson have made a significant contribution to both counseling and gifted education." **—Nicholas Colangelo, PhD, Dean and Director Emeritus, College of Education, University of Iowa**

Despite the attention paid to diversity and inclusiveness, counselor education programs often overlook the gifted population, resulting in a training gap that complicates school counselors' awareness of—and ability to appropriately respond to—the unique needs of gifted individuals. This book appears tailor-made to rectify that oversight. Wood and Peterson have created both a research-informed text counselor educators can seamlessly incorporate into their coursework *and* a practical manual school counselors may use to improve the services they offer their gifted and talented students. **—Christopher Lawrence, PhD, LPCC, Assistant Professor, Department of Counseling, Social Work, and Leadership, Northern Kentucky University**

As both a stepparent of gifted children and a counselor educator, this new text is a welcome addition to my professional library. Too often, gifted children are punished for behaviors common to them, such as fidgeting in class or being "off-task" when they are actually under-stimulated in the classroom. This text will help school counselors and other school personnel learn more about gifted students, and how to better serve them at school. Parents of gifted students would do well to read it, also. Wood and Peterson have written a very interesting and helpful book, full of research yet balanced with practical suggestions. **—Catherine Tucker, PhD, LMHC, RPTS, Research Director, The Theraplay Institute**

This book makes the case that serving these students to the best of our ability is required of us as professionals. And fortunately for all of us, the authors provide a clearly articulated road map for helping us live up to our professional responsibilities. **—Tracy L. Cross, PhD, Jody and Layton Smith, Professor of Psychology and Gifted Education, Executive Director, Center for Gifted Education & Institute for Research on the Suicide of Gifted Students, College of William & Mary**

Counseling Gifted Students is a complete handbook for understanding and meeting the needs of gifted students. Combining a conceptual foundation, research, and relatable vignettes, Dr. Wood and Dr. Peterson teach us everything we need to know about creating gifted programs, identifying gifted students, collaborating with educators, and, equally if not more critical, understanding the unique developmental needs of gifted students. This book gets to the essence of the "whole" gifted student and how critical it is to foster not only intellectual and academic growth, but also healthy identity developmental and mental well-being. **—Dan Peters, PhD, Licensed Psychologist, Co-founder/Executive Director, Summit Center**

Counseling Gifted Students: A Guide for School Counselors is an exceptional book meshing the best in counseling theory and practice with gifted research for professional school counselors and professors of school counseling and gifted education. This thorough presentation of theory and research, impactful case studies, specific strategies, and excellent supplemental resources is a welcome and much-needed addition to both fields. Dr. Peterson and Dr. Wood have been outstanding leaders in counselor education, school counseling, and gifted education for many years, and it is exciting to have their combined wisdom, and that of their select and notable contributors, now available to both novice and seasoned school counselors, counselor educators, and the gifted community. I can't wait to share this book with my colleagues and students! — **Debra Mishak, PhD, PSC, Winona State University**

Counseling Gifted Students is a timely and much needed text for any school counseling program. This comprehensive text covers important issues such as identification and understanding the emotional needs of the gifted, theories of giftedness to classroom and parental support. It aligns nicely with the ACSA National Model and even provides insight into the unique mental health needs of the gifted student. The key concepts and references for each chapter make it a useful reference beyond the classroom setting as well. Every counselor should own a copy! **—Anna M. Viviani, PhD, LMHC, NCC, ACS, Indiana State University**

I applaud Wood and Peterson for filling a critical void in the school counseling literature with their book, *Counseling Gifted Students*. . . . Addressing the many myths held about this often-overlooked population of youth, the editors and their colleagues provide the reader with research-based information from which to thoroughly understand this population's unique social, emotional, academic, and career development characteristics and needs within the context of the school culture. Concurrently, this well-rounded text gives concrete school counseling strategies that can be easily implemented by school counselors within the school day to effectively support and guide these students. **—Amy H. Gaesser, PhD, NCC, Purdue University**

Counseling Gifted Students is an overdue piece of work within the counseling profession, as it fills a much-needed gap in the literature. This piece is unique in that it specifically explores the role of professional school counselors when working with gifted students. . . . I applaud Dr. Wood and Dr. Peterson for providing this professional school counseling–specific work which helps to illuminate the voices of students often unheard! **—Janice A. Byrd, PhD, Assistant Professor, Counselor Education & Supervision, College of Education, Health & Human Services, Kent State University**

Counseling Gifted Students

Susannah M. Wood, PhD, is currently an associate professor in the Department of Rehabilitation and Counselor Education at the University of Iowa. She is also a faculty partner with the Connie Belin and Jacqueline N. Blank International Center for Gifted Education and Talented Development, where she provides professional development opportunities for undergraduate students, graduate students, and practicing educators related to the social and emotional concerns of gifted students. She has received numerous accolades for her teaching, including the University of Iowa's collegiate teaching award in 2012 and the Association for Counselor Education and Supervision (ACES) award for outstanding teaching in 2015. Her research interests encompass preparing school counselors for practice, with a particular focus on serving the gifted population in collaboration with other educators and professionals. Dr. Wood's research has been published in such peer-reviewed publications as *Gifted Child Quarterly, Roeper Review, Journal of the Education of the Gifted, Journal of School Counseling, Journal of LGBT Issues in Counseling*, and *Journal of Counselor Leadership and Advocacy*. In 2015, Dr. Wood coedited with Dr. Nicholas Colangelo a special section in the *Journal of Counseling & Development* dedicated to counseling the gifted individual. With Dr. Tamra Stambaugh, she coedited the book *Serving Gifted Students in Rural Settings: A Framework for Bridging Gifted Education and Rural Classrooms*. She regularly presents at professional organizations conferences such as the American Counseling Association, the National Association for Gifted Children, and ACES and various state conferences related to the topics of school counseling and/or gifted and talented, and counselor education.

Jean Sunde Peterson, PhD, professor emerita and former director of school counselor preparation at Purdue University, was a classroom and gifted-education teacher for 24 years and was involved concurrently in teacher education prior to obtaining her master's degree in school counseling and doctorate in counselor education at The University of Iowa. A licensed mental health counselor with considerable clinical experience with gifted youth and their families, she is a veteran consultant and presenter nationally and internationally and conducts school-based workshops on social and emotional development of high-ability students, academic underachievement, bullying, parenting gifted children and adolescents, cultural values related to selection for gifted-education programming, prevention-oriented counseling curriculum, and listening skills for educators—all of these related to her research and clinical work. She has been an active researcher and author in her second career, publishing 9 books, 45 refereed journal articles, 44 invited book chapters, 16 articles in practitioner journals, and countless smaller articles in other professional publications. Her research has been presented in journals such as *Journal of Counseling & Development, Journal for the Education of the Gifted, Professional School Counseling, Roeper Review, Gifted Child Quarterly, Journal for Specialists in Group Work*, and *Counselor Education and Supervision*. Her *Talk with Teens* books are used in many countries and are often on resource lists related to working with youth. Specific to working with gifted individuals are *Models of Counseling Gifted Children, Adolescents, and Young Adults* and *The Essential Guide to Talking With Gifted Teens: Ready-to-Use Discussions About Identity, Stress, Relationships, and More*. She served two terms on the board of directors of the National Association for Gifted Children. She has received 9 national awards and 12 awards at Purdue University, evenly divided among research, teaching, and service.

Counseling Gifted Students

A Guide for School Counselors

Susannah M. Wood, PhD

Jean Sunde Peterson, PhD

Editors

SPRINGER PUBLISHING COMPANY

Springer Publishing Company, LLC
11 West 42nd Street
New York, NY 10036
www.springerpub.com

Acquisitions Editor: Sheri W. Sussman
Compositor: diacriTech, Chennai

ISBN: 978-0-8261-3654-1
ebook ISBN: 978-0-8261-3655-8

17 18 19 20 21 / 5 4 3 2 1

The author and the publisher of this Work have made every effort to use sources believed to be reliable to provide information that is accurate and compatible with the standards generally accepted at the time of publication. The author and publisher shall not be liable for any special, consequential, or exemplary damages resulting, in whole or in part, from the readers' use of, or reliance on, the information contained in this book. The publisher has no responsibility for the persistence or accuracy of URLs for external or third-party Internet websites referred to in this publication and does not guarantee that any content on such websites is, or will remain, accurate or appropriate.

Library of Congress Cataloging-in-Publication Data
Names: Wood, Susannah M., author. | Peterson, Jean Sunde, 1941- author.
Title: Counseling gifted students : a guide for school counselors/
    Susannah M. Wood, PhD, and Jean Sunde Peterson, PhD.
Description: New York, NY : Springer Publishing Company, LLC, [2018] |
    Includes bibliographical references and index.
Identifiers: LCCN 2017034522 | ISBN 9780826136541
Subjects: LCSH: Gifted children—Education—United States. | Gifted
    children—Counseling of—United States. | Educational counseling—United
    States.
Classification: LCC LC3993.9 .W66 2018 | DDC 371.95—dc23LC record available at
https://lccn.loc.gov/2017034522

Printed in the United States of America by Gasch Printing.

Contents

Contributors   ix

Preface   xi

1. Counseling Gifted and Talented Students   01
Susannah M. Wood and Jean Sunde Peterson

2. Aligning Service to Gifted Students With the ASCA National Model   15
Susannah M. Wood

3. Characteristics and Concerns of Gifted Students   31
Jean Sunde Peterson

4. Diverse Gifted Students: Intersectionality of Cultures   47
Renae D. Mayes, SaDohl Goldsmith Jones, and Erik M. Hines

5. Theories That Support Programs and Services in Schools   65
Jean Sunde Peterson

6. Identifying Gifted and Talented Learners in Schools: Common
Practices and Best Practices   83
Tamra Stambaugh and Susannah M. Wood

7. Working With Classrooms and Small Groups   103
Jean Sunde Peterson

8. Academic Advising and Career Planning for Gifted and Talented Students   121
Michelle Muratori and Carol Klose Smith

9. Personal/Social Counseling and Mental Health Concerns   139
Jean Sunde Peterson

10. Collaboration, Consultation, and Systemic Change: Creating a Supportive School
Climate for Gifted Students   157
Susannah M. Wood

11. Empowering Parents of Gifted Students   173
Susannah M. Wood and Carrie Lynn Bailey

12. School Counselors as Leaders and Advocates for Gifted Students   191
Susannah M. Wood, Erin M. D. Lane, and Matthew J. Beck

13. Concluding Thoughts   211
Jean Sunde Peterson

Appendix: Resources by Topic and Type   217

Index   237

Contributors

Carrie Lynn Bailey, PhD, NCC, LPSC, LPC
Core Faculty
School of Counseling
Walden University
Minneapolis, Minnesota

Matthew J. Beck, PhD
Assistant Professor
Western Illinois University–Quad Cities
Department of Counselor Education
Moline, Illinois

Erik M. Hines, PhD
Assistant Professor
School Counseling Program
Department of Educational Psychology
University of Connecticut
Storrs, Connecticut

SaDohl Goldsmith Jones, PhD, LPC, NCC, ACS, CPCS
Assistant Professor
School Counseling Program
Argosy University
Atlanta, Georgia

Erin M. D. Lane
Doctoral Candidate
Department of Rehabilitation and Counselor Education
The University of Iowa
Iowa City, Iowa

Renae D. Mayes, PhD, NCC

Assistant Professor
Director, School Counseling Program
Department of Educational Psychology
Ball State University
Muncie, Indiana

Michelle Muratori, PhD

Senior Counselor/Researcher, Center for Talented Youth
Faculty Associate, School of Education
Johns Hopkins University
Baltimore, Maryland

Jean Sunde Peterson, PhD

Professor Emerita
Former Director of School Counselor Preparation
Purdue University
Lafayette, Indiana

Carol Klose Smith, PhD

Clinical Associate Professor
Department of Rehabilitation and Counselor Education
The University of Iowa
Iowa City, Iowa

Tamra Stambaugh, PhD

Assistant Research Professor of Special Education
Executive Director, Programs for Talented Youth
Vanderbilt University,
Nashville, Tennessee

Susannah M. Wood, PhD

Associate Professor
Department of Rehabilitation and Counselor Education
University of Iowa
Iowa City, Iowa

Preface

As we became increasingly involved with gifted children and adolescents through our work as school counselors, researchers, educators of counselors, and counselors of gifted students and their families, we became more and more aware that administrators, teachers, and counselors do not usually associate giftedness with counseling concerns. Invariably, when we teach gifted-education licensure courses focused on social and emotional development, the educational psychology graduate students, teachers pursuing licensure, and undergraduate education majors indicate that they had not previously considered counseling concerns. After we speak at gifted-education conferences, we hear similar comments from school administrators, gifted-education coordinators, and gifted-education teachers in our audiences. Those responses are also typical when we include attention to gifted students as a special population in coursework for counseling-in-training. That feedback, and our realization that it reflected a major gap in both counselor education and gifted education, led us finally to this book project.

In professional dialogue in most arenas of education, it is typically academic rigor, appropriate challenge, motivation to achieve, and performance that take precedence over the complexities of career development for this population and these children's potential social and emotional concerns. Though the well-being of the whole gifted child has received increasing attention in the gifted-education field in recent decades, social and emotional development is still not considered routinely, including in connection with motivation and performance. Especially important is the reality that most research, coursework, and discussion about social and emotional development does not reflect, is not informed by, and is not driven by a counseling perspective.

At least some coursework preparing educators for licensure or certification in gifted education may be housed in departments focused on policy, leadership, and curriculum and instruction—fields likely to emphasize measurement and teaching more than exploration of how giftedness, which affects all areas of life, is experienced. That exploration aligns well with the work of school counselors, who not only have access to gifted children and teens, but also possess rare and crucial school-related skills, professional preparation encouraging openness to learning about the internal world, and instincts keeping them alert to concerns—even when the public image of a gifted student is solidly and invulnerably positive.

Representing omission in the other direction, the American Counseling Association (ACA) and the American School Counselor Association (ASCA) have tended not to acknowledge giftedness as a high-impact demographic variable. ASCA does have a role statement, and the Council for Accreditation of Counseling and Related Educational Programs, the national accreditation body, refers to ability in its standards. However, national organizations do not admonish or require counselor educators to expose counselors-in-training to the idea that gifted students are a special population requiring specific knowledge, awareness, and skills, as well as differentiated counseling approaches. In contrast, the American Psychological Association has a subdivision dedicated to gifted and talented youth.

Gifted kids are indeed different—different enough to be labeled as eligible for special services. The wide range of measured giftedness, stretching potentially far beyond two standard deviations from the mean, encompasses a population that should be understood like any other nonmainstream, minority culture—with characteristics, norms, behaviors, interests, and experiences with microaggressions that contribute to "felt differentness." Probably few school personnel consider the potential impact of differences associated with extreme capability on everyday school life, except, perhaps, to note "odd" behaviors. Even students who are "just" two standard deviations above the mean— sometimes the minimum for eligibility to participate—probably feel that others do not or cannot understand them at times. School counselors may miss the vulnerability, discomfort, and distress felt by children and teens in this population because those concerns are often hidden.

We therefore invested in this book project—mostly to inform school counselors and counselor educators about gifted kids as a special population and to offer guidance for responding with appropriate counseling services. However, we also hope to inform the gifted-education field about pertinent counseling dimensions as well as how school counselors can play a vital role in the lives of gifted students. Professional school counselors not only have ready access to them, but also have valuable skills and perspectives that can support these students in a uniquely satisfying way.

Susannah M. Wood
Jean Sunde Peterson

Counseling Gifted and Talented Students

SUSANNAH M. WOOD AND JEAN SUNDE PETERSON

Why a book on counseling gifted students in the schools? A professional school counselor or someone in a school counseling preparation program might see such a book as unnecessary at best, or insulting at worst. School counselors wear numerous hats, and their days are filled with calls to and from parents, grandparents, and guardians, crisis intervention, meetings involving students with disabilities, classroom guidance, "other duties as assigned," and frequent unexpected turns. They are responsible for the academic success, career and college preparation, and personal–social well-being of *all* their students. School counselors collaborate, consult, and coordinate resources. They partner with community agencies, empower parents and families, advocate for students, and are probably part of the leadership team in their schools. There is no "ordinary" day for a school counselor.

• • •

THE RATIONALE BEHIND *COUNSELING GIFTED STUDENTS*, PART 1

Every day, school counselors probably make lists of tasks that must be accomplished and then prioritize those according to level of urgency. Today the needs of K–12 students, collectively, seem to be increasingly numerous and serious. The general population in public schools is more diverse, creating an urgent need for a safe, supportive, and respectful school culture in every school. Students come to school with an array of concerns, such as unstable homes, mental health diagnoses, aftereffects of trauma, and challenges related to poverty, all of which require school counselors to connect parents with community resources, provide school supplies and clothing, and provide individual counseling. The educational reform movement has emphasized academic success, standardized test scores, and, recently, an intense focus on college and career preparation. The reform movement has also provoked reexamination of traditional roles and responsibilities of school counselors, expanding them to include data manager, program developer, and systems change agent. Above all, whether it be providing research-based interventions, engaging in 4-year planning toward high school graduation, or attending a child-study meeting, *school counselors make students their top priority*. On many days, school counseling feels like an impossible job.

We understand this experience. We know the feeling of being pulled in too many directions, frustrated at not being able to do any one thing as well as we would like. Because we were school counselors, we can empathize with school counselors. Because we are counselor educators, in close touch with our students during their clinical experiences, we are familiar with the range of challenges across school levels and sizes. Whether you are a practicing school counselor or a counselor-in-training, we want you to know that you have our respect and admiration. The content of this book is not designed to be "just one more thing" for you to master. Nor is it meant to imply that counselors are not doing enough. We know they are doing their best with the resources they have. We can also probably safely assume that school personnel, students, and other residents of your community are not aware of the scope of your work—and make assumptions accordingly.

Why a book about counseling gifted students at school? We developed this book because we know school counselors care deeply about students and that school counselors must do what they can with the time they have. The student who is talking about suicide, the student who has episodes of explosive anger, the student who has just reported abuse at home, and the student who is danger of not graduating—we know these situations take priority. We commend school counselors for the work that they do in distressing and challenging situations, when they feel powerless to change the circumstances. We developed this book especially to encourage counselors to consider the reality that these students—the students in crisis, angry adolescents, the almost-high-school dropouts—can be gifted. And *because they are gifted, the way they experience the world and their own development is far different from the norm. What they need from school counselors is also different.*

Common Mythology Surrounding Gifted Students

When prioritizing student needs, the needs of gifted students may not rise to the top in the mind of the school counselor. We recognize this. Most educators equate "gifted" with high-achieving, perfectionistic, perhaps slightly eccentric students, and highly involved helicopter parents. Depending on the educator being asked, the "typical" gifted student is often *also* a well-behaved, White female student. Yet gifted students (a) come from a variety of races and ethnicities (Kitano, 2012) and backgrounds, including poverty, both urban and rural (Howley & Howley, 2012; Worrell & Young, 2012); (b) are members of widely varying family constellations, including in foster homes, or have no home at all (Hermann & Lawrence, 2012); (c) sometimes have disabilities such as attention deficit hyperactivity disorder (ADHD) or an autism spectrum disorder (Foley-Nicpon & Assouline, 2015); and (d) identify as lesbian, gay, bisexual, transgender, or queer (Peterson & Rischar, 2000). As Robinson (2002) wrote, "there is no more varied group of young people than the diverse group known as gifted children and adolescents" (p. xi). *In other words, gifted students can look and act like any other students, but they are otherwise unique and highly idiosyncratic, both individually and collectively.*

Even when this complexity is acknowledged, school counselors can encounter common myths and stereotypes that discourage educators from helping gifted students—misconceptions and biases that even school counselors can fall prey to. A problem with automatically equating giftedness with achievement, for instance, is that with this assumption come corollary beliefs: (a) if they are achieving, then these students need "less"; and (b) because they are gifted, they will automatically get "it." "It" can mean academic content, college entrance, support, or a happy, meaningful, satisfying life. "Less" can be applied to counseling services, preparation for college, or academic coursework appropriate for their ability level. According to Plucker and Levy (2001), "even the happiest, most talented individuals must face considerable personal and professional roadblocks emanating from their talent. The process of achieving professional success and personal happiness and adjustment involves overcoming many interrelated challenges" (p. 75).

The second problem is rooted in what Americans believe about gifts and giftedness within a general cultural paradigm. Historically there have been two conflicting beliefs about giftedness in the United States: "a distrust of the intellect and an assumption that people should be allowed to develop to their full potential" (Office of Educational Research and Improvement, 1993, p. 13). This distrust, or anti-intellectualism, is engrained in our culture to the extent that public school education often discounts the activities of the mind and the students who are high performers (Colangelo, 2009). The era of educational reform, with its emphasis on closing the achievement gap, has only exacerbated this phenomenon, leading to the claim that high achievers, including gifted students, are actually being "left behind" (Gentry, 2006; Thomas B. Fordham Institute, 2008).

Distrust also stems from common negatives associated with intellectual giftedness. Unlike students with other kinds of special needs, gifted students do not typically garner sympathy or public support (Thompson, April, 1998), although "by virtue of being ahead in one or more domains, the degree of internal differences gifted children experience is usually greater than those encountered by any average child who does not have a disability" (Robinson, 2002, p. xvii). Indeed, Robinson, Zigler, and Gallagher (2000) have suggested that "individuals who are intellectually challenged or gifted share the burden of deviance from the norm in both a developmental and statistical sense" (p. 1413). If it is a gift, then it was not paid for hence, "if you are gifted, you shouldn't deserve any credit for something that was only a gift" (Thompson, 1998, para. 46), even though all educators would probably acknowledge that students must be self-disciplined enough to study, practice, and have the internal drive and commitment to transform an inborn "gift" into a recognizable talent (Gagné, 2013; Olszewski-Kubilius, Subotnik, & Worrell, 2015).

The third problem is the argument that all students are "gifted in their own way." Yet, if *gifted* is replaced by various factors in the following passage, the implication becomes humorous:

> [Then] everyone is Michael Jordan in their own way. Everyone is exhausted in their own way. Everyone is female in their own way. Everyone does calculus in their own way. Everyone is a great writer in their own way... It is only when giftedness is discussed that someone feels the need to make it a universal attribute; someone may not be gifted—everyone must be. But just as everyone is not tall, even in their own way, everyone is not gifted, even when we twist the idea by saying, *in their own way* [emphasis added]. Everyone is not gifted. It isn't true. (Thompson, 1998, para. 20, 24–27)

A gifted student's "gift," whether it be far-above-average intelligence or creativity, does not inoculate that student against life's stressors. *Gifted students, like all students, can struggle with death and loss, divorce, difficulties with friendships, neglect, or substance abuse (Moon, 2009)—struggles school counselors help students with daily. Gifted students also develop as any other student does, but they do so differently because of giftedness and characteristics associated with it.*

We are often asked if gifted students are relatively more likely to encounter mental health issues or psychopathology. Our response is this: *Gifted students are no more nor less likely than their chronological peers to have these concerns* (Peterson, 2009). However, Peterson also believes—and has written extensively about—the fact that giftedness may be a risk factor for poor personal and educational outcomes. Giftedness is both asset and burden when responding to life's challenges, including even developmental tasks and transitions (Peterson, 2012; Peterson, Duncan, & Canady, 2009).

KEY CONCEPT

The Asset–Burden Paradox of Giftedness

When gifted children and teens are asked what it is like to be "smart," they often mention being able to get good grades and excel elsewhere. However, based on the author's experiences with school and summer-program small-group discussions, they then mention feeling different, having difficulty with conversation, feeling that teachers do not like them, talking too much (or being extremely shy), caring too much, being easily upset, not having a readily available peer with similar interests, or having difficulty stopping their minds so that they can fall asleep. Their comments reflect the asset–burden paradox of giftedness.

A longitudinal case study (Peterson, 2012, 2014) that followed an unusually gifted young woman from age 15 through 30 examined how she experienced development. After she revealed multiple traumas, including sexual abuse within the family, the focus of the study shifted to the individual's development in the wake of trauma. One overarching theme that emerged in her oral and written communication was that giftedness was both asset and burden as she struggled with developmental tasks, coped with posttraumatic stress, reacted to situations sensitively and intensely, and used her intuitive intelligence to make sense of people, relationships, institutional and family systems, and herself.

Perhaps most interesting and pertinent here, asset and burden were represented almost equally in a table of experiences during adolescence and young adulthood (e.g., has a strong presence in family, but is blamed for family difficulties; reads self-help books and is assertive in finding adult support elsewhere, but becomes mother's adult-like confidante; highly invested as a teacher, but emotionally drained by students' needs and colleagues' high expectations). She credited her emotional and sensual overexcitabilities (see Chapter 3) for driving her forward and helping her survive until intellectual strengths could help her make sense of her experiences and emotions.

• • •

THE RATIONALE BEHIND *COUNSELING GIFTED STUDENTS*, PART 2

Given the many priorities school counselors already have, why attend to gifted students? Why consider them a special population that requires specific knowledge and awareness in those who work with them? We have been asked this question frequently. We respond with the following:

1. **Because school counselors serve all students, including gifted students, and they have an ethical mandate to do so.** According to the preamble of American School Counselor Association's (ASCA) Ethical Standards, students have rights:

   > [to] be respected, be treated with dignity and have access to a comprehensive school counseling program that advocates for and affirms all students from diverse populations including but not limited to: ethnic/ racial identity, nationality, age, social class, economic status, abilities/ disabilities… (ASCA, 2016, p. 1)

   In addition, the ethical standards require that school counselors advocate for "the equal right and access to free, appropriate public education for all youth, in which students are not stigmatized or isolated" based on specific labels or identifiers, including "any other exceptionality or special need" (p. 5, A-10-f). School counselors are to "affirm the abilities of and advocate for the learning needs of all students. School counselors also should support the provision of appropriate accommodations and accessibility" (B-2-k, p. 7). Accommodations might include acceleration, for example. In addition, the ethical standards include specifics about testing and interpretation that have bearing on identifying gifted students.

2. **Because school counselors are working with gifted students anyway, by virtue of their role and function.** A middle school counselor working with a student who is struggling with anxiety and cutting may find in the cumulative file that the student scored at or above the 97th percentile in every area of a standardized test. A high school counselor helping a ninth-grade student new to the district with a 4-year plan may find that the student was accelerated a whole grade in the previous middle school. An elementary school counselor may be playing a game with a second-grader and realize that the student has a working vocabulary equivalent to a seventh-grade student. According to the Office of Civil Rights (2014), approximately 3,329,544 students were identified as gifted students in 2014. Based on that number, the National Association for Gifted Children (NAGC; n.d.) estimates that gifted students comprise 6% of public school students.

3. **Because gifted students are different from most age peers.** Typically, gifted students are more cognitively advanced than others their age. This precocity is often not the same in other areas of development, such as emotional, social, and psychomotor. The experience of discrepancies between these areas of development is referred to in the gifted-education field as *asynchronous development* (Silverman, 2012). Characteristics often associated with giftedness are advanced reasoning, rapid assimilation of information, intensity, sensitivity, creativity, and goal-driven behavior, among others (Daniels & Piechowski, 2009; Hoh, 2008). Gifted students may question rules and challenge authority one minute, and the next minute become overwhelmed by environmental stimuli, such as large crowds, scratchy clothing, or specific smells and sounds (Mendaglio, 2007; Peterson, 2015). School counselors have undoubtedly seen the fallout of this uneven development in their offices. These are the students who can speak at an adult level yet have emotional "meltdowns" over a misspelled word or a seemingly innocuous interaction with another student. School counselors, teachers, and parents are probably concerned and want to help them relax, but giftedness may not allow them to do that (Piechowski, 2013).

4. **Because gifted students can be considered a special population.** Levy and Plucker (2008) suggested that "because of differential abilities and expectations associated with those abilities, gifted children constitute a unique subculture that necessitates understanding and application of specialized skills by helping professionals, including school counselors" (p. 4). Counselor preparation programs emphasize developing and refining counselors' awareness, knowledge, and skills so that counselors can continue to enhance their cultural competence (Sue & Sue, 2013). Counselors who do not attend to their client's unique cultural, gender, or sexual identities risk their client's distrust and possible early termination of counseling services (Sue & Sue, 2013). If gifted students constitute a special population or subculture, then school counselors should have a firm understanding of that population's characteristics, development, and needs to be able to provide appropriate services.

● ● ●

NEXT STEPS

If school counselors agree that they are in fact working with gifted students and that gifted students may require a differentiated counseling approach, how do they proceed? School counselors can consult the ASCA (2013) position statement entitled "The School Counselor and Gifted and Talented Student

Programs," which gives a brief rationale for school counselors' awareness of characteristics and developmental concerns of gifted students. Earlier drafts (ASCA, 2007) of the statement included specific roles of school counselors: (a) identifying gifted students; (b) advocating for counseling activities that address academic, career, and personal/social needs of gifted students through individual and group guidance; (c) providing resources and materials; (d) raising awareness of issues related to giftedness; and (e) engaging in professional development activities pertaining to giftedness.

School counselors might also peruse NAGC's (2009) position statement entitled "Position Statement: Nurturing Social and Emotional Development of Gifted Children," which includes the following assertion:

> Gifted youth deserve attention to their well-being and to their universal and unique developmental experiences—beyond academic and/or talent performance or non-performance. Gifted education programs, teachers, administrators, and school counselors can and should intentionally, purposefully, and proactively nurture socio-emotional development in these students (para. 2).

The NAGC "Pre-K–Grade 12 Gifted Education Programming Standards" (2010a) outlines areas for integrating social and emotional learning into gifted programs and curricula. An Internet search for books may also yield several titles that school counselors could utilize. However, very few texts address how school counselors can support gifted students specifically with school counselor roles and responsibilities in mind. Because there are so few pertinent journal articles and books specifically for school counselors (versus those written for school psychologists, educational psychologists, or mental health counselors or psychotherapists), we wrote this book.

We know that school counselors receive very little, if any, training during their preparation that addresses the uniqueness of gifted students as a special population (Peterson & Wachter Morris, 2010). In general, school counselors may receive 1 to 2 clock hours of training, at most, regarding gifted students. By contrast, preparation programs (and many state departments of education) typically require at least one 3-credit-hour class (approximately 45 hours of class time plus outside assignments) focused on graduation or licensure eligibility for students with special needs. *Hence, we believe that school counselors, both in practice and in training, need a guide to help them work with the gifted students. This book is designed to be that guide.*

Our *Counseling Gifted Students: A Guide for School Counselors* is divided into three primary sections. The first is foundational knowledge—what we believe every school counselor should know about gifted students, including characteristics, developmental patterns, theories of giftedness and talent development, identification, and the intersection between giftedness, culture, and race. We preface this section with a chapter about how school counselors can use the ACSA National Model to frame their work with gifted students. The second section focuses on service delivery and how school counselors can address needs and concerns of gifted students, including academic and career planning individual counseling, small groups, and through classroom guidance. Information and attention to personal development with considerations regarding gifted students' mental health issues are also provided. The final section presents ways school counselors can engage in consultation, collaboration, leadership, and advocacy around issues of gifted students and their parents. Last, we offer a master list of resources: websites, books, journal articles, and other resources, organized by chapter.

Throughout this volume we use the term *gifted*. We are aware of a variety of other terms available to describe the population we are discussing: *creative*, *talented*, and *high ability*, for example. Many theories of giftedness exist as well (as discussed in Chapter 5), which utilize various terms and definitions. NAGC (2010b, para 1) offered some clarification:

> Gifted individuals are those who demonstrate outstanding levels of aptitude (defined as an exceptional ability to reason and learn) or competence (documented performance or achievement in top 10% or rarer) in one or more domains. Domains include any structured area of activity with its own symbol system (e.g., mathematics, music, language) and/or set of sensorimotor skills (e.g., painting, dance, sports).

However, every state has its own definition of *gifted* or *gifted and talented*, which drives how students are identified (see Chapter 6). We have elected to use the term *gifted* for reasons of expediency and because that is the most commonly used term at various levels in the field—and in education in general. *Talent* continues to be somewhat confusing to readers and consumers because of how it is used and interpreted, at various ages, regarding specific nonacademic talent areas (e.g., music, athletics, arts, chess, leadership, and communication), academic strengths, "natural endowment," and demonstrations of strengths through performance.

We also need to clarify other terms. *Grades* refers to one point of data that can be used to identify gifted students. *Grade-point average* (GPA) is generally a quantitative term, versus classroom-performance *grades*, which refer to levels of achievement denoted by a letter of the alphabet (e.g., A, B, C, D, and F, with A the highest). We realize that these are terms commonly used in the United States; *mark* may be the term in another country, and numbers may be used in others. *GPA* and *grades* may be used interchangeably to reflect composite level of academic performance. We also know that, depending on the U.S. state, school counselors may be present at every building level or not in all. In some districts school counselors divide their time between or among schools. In this text, we provide suggestions for practice for school counselors regardless of grade level (or other designation) served. In essence, we wanted to provide research-based best practices for counseling gifted children and teens while still respecting individual state and school cultures and norms. This book is, in part, based in the ASCA's National Model, making it geared toward school counselors in the United States. However, we hope both U.S. school counselors and their counterparts in other countries will find this book worthwhile and informative.

* * *

CONCLUDING THOUGHTS AND RECOMMENDATIONS

School counselors work with gifted students on a regular basis. These students come with a variety of concerns, ranging from typical developmental needs to mental health concerns that warrant immediate attention and service. While gifted students are no more or less likely to experience concerns tied to mental health, they do experience the world differently because they are gifted. Gifted students are a special population, but they are not a protected class of students; hence there is no guarantee that they will receive differentiated academic, career, or personal/social supports.

School counselors are trained to listen, empower, and advocate. However, many are not trained to work specifically with issues pertaining to giftedness. Thus, we have written this book to help school counselors gain information they need to provide effective services. We encourage school counselors-in-training to utilize this book as well, as a supplement to the content and skills already emphasized in their preparation.

We applaud school counselors for all they do, every day, for the students in their care and humbly offer this book as a resource for their work with gifted students.

This book is only the first step. We recommend that school counselors seek out additional training and professional development and suggest that ASCA could take the lead in providing that training. In addition, ASCA and NAGC could benefit from a partnership that would facilitate collaboration between the school counseling and gifted-education fields as well as be a model for a positive working alliance between gifted-education teachers and school counselors.

* * *

REFERENCES

American School Counselor Association. (2007). *Position statement: Gifted programs.* Alexandria, VA: Author.

American School Counselor Association. (2013). *The school counselor and gifted and talented Programs.* Alexandria, VA: Author. Retrieved from https://www.schoolcounselor .org/asca/media/asca/PositionStatements/PS_Gifted.pdf

American School Counselor Association. (2016). *Ethical standards for school counselors.* Alexandria, VA: Author. Retrieved from https://www.schoolcounselor.org/asca/ media/asca/Ethics/EthicalStandards2016.pdf

Colangelo, N. (2009). Anti-intellectualism. In B. Kerr (Ed.), *Encyclopedia of giftedness, creativity and talent* (pp. 42–43). Thousand Oaks, CA: Sage.

Daniels, S., & Piechowski, M. M. (2009). Embracing intensity: Overexcitability, sensitivity, and the developmental potential of the gifted. In S. Daniels & M. M. Piechowski (Eds.), *Living with intensity* (pp. 3–29). Tucson, AZ: Great Potential Press.

Foley-Nicpon, M., & Assouline, S. G. (2015). Counseling considerations for the twice-exceptional client. *Journal of Counseling and Development, 93*, 202–211. doi:10.1008/j.1556-6676.2015.00196.x

Gagné, F. (2013). Differentiated model of giftedness and talent. In T. L. Cross & J. R. Cross (Eds.), *Handbook for counselors serving students with gifts and talents: Development, relationships, school issues, and counseling needs/interventions* (pp. 3–20). Waco, TX: Prufrock Press.

Gentry, M. (2006). No child left behind: Gifted children and school counselors. *Professional School Counseling, 10*(1), 73–81. doi:10.5330/prsc.10.1.x68mv737r1203v57

Hermann, K. M., & Lawrence, C. (2012). Family relationships. In T. L. Cross & J. R. Cross (Eds.), *Handbook for counselors serving students with gifts and talents: Development, relationships, school issues, and counseling needs/interventions* (pp. 393–408). Waco, TX: Prufrock Press.

Hoh, P. S. (2008). Cognitive characteristics of the gifted. In J. A. Plucker & C. M. Callahan (Eds.), *Critical issues and practice in gifted education* (pp. 57–83). Waco, TX: Prufrock Press.

Howley, A., & Howley, C. (2012). Counseling the rural gifted. In T. L. Cross & J. R. Cross (Eds.), *Handbook for counselors serving students with gifts and talents: Development, relationships, school issues, and counseling needs/interventions* (pp. 121–136). Waco, TX: Prufrock Press.

Islas, M. René. (2016). *Change the narrow focus on grade-level proficiency.* Retrieved from https://www.nagc.org/blog/change-narrow-focus-grade-level-proficiency

Kitano, M. (2012). Social-emotional needs of gifted students of color. In T. L. Cross & J. R. Cross (Eds.), *Handbook for counselors serving students with gifts and talents: Development, relationships, school issues, and counseling needs/interventions* (pp. 209–226). Waco, TX: Prufrock Press.

Levy, J. L., & Plucker, J. A. (2008). A multicultural competence model for counseling gifted and talented children. *Journal of School Counseling, 6*(4), 1–45. Retrieved from http://jsc.montana.edu/articles/v6n4.pdf

Mendaglio, S. (2007). Introduction. In S. Mendaglio & J. S. Peterson (Eds.), *Models of counseling: Gifted children, adolescents, and young adults* (pp. 1–6). Waco, TX: Prufrock Press.

Moon, S. M. (2009). Myth 15: High-ability students don't face problems and challenges. *Gifted Child Quarterly, 53*, 274–276. doi:10.1177/0016986209346943

National Association for Gifted Children. (n.d.). Frequently asked questions about gifted education. Retrieved from http://www.nagc.org/resources-publications/resources/frequently-asked-questions-about-gifted-education

National Association for Gifted Children (2009). Nurturing social and emotional development of gifted children. Retrieved from https://www.nagc.org/sites/default/files/Position%20Statement/Affective%20Needs%20Position%20Statement.pdf

National Association for Gifted Children. (2010a). 2010 pre-K–grade 12 gifted programming standards. Retrieved from http://www.nagc.org/sites/default/files/standards/K-12%20programming%20standards.pdf

National Association for Gifted Children. (2010b). Redefining giftedness for a new century: Shifting the paradigm. Retrieved from http://www.nagc.org/sites/default/files/Position%20Statement/Redefining%20Giftedness%20for%20a%20New%20Century.pdf

Office of Civil Rights. (2014). 2013–2014 gifted and talented enrollment estimations, 2013–2014. Retrieved from https://ocrdata.ed.gov/StateNationalEstimations/Estimations_2013_14

Office of Educational Research and Improvement. (1993). *National excellence: A case for developing America's talent* (Report No. ED 359743). Washington, DC: U.S. Government Printing Office.

Olszewski-Kubilius, P., Subotnik, R. F., & Worrell, F. C. (2015). Conceptualizations of giftedness and the development of talent: Implications for counselors. *Journal of Counseling & Development, 93*, 143–152. doi:10.1002/j.1556-6676.2015.00190.x

Peterson, J. S. (2009). Myth 17: Gifted and talented individuals do not have unique social and emotional needs. *Gifted Child Quarterly, 53*, 280–282. doi:10.1177/0016986209346946

Peterson, J. S. (2012). The asset–burden paradox of giftedness: A 15-year phenomenological, longitudinal case study. *Roeper Review, 34*, 1–17.

Peterson, J. S. (2014). Giftedness, trauma, and development: A longitudinal case study. *Journal for the Education of the Gifted, 37*, 295–318.

Peterson, J. S. (2015). School counselors and gifted kids: Respecting both cognitive and affective. *Journal of Counseling & Development, 93*, 153–162. doi:10.1002/ j.1556-6676.2015.00191.x

Peterson, J. S., Duncan, N., & Canady, K. (2009). A longitudinal study of negative life events, stress, and school experiences of gifted youth. *Gifted Child Quarterly, 53*, 34–49.

Peterson, J. S., & Rischar, H. (2000). Gifted and gay: A study of the adolescent experience. *Gifted Child Quarterly, 44*, 149–164. doi:10.1177/001698620004400404

Peterson, J. S., & Wachter Morris, C. (2010). Preparing school counselors to address concerns related to giftedness: A study of accredited counselor preparation programs. *Journal for the Education of the Gifted, 33*, 311–366.

Piechowski, M. M. (2013). *Mellow out, they say. If I only could: Intensities and sensitivities of the young and bright* (2nd ed.). Unionville, NY: Royal Fireworks Publishing.

Plucker, J. A., & Levy, J. J. (2001). The downside of being talented. *American Psychologist, 56,* 75–76.

Robinson, N. M. (2002). Introduction. In M. Neihart, S. M. Reis, N. M. Robinson, & S. M. Moon (Eds.), *The social and emotional development of gifted children: What do we know?* (pp. xi–xxiv). Waco, TX: Prufrock Press.

Robinson, N. M., Zigler, E., & Gallagher, J. J. (2000). Two tails of the normal curve: Similarities and differences in the study of mental retardation and giftedness. *American Psychologist, 55,* 1413–1424.

Silverman, L. K. (2012). Asynchronous development: A key to counseling the gifted. In T. L. Cross & J. R. Cross (Eds.), *Handbook for counselors serving students with gifts and talents: Development, relationships, school issues, and counseling needs/interventions* (pp. 261–280). Waco, TX: Prufrock Press.

Sue, D. W., & Sue, D. (2013). *Counseling the culturally diverse: Theory and practice.* Hoboken, NJ: Wiley.

Thomas B. Fordham Institute. (2008). Executive summary. In *High-achieving students in the era of NCLB.* Retrieved from: http://www.nagc.org/sites/default/files/key%20 reports/High_Achieving_Students_in_the_Era_of_NCLB_Fordham.pdf

Thompson, M. C. (1998, April). *Is everyone gifted?* Address presented at Indiana Association for the Gifted in Indiana. Retrieved from https://www.rfwp.com/pages/ is-everyone-gifted-in-their-own-way

Worrell, F. C., & Young, A. E. (2012). Gifted children in urban settings. In T. L. Cross & J. R. Cross (Eds.), *Handbook for counselors serving students with gifts and talents: Development, relationships, school issues, and counseling needs/interventions* (pp. 137–152). Waco, TX: Prufrock Press.

Aligning Service to Gifted Students With the ASCA National Model

SUSANNAH M. WOOD

Tosha and Erik are the two school counselors in a large suburban elementary school. For 5 years, they have worked to create a school counseling program aligned with their state's framework, which was developed with the ASCA National Model in mind. This year, they are hosting a school counseling intern, Tony, from a program in the school of education at a local university. Although the school counselors are grateful to have an intern with fresh eyes and new ideas, they wonder whether the supervision will require too much time and divert their attention from the report they must write prior to a visit by the state department of education later in the year. At the initial interview, Tosha and Erik learn that because Tony had already had several education classes, his program advisor suggested that he take some electives in areas of interest. During his student-teaching experience, he had been intrigued by creative and artistic students and therefore opted to take a few courses in gifted education. He is excited to be working with Tosha and Eric and wants to know if he might work with gifted students and find out how the gifted-education program is currently serving them.

Like most practicing school counselors, Erik and Tosha have worked hard to develop a comprehensive, developmental school counseling program. On a daily basis, their responsibility is not only to serve students with pressing needs but also to provide preventive services through small groups and classroom guidance. Erik and Tosha collaborate with administration, consult with teachers, and work to establish strong partnerships with parents and community agencies. Weekends, planning days, and summers have been dedicated to documenting their program, putting data collection points in place, and revisiting the program mission and vision. Having a new intern means that Tosha and Erik have another pair of hands to help in their efforts. Tony has a grasp of the state framework and the American School Counseling Association (ASCA) National Model and is willing to work on whatever Tosha and Erik have in mind, but the two are wondering how to best provide Tony opportunities to work with gifted students. Tony asks if they would be willing to sit down with him and talk about how they see the current program fitting with the needs of those students. Given that the school counselors need to review the program before the upcoming district administrators' visit, talking with Tony is a place to start that process.

● ● ●

SCHOOL COUNSELING AND GIFTED STUDENTS: WHAT DO WE KNOW?

Research Related to School Counselors and Gifted Students

If Tosha, Erik, and Tony were to do a quick Internet search with the terms *counseling* and *gifted students* the results would yield a variety of resources. However, locating studies requires searching databases from widely differing fields (e.g., general education, gifted education, social work, counseling, psychiatry, and educational psychology). The field of gifted education has long demonstrated a need for counseling services for this population, yet the counseling profession—and school counseling specifically—has generated relatively little pertinent dialogue. A coherent understanding comes only after patiently piecing together information from articles and books published over multiple decades. In general, most of the literature specific to counseling gifted individuals is conceptual, with the majority of books and articles referring to a need for counseling and presenting various theories and interventions for addressing concerns.

Empirical research—that is, studies that investigate an issue using quantitative, qualitative, or mixed methods—pertinent to counseling the gifted can also be found. Quantitative studies generally focus on a specific area or issue, such as self-concept, underachievement, motivation, application of a specific career theory, anxiety and depression, and bullying or other social concerns, as well as comparisons of gifted and nongifted participant groups (Colangelo & Wood, 2015). Qualitative studies frequently focus on the experiences of gifted students, families, or service providers when an issue or phenomenon such as trauma, substance abuse, or twice-exceptionality is of interest. Participants in these studies are typically gifted students, families of gifted students, psychologists, and school personnel. Some books act as compendia of research on these topics and present ideas for application in counseling. Several can be found in the resources section of this volume.

Jean and I, the editors of this book, have been privileged to work with gifted students as school counselors, mental health counselors, and residential counselors. We have also spent years formally studying this population and how school counselors can best serve it. Other researchers have also examined how school counselors work with gifted students, but that body of literature is small. What we do know is that school counselors *are* working with gifted students. Unfortunately, the literature of the school counseling field falls short in capturing the amazing work these counselors are doing and the positive effects of their work. Furthermore, findings in the empirical studies published in academic journals and dissertations are not consistent. Sometimes, conclusions in one study conflict with those of other studies. Some that seem firm and are important for school counselors follow here.

First, *a relationship exists between school counselors' knowledge of gifted students and their reported involvement with those students* (Carlson, 2004; Carlson, Holcomb-McCoy, & Miller, 2017). School counselors with the most years of experience are more likely to report relatively more knowledge about these students. School counselors who are aware of and knowledgeable about the unique needs and development of gifted students report more frequent involvement, including advocacy, with these students (Carlson, 2004; Carlson, Holcomb-McCoy, & Miller, 2017). School counselors interviewed by Wood (2010b) reported that their recognition of traits and characteristics associated with giftedness during their experiences added a new dimension to their counseling services.

Training and professional development make a difference. As a result of training, small-group guidance activities, and debriefings, school counselors who participated in Project HOPE, a summer program for young gifted children, reported that they "had not expected such obvious 'differentness' in gifted children" (Peterson, 2013, p. 199). These school counselors received training focused on development and needs of gifted students so that they would be prepared not only to facilitate guidance activities with high-ability students from low-income backgrounds, but also to assist in economically heterogeneous classrooms. As a result of their experiences in the program, the *counselors began to perceive high-ability students in new ways and became more aware of the importance of the role of school counselors in the lives of gifted students across a wide socioeconomic spectrum.*

Knowledge about giftedness and counselor self-efficacy predict a school counselor's advocacy for gifted students (Goldsmith, 2011). Elementary school counselors tend to report a higher level of knowledge about giftedness than counselors at other building levels (Goldsmith, 2011). However, Goldsmith did not find a relationship between school counselors' years of experience and their level of advocacy for this population. Dockery (2005) interviewed school counselors and found that they had identified several social and emotional needs of gifted students, but demonstrated "a lack of awareness of the developmental and critical social and emotional needs typical of gifted students" in their school (p. 275).

Second, *certain counseling behaviors* (e.g., providing appropriate assessment of gifted students, advocating for appropriate curricular modifications, guiding career development, facilitating interpersonal relationships and individual growth, and helping students understand their gifts in multiple contexts) *facilitate school counselors' work with gifted students* (Earle, 1998). School counselors in special schools for gifted students worked with students on academic and career planning as well as on issues related to healthy self-image, self-esteem, and study skills and goal-setting (Dockery, 2005). Public school counselors interviewed by Wood (2010b) reported that they helped gifted students with concerns that seemed to stem from *the interplay between them and the degree of challenge and academic rigor provided in the educational environment.* Some school counselors are helping gifted students find a healthy balance between being challenged by school and paying attention to self-care (Wood, 2010b).

Third, *school counselors feel they are more effective when they differentiate their counseling in terms of pace, depth, novelty, and complexity to match their gifted students' developmental level* (Earle, 1998). School counselors in Wood's study (2010b) utilized various types of services such as individual academic counseling, career and college counseling, group counseling, enrichment opportunities and other programming, and community partnerships. However, Dockery (2005), in a qualitative dissertation, found that school counselors did not believe that gifted students were any different from other adolescents and thus were not in need of differentiated counseling. She *did* find that school counselors who worked in specialized schools for gifted students responded to needs pertaining to elevated levels of stress and depression, but the counselors attributed those needs to the unique educational setting.

Fourth, although *some gifted students access school counselors, others feel that counseling services are not for students like them* but for other students instead (Peterson, 2003; Wood, 2009). Gifted students do experience concerns related to multipotentiality, social acceptance, perfectionism, and fear of failure (Wood, 2009) and they have a wide variety of negative life experiences (Peterson, Duncan, & Canady, 2009), but fewer than half of them access a school counselor for help. According to Wood's (2010a) study, those who do contact a school counselor perceive that their relationship with the counselor is mostly strong and positive and that their time is well spent. Most reported that the school counselors did understand their drive to achieve and their love of learning. However, almost half of the gifted students surveyed felt that the school counselor misunderstood them and that their concerns were dismissed. More worrisome was their reporting that the majority of skills and topics that scholars suggests are part of best counseling practices were not being experienced (Wood, 2010a), although there were notable exceptions. Gifted students reported that school counselors worked with them on options and choices, strengths and talents, self-expectations, and (briefly) leadership (Wood, 2010a).

Fifth, *school counselors do encounter difficulty when attempting to serve gifted students*. Dockery (2005) found that school counselors reported difficulty accessing students due to limited time available outside of classes. School counselors in Wood's (2010b) study noted that constraints such as time, high student–counselor ratios, and lack of resources had a negative impact on their ability to work with gifted students. Additional obstacles were value conflicts between them as counselors and the culture and climate of their schools regarding gifted students and colleagues' perceptions about the need for services (Wood, 2010b).

Sixth, findings from these studies suggest that *school counselors may feel unprepared to address the needs of these students*. Lack of preparation affects what school counselors believe about gifted students and how they serve them (Carlson, 2004; Dockery, 2005; Earle, 1998; Wood, 2010b, 2012). School counselors in Wood's (2010b) study reported that they were not prepared to work with some of the unique issues gifted students brought to counseling sessions. The counselors wished they had additional training related to characteristics associated with giftedness and gifted students' development in their school counseling preparation program. These findings support conclusions in past studies that *school counselors are not traditionally trained in issues pertaining to gifted learners* (Peterson & Wachter Morris, 2010). Unfortunately, this lack of training contributes to two problems: "First, very few mental health professionals know how to adapt their counseling strategies to better meet the needs of individuals with high abilities, and second, untrained counselors may pathologize normal characteristics of gifted individuals" (Moon, 2002, p. 218).

This review of the counseling literature indicates that school counselors need training in gifted education if they did not receive it in their preparation programs, and that the degree of exposure does make a difference in their service. However, this conclusion does not provide school counselors with ideas for serving gifted students that can complement their general counseling program. The following section briefly describes how school counselors can continue what they are already doing and incorporate specific services for gifted students and their families into it. Subsequent chapters will take these initial concepts and scaffold them with both current research and applications for practice. *The emphasis will not be on what school counselors need to do more of, further complicating their heavy workloads. Instead, counselors can consider adding a layer of specificity to what they are already doing. Later chapters offer suggestions for making the ASCA National Model work for them and for the gifted students for whom they are responsible.*

• • •

THE ASCA NATIONAL MODEL AND SCHOOL COUNSELORS' WORK WITH GIFTED STUDENTS

In 2003, ASCA produced the National Model largely in response to the accountability and educational reform movements in the United States. The model was designed to provide a template for creating preventive, comprehensive, developmental guidance, and counseling programs. The model not only provided an answer to the ubiquitous question "What do school counselors actually do?" by providing a clear and comprehensive list of roles, functions, and responsibilities, but also challenged school counselors to consider how students and schools differed and, ideally, improved as a result of their services. The ASCA National Model has been updated at least three times since its inception and includes four distinct components: (a) foundation and philosophy, (b) service delivery, (c) management systems, and (d) accountability (ASCA, 2012).

In 1998, ASCA adopted a position statement on school counselors' involvement with gifted education and their service to gifted students. The position statement has been updated several times since then, most recently in 2013. An excerpt follows here.

> The school counselor delivers a comprehensive school counseling program as an integral component of the school's efforts to meet the academic and developmental needs of all students. Gifted and talented students have unique and diverse needs that are addressed by school counselors within the scope of the comprehensive school counseling program and in collaboration with other educators and stakeholders. (p. 28)

The position statement also provides a rationale for service and outlines specific roles and functions for school counselors pertinent to serving gifted students. Because the statement does not align these roles directly with the ASCA National Model, the next sections present our suggestions for each of the four components.

Foundation

The foundation component of the model comprises three areas: the focus of the school counseling program, student competencies, and school counselor competencies. The focus of the program is presented in documents such as mission and vision statements, philosophy statements, program goals, and plans for measuring progress toward those goals. To develop these, school counselors take time to consider their own personal beliefs and values about education, student learning, and school counseling programs and then develop the documents on their own or in collaboration with counselor colleagues.

Beliefs and Vision

Tosha and Erik already have a mission statement that guides their program and is aligned with their school and district mission statements. But when preparing to review it with Tony, the school counselors are considering how it specifically guides service delivery to gifted students in this school. They ask themselves, *"How are the gifted students—identified or not—different as a result of what we do?"* If their answer is uncertain or vague, it may be time to reevaluate the program. The program likely does not have specified goals or services that have direct impact on, or relevance for, this population. Tosha and Erik, given their large caseloads, may simply not have thought about direct services targeting gifted students. The Key Concept Exploring Beliefs About Gifted Students offers a series of questions school counselors might ask as they consider their own beliefs and attitudes toward gifted students. Once those beliefs are explored and discussed, Tosha and Erik can revisit their foundational statements to determine whether they reflect their discussion.

KEY CONCEPT

Exploring Beliefs About Gifted Students

As mentioned previously, counselor preparation programs that include more than minimal information and training about working with gifted students are not typical. Lack of exposure to concepts pertaining to giftedness, talent development, or high ability may mean that practicing school counselors have not thought about these concepts. If school counselors believe that gifted students are indeed a special population, then they should consider some of the many myths and stereotypes that surround giftedness (see Chapter 1). All human interactions have overlays of beliefs, values, and expectations. Interactions between a school counselor and a gifted student are no different; each has beliefs and expectations of the other. The purpose of the following questions is to encourage school counselors to explore what they believe about gifted students and gifted-education services. These questions are adapted from Questions for Raising Awareness of Attitudes About Gifted Students (Wood & Peterson, 2014, p. 641).

(continued)

- What are my experiences with gifted students in my current role? In my past as a student? What kinds of emotions does the word *gifted* evoke? Are these emotions positive? Negative? Both?
- When I think of "gifted students," which images come to mind? What do "gifted students" look like? What do they do? What don't they do? What types of families do they come from? What is their academic profile?
- What do I believe about programming for gifted students? Should gifted-education programming be only for students "who deserve it" or for all students with exceptionally high ability, regardless of academic performance?
- How willing am I to fight for optimal learning experiences for all gifted students? How willing am I to investigate and advocate for more "controversial" types of programming, including acceleration?
- Which do I know about gifted education in my district? How are students currently being identified? What kind of relationships do I have with gifted-education teachers and coordinators?
- Which types of gifted programming exist (e.g., pull-out, self-contained gifted-education classrooms at the elementary level, honors or enrichment courses at many levels, Advanced Placement)? How well does the programming fit the various strengths, limitations, and needs of highly able students? To what extent am I prepared to investigate and advocate for changes in the programming if changes are needed?
- Which, if any precedents exist for gifted students in need of more specialized programming (e.g., grade-skipping, dual-enrollment arrangements with local institutions of higher education, early entrance to college)? What have the outcomes been?
- Is current programming accessible to all eligible gifted students, including those in remote communities and students living in poverty? If not, to what extent am I prepared to investigate contexts and advocate for access, including through technology?
- To what extent do I have the resources and contacts needed to connect students and families to additional resources such as national talent searches or summer enrichment programs at universities and colleges? What does my community offer in the form of mentors, job-shadowing opportunities, or additional arts and science opportunities?

(continued)

- To what extent am I prepared to help gifted students with anxiety; sexual orientation; microaggressions related to race, ethnicity, and socioeconomic status; or cyberbullying? Or parents or guardians of gifted students who are concerned about their child or teen or parenting? Which helping professionals in my community are knowledgeable about gifted students and their families?

Student Competencies

The second foundation component is the student competency section. Student competencies drive how school counselors map their classroom guidance delivery and small-group offerings. Past versions of the model organized student competencies, or what students should be able to do after completing the K–12 school counseling curriculum and programming, around three distinct areas: academic, career, and personal/social. In 2014, ASCA updated these competencies to reflect the need for college- and career-readiness and produced the *ASCA Mindsets & Behaviors for Student Success: K-12 College- and Career-Readiness Standards for Every Student*. The ASCA (2013) position statement on gifted and talented student programs aligns with the emphasis on readiness in those areas by stating that "purposeful gifted and talented education programs include several benefits: assisting the gifted student in college and career goals, defining post-secondary and career plans and increasing achievement levels" (p. 28).

School counselors assume that guidance related to college and career choice simply happens for gifted students, perhaps by osmosis, in the context of educated parents and abundant enrichment opportunities and models. Actually, due to their unique traits and talents, gifted students not only need specific college and career guidance, but may also require differentiated assessments such as adult-level career inventories. Chapter 8 discusses these concerns in more detail.

Professional Competencies

The last component, professional competencies, includes two documents: ASCA School Counselor Competencies and the ASCA Ethical Standards for School Counselors. Neither directly specifies competencies for working with gifted and talented students. However, the school counselor competencies, which "outline the knowledge, attitudes and skills that ensure school counselors are equipped to meet the rigorous demands of the profession" (ASCA, n.d., p. 2), do include language related to school counselors' understanding and knowledge of developmental and learning theory (I-A-8, II-A-3). Chapter 5 details theories specific to the development of gifted and talented students. Two competencies specific to one of the many essential skills is the ability to identify and address educational barriers (I-A-3, III-B-3b) and to find resources for students who are not successful in school (III-B-3f) (ASCA, 2016). According to the ASCA's Ethical Standards, school counselors have a responsibility to serve all students. The ethical standards require that school counselors advocate for "the equal right and access to free, appropriate public education for all youth, in which students are not stigmatized or isolated" based on specific labels or identifiers, including "any other exceptionality or special need" (p. 5, A-10-f). School counselors are to "affirm the abilities of and advocate for the learning needs of all students. School counselors also should support the provision of appropriate accommodations and accessibility" (B-2-k, p. 7).

Finally, school counselor competencies refer to the *need for school counselors have access to professional development opportunities so that they can stay current with research and policy affecting their practice.* The ethical standards (B.3.e) also mandate that school counselors participate in professional development via state and national conferences, reading journal articles, and training in ethical responsibilities. The ASCA position statement echoes this mandate:

> School counselors also seek to keep current on the latest gifted and talented programming research and recommendations to employ best practices to meet the needs of identified students and collaborate with other school personnel to maximize opportunities for gifted and talented students. (ASCA, 2013, p. 28)

For professional development, Tosha and Erik could attend the annual conference of their state gifted and talented association or engage in webinars provided by the National Association for Gifted Children. At the end of this book is a list of resources (e.g., books, articles, websites) to help school counselors identify areas of interest and need.

Delivery

According to the executive summary of the ASCA National Model, the delivery component accounts for 80% of this model (ASCA, n.d.). In other words, school counselors are to spend the majority of their time in actual service delivery (both direct and indirect) to students. Direct service includes engaging in individual student counseling sessions or academic advising, facilitating small groups, and conducting classroom guidance sessions. Delivery also includes indirect services such as community and agency referrals, collaboration with families, and consultation with teachers and administration. Attending to school climate concerns may be considered indirect service as well, because identifying environmental barriers to student connectedness is essential for a healthy school culture and future student success, including for gifted students. Chapter 10 discusses school climate and its influence on gifted students in more detail.

The ASCA position statement on programs for gifted and talented students also refers to components for service delivery to gifted students: (a) facilitating identification of gifted students, (b) including and participating in activities that "effectively address the academic, career and social/emotional needs of gifted and talented students" (2013, p. 28), (c) providing small-group and individual counseling, and (d) serving as a resource for high-ability students and their families. Chapter 9 highlights the importance of personal–social counseling for gifted students for preventing and addressing mental health concerns, and Chapter 11 offers strategies for school counselors working with families of gifted students.

The ASCA position statement does not specifically address classroom guidance activities for gifted students. However, *school counselors can collaborate with classroom teachers to differentiate guidance lesson plans and integrate affective elements into core academic content.* Collaboration potentially allows teachers to focus on the core content and school counselors to emphasize skills such as critical thinking, problem identification, and solution creation, which the ASCA Mindsets/Behaviors document addresses. Chapter 7 provides suggestions for small groups and classroom guidance lessons specific to high-ability students.

Delivery can also include professional development provided to staff by school counselors. Tosha and Erik have found it difficult to get "time" with fellow educators as a large group to explain their role and program. However, they are considering partnering with the gifted-education coordinator to provide training to other educators. The ASCA position statement suggests that "school counselors assist in promoting understanding and awareness of the unique issues that may affect gifted and talented students" (p. 28) and offers suggestions for discussion topics (e.g., stress management, perfectionism, and social issues). Chapter 3 provides an overview of characteristics and development pertinent to giftedness for school counselor consideration.

Management

Of the four parts of the model, the management component requires the most effort regarding organization and documentation. The management section details types of documentation school counselors might consider for assessing their program and progress toward goals. These documents can include but are not limited to (a) use-of-time assessments; (b) annual agreements and contracts developed by school counselors and administrators; (c) data points that help to determine need for growth, educational barriers, and areas that require systemic change; (d) curriculum plans for classroom guidance and small groups; (e) action plans for closing achievement gaps; and (f) annual calendars documenting program activity. The management component also includes an advisory council to help meet program goals, act as a measure of accountability, and provide recommendations for the program.

School counselors can utilize these types of documentation to determine the current level of interface with the gifted-education program in their building, beginning with a program audit. The ASCA position statement does not specify ideas for management. The closest approximation is an admonition that the school counselor, in collaboration with the gifted-education specialist, use a multic-riterion method of assessment when identifying gifted students. The position statement stipulates that the school counselor is not responsible for administering or overseeing the identification process, but is involved in consultation and data analysis as needed. Chapter 6 details the parts of a research-based best-practice approach to identifying gifted students.

Tosha and Erik work at a middle school where a formal, whole-school identification process for determining eligibility for the gifted-education program (i.e., advanced classes only) does not exist. However, they can review student cumulative files. Perusing the files of students who come to their attention as perhaps needing gifted-education services may confirm that some do appear to warrant services and should be evaluated accordingly. If the records show that a student was identified in earlier grades, but chose not to be involved because services were not a good fit or for other reasons, these counselors can offer supportive contact and discuss options with the student. The same approach would apply if a student was not allowed to continue in a narrowly focused program. Certainly, from a counseling perspective, children should not be labeled "gifted" and then later be made "ungifted." In the intervening years, social and emotional development, other kinds of changes, and having more academic choices may argue for reconsideration.

Achievement gap action plans have not traditionally addressed the needs of gifted students. However, gifted students can and do underachieve and even drop out of school for reasons that are explored throughout this book. Use-of-time assessments can help Tosha and Erik determine where they spend their service time and to what extent that service extends to gifted students in their building. Annual calendars could include dates for talent-search participation, summer enrichment opportunities or visits to universities, and schedules for local businesses that might offer job-shadowing opportunities.

Accountability

The concept of accountability is the focus of only one section of the model, but accountability should permeate the entire school counseling program. From developing programmatic goals to creating specific closing-the-gap plans, accountability and attention to data help school counselors determine what the program is doing, which services it provides, and how effective those services are. Erik and Tosha are already comfortable with the assessment points they have established during the academic year. They collect data from teachers, students, parents, and administration. They use district data and state assessment tools. They are highly attuned to issues pertaining to race and ethnicity in course enrollment, behavioral referrals, and identification of special needs. As a result of their emphasizing cultural competence for all educators, behavioral referrals of students of color were reduced by 10% last year, although needs in that arena continue.

Regarding gifted education, mining data and planning for assessment are slightly more nuanced. Tosha and Erik, now with Tony's help, could begin with a program audit, using an ASCA template, to help them not only prepare for the upcoming visit by the state department of education administrators, but also determine how they are working with gifted students and what could be changed. They might examine enrollment patterns in honors classes to determine if they reflect district norms related to identified gifted learners, diversity, and gender. In a culturally diverse middle school, having no students of color in seventh-grade algebra, which is considered an advanced course, should raise a warning flag. A low percentage of females in eighth grade moving to honors biology in ninth grade is also cause for concern. Teacher consultation in tandem with reviewing students' files may reveal students whose giftedness has been overlooked because of a learning disability (i.e., "twice exceptional"). Chapter 3 discusses the intersection of cultural identity and giftedness.

Even during early elementary school years, a routine meeting with a parent or a teacher or a regular check of academic performance (grade-point average [GPA]) or standardized-testing data might unexpectedly call attention to students who are ready for more advanced coursework. Student data may also reveal students who have typically had a stellar GPA (e.g., 4.0) but now have lower marks. Although school counselors may not view students with a 3 or 3.5 GPA as a priority when others are at risk for academic failure, even a 0.5 to 1 percentage point drop in GPA may indicate a serious personal concern. Participation in multiple student activities and organizations, in addition to advanced coursework, in an effort to bolster chances for admission to the "right college" can result in exhaustion and medical concerns. However, emotional and physical overload may not be noticed until an obvious crisis occurs. Research has shown that gifted students are often reluctant to seek help from school counselors (Peterson, 2003; Wood, 2009). In addition, *high academic performance and exemplary test scores, coupled with few disciplinary referrals and high involvement in activities, may hide symptoms of bullying, anxiety, depression, posttraumatic stress, disordered eating, or substance misuse.*

School Counselor Skills and Dispositions

Consultation, collaboration, and coordination have long been fundamental to school counseling, but the roles of leader and advocate are relatively new to the profession. School counselors now use data to identify systemic barriers to academic achievement, and they daily advocate for change for their students. In some cases, according to Ratts, DeKruyf, and Chen-Hayes (2007), the system—not the student—may need to change, such as when the system is not prepared to respond to a young child's need for more advanced coursework. These scholars offered examples of school counselors engaged in social justice advocacy for high-ability students and suggested ways counselors can intervene. The suggestions provided by Ratts et al. highlight the importance of identifying curricular areas of concern and students who need advocacy based on data. Thus, *leadership, advocacy, delivery, and accountability are all intertwined.* The ASCA position statement does mention using advocacy to ensure that services and activities address personal/social, academic, and career needs of gifted students. Chapter 12 provides suggestions for school counselor advocacy and leadership with regard to gifted-education programming.

•   •   •

CONCLUDING THOUGHTS AND RECOMMENDATIONS

Tony has energized Erik and Tosha to rethink their approach to working with gifted students and to consider how their current interface with the gifted-education program in their school is working. Taking a divide-and-conquer approach that does not interfere with addressing Tony's needs as an intern, each of the three will examine a component of the ASCA model. Erik will review the mission and vision and determine a time for the counseling team to meet with the administration to talk about current service to gifted students. Tosha has been the mastermind behind the databases the counseling program has been utilizing and will scrutinize 4-year plans and eighth- and ninth-grade enrollment patterns in advanced courses. Tony is doing what he loves, meeting individually with identified gifted students to talk about their experiences in the school and with their parents to discuss what they would like the program to do in the future. Tosha, Eric, and Tony will also present their findings to their advisory board and ask for recommendations. Together, as a team, they are making the ASCA National Model work for them and for the gifted and talented students at the school.

Current school counseling practitioners can utilize this chapter as a guide for evaluating and reenvisioning their school counseling program with specific attention to how the program serves gifted students. By analyzing current practices in each of the four areas of the national model, school counselors can identify programming that is benefiting their gifted learners and areas that need improvement. Using the model to guide their thoughts, school counselors can also create new components of their program that can address the career, personal–social, and academic needs of gifted students in a more strategic manner.

● ● ●

REFERENCES

American School Counselor Association. (n.d.). Executive summary. Retrieved from https://www.schoolcounselor.org/asca/media/asca/ASCA%20National%20 Model%20Templates/ANMExecSumm.pdf

American School Counseling Association. (2012). *The ASCA National Model: A framework for school counseling program* (3rd ed.). Alexandria, VA: Author.

American School Counselor Association. (2013). *The school counselor and gifted and talented programs*. Alexandria, VA: Author.

American School Counselor Association. (2014). *Mindsets & behaviors for student success: K-12 college-and career-readiness standards for every student*. Retrieved from https://www.schoolcounselor.org/asca/media/asca/home/MindsetsBehaviors.pdf

American School Counselor Association. (2016). *Ethical standards for school counselors*. Alexandria, VA: Author. Retrieved from https://www.schoolcounselor.org/asca/media/asca/Ethics/EthicalStandards2016.pdf

Carlson, N. N. (2004). *School counselors' knowledge, perceptions, and involvement concerning gifted and talented students* (Doctoral dissertation, University of Maryland, College Park, 2004). Dissertation Abstracts International, 65(04), 04B. (UMI No. 3128875).

Carlson, N. N., Holcomb-McCoy, C., & Miller, T. R. (2017). School counselors' knowledge and involvement concerning gifted and talented students. *Journal of Counselor Leadership and Advocacy*, 1–13. doi:10.1080/2326716X.2017.1294122

Colangelo, N., & Wood, S. M. (2015). Counseling the gifted: Past, present, and future Directions. *Journal of Counseling & Development*, *93*, 193–142. doi:10.1002/j.1556-6676.2015.00189.x

Dockery, D. A. (2005). *Ways in which counseling programs at specialized high schools respond to social and emotional needs of gifted adolescents* (Doctoral dissertation, University of Virginia, 2005). Available from ProQuest Dissertations and Theses: AAT 3161256.

Earle, S. (1998). *A critical incident study of the school guidance counselor's interactions with gifted students* (Doctoral dissertation, Kent State University). Dissertation Abstracts International 59, 07A. (UMI No. 9842490).

Goldsmith, S. K. (2011). *An exploration of school counselors' self-efficacy for advocacy of gifted students* (Doctoral dissertation, University of Iowa). Available from ProQuest Dissertations and Theses. (UMI No. 3494154).

Moon, S. M. (2002). Counseling needs and strategies. In M. Neihart, S. Reis, N. Robinson, & S. Moon (Eds.), *The social and emotional development of gifted children: What do we know?* (pp. 213–222). Waco, TX: Prufrock Press.

Peterson, J. S. (2003). An argument for proactive attention to affective concerns of gifted adolescents. *Journal of Secondary Gifted Education, 14*(2), 62–70.

Peterson, J. S. (2009). Myth 17: Gifted and talented individuals do not have unique social and emotional needs. *Gifted Child Quarterly, 53*, 280–282. doi:10.1177/0016986209346946

Peterson, J. S. (2013). School counselors' experiences with a summer group curriculum for high-potential children from low-income families: A qualitative study. *Professional School Counseling, 16*(3), 194–204.

Peterson, J. S., Duncan, N., & Canady, K. (2009). A longitudinal study of negative life events, stress, and school experiences of gifted youth. *Gifted Child Quarterly, 53*, 34–49.

Peterson, J. S., & Wachter Morris, C. (2010). Preparing school counselors to address concerns related to giftedness: A study of accredited counselor preparation programs. *Journal for the Education of the Gifted, 33*, 311–366.

Ratts, M. J., DeKruyf, L., & Chen-Hayes, S. F. (2007). The ACA advocacy competencies: A social justice advocacy framework for school counselors. *Professional School Counseling, 11*(2), 90–97. doi:10.5330/PSC.n.2010-11.90

Wood, S. M. (2009). Counseling concerns of gifted and talented adolescents: Implications for school counselors. *Journal of School Counseling, 7*(1). Retrieved from http://www.jsc.montana.edu/articles/v7n1.pdf

Wood, S. M. (2010a). Best practices in counseling the gifted in schools: What's really happening? *Gifted Child Quarterly, 54*, 42–58.

Wood, S. M. (2010b). Nurturing a garden: A qualitative investigation into school counselors' experiences with gifted students. *Journal for the Education of the Gifted, 34*(2), 261–302.

Wood, S. M. (2012). Rivers' confluence: A qualitative investigation into gifted educators' experiences with collaboration with school counselors. *Roeper Review, 34*(4), 261–274.

Wood, S. M., & Peterson, J. S. (2014). Superintendents, principals, and counselors: Facilitating secondary gifted education. In F. A. Dixon & S. M. Moon, (Eds.), *The handbook of secondary gifted education* (2nd. ed., pp. 627–649). Waco, TX: Prufrock Press.

Characteristics and Concerns of Gifted Students

JEAN SUNDE PETERSON

Thomas (pseudonym for a composite student profile), in his final K–12 year, participates in five components of a multidimensional program for gifted students in a large school: Future Problem Solving (FPS), Advanced Placement (AP) courses, a noon-hour philosophy course taught by a retired professor, after-school lectures by community members, and small discussion groups focused on nonacademic development. He has an extremely high IQ, is known as an excellent musician, and recently was named a semifinalist in the Preliminary SAT (PSAT) merit-scholar competition. However, his only-average academic record has long frustrated teachers, who seem offended by his seemingly limp investment and who see an "attitude problem" in his lack of oral engagement and absent homework. Thomas has a quiet personality, typically avoids eye contact, and seems older than his age. He has taken no steps toward postsecondary education, and he will need financial aid if that is his direction. One of his teachers asks the school counselor to meet with him to assess needs and concerns, including those related to college applications. Before she meets with Thomas, the counselor arranges conversations with his current teachers, his single-parent mother, the orchestra teacher/conductor, and the gifted-education program coordinator. Only the one teacher has ever referred Thomas to the counselor.

The AP American Literature and AP American History teachers both focus mostly on the missed assignments but note his serious alertness during class and brilliant insights on the papers he has submitted. The chemistry teacher expresses concern about Thomas's sad demeanor but notes that he pays attention in class and does "OK" academically. The orchestra director, who has worked with Thomas since elementary grades, calls him one of the most gifted and highly invested musicians he has known. He reacts emotionally when he listens to classical music.

The gifted-education teacher has learned that Thomas struggles with perfectionism— with essays stalled after he has discarded several eloquent thesis statements. He has told her that he doubts he can follow through worthily. About eye contact, Thomas once said he could not hear peers' comments when distracted by the visual stimuli of faces. He despairs over circumstances in distressed countries. Nevertheless, he is a quiet leader on his FPS team. His mother describes her acrimonious divorce and the depression Thomas has struggled with since middle school. She worries about him, especially now, with his inertia about applications. She hopes, given the PSAT results, that he will now invest in the process, securing a scholarship. She feels incapable of helping him.

• • •

PERTINENT RESEARCH AND CLINICAL LITERATURE

The vignette reflects several elements related to the social and emotional development of gifted students, according to scholars and clinicians: heightened sensitivity, intensity, asynchronous development, anxiety, perfectionism, introversion, existential depression, denied emotions, academic underachievement coupled with excellence in a talent area, career indecision, a desire to learn, the asset–burden paradox of giftedness, multipotentiality, and a strong sense of justice and fairness. Most of these areas have had research attention; existential depression, sensitivity, intensity, asynchrony, denied emotions, and a strong sense of justice have been discussed mostly by clinical professionals in the gifted-education literature. A discussion of various characteristics associated with giftedness follows here. However, since this population is so idiosyncratic, making assumptions about *all* gifted students on the basis of any one element or person is unwise.

Heightened Sensitivity

For several decades (e.g., Hollingworth, 1926), clinicians working with gifted youth have maintained that heightened sensitivity is associated with giftedness—a *cognitive* sensitivity. According to Mendaglio (2007), the rapidly processing brain of a gifted person contributes to thinking more and feeling more, to strong awareness of emotions, to self-criticism, and to emotional lability. The brain is hyperalert to environmental stimuli, and some gifted individuals have intense and even pained responses to visual stimuli, smells, sounds, tastes, and textures. Whether and how they express emotional responses outwardly depends on how they were socialized.

School counselors should be aware that sensitivity can have positive effects, but can also exacerbate struggles related to individual and family developmental transitions, change and loss, and relationships with peers and authority. Findings in Peterson, Duncan, and Canady's (2009) study of negative life events suggest that sensitivity contributes to increasing stress during the school years, as well as lack of confidence, shyness, fears, sensitivity to criticism, awkwardness, feelings of inferiority, and self-consciousness. In addition, sensitivity to social injustice may be unsettling, especially when gifted youth are not yet equipped emotionally to deal with that.

Intensity

In the view of clinical professionals who work with gifted persons, intensity also is common (e.g., Daniels & Piechowski, 2009)—for example, intense responses to sensory stimuli; intense empathy; intense interests ("passion areas"); intense responses to unfairness, rejection, and inclusion; intense engagement with technology, discussion, or activities; and intense investment in learning. Peers' and family members' responses to the intensity may affect the gifted child's sense of self (Peterson & Moon, 2008), and intense responses to sensory stimuli may affect how normal developmental transitions, life events, and competitive and stimulus-rich classroom and work environments are experienced. School counselors who recognize that gifted students may struggle with intensity can normalize strong feelings and dramatic behaviors for these students, who may actually fear they are "crazy," and help them develop coping strategies.

Overexcitabilities

Connected to heightened sensitivity and intensity is the concept of overexcitabilities (OEs), part of Dabrowski's (1967; see also Mendaglio, 2007; Probst & Piechowski, 2012) theory of positive disintegration (TPD). An OE can be intellectual, sensual, imaginational, emotional, or psychomotor. Piechowski (1999) brought the OE concept to the gifted-education field, noting that OEs might be connected to creativity, passionate interests, constant movement, and perfectionism, in addition to the responses mentioned earlier here.

TPD asserts that struggle is related to growth and development, and that advanced development is not possible without struggle. When previous learning is applied unsuccessfully to difficult, uncontrollable situations, psychological disintegration is possible. However, advanced development can occur through self-education and self-correction, empathy and a sense of justice, consciously applying higher values, and assuming responsibility for self and others.

School counselors who are familiar with OEs and TPD can introduce despairing children and adolescents to them, helping them make sense of complex and deeply unsettling feelings and survive horrendous experiences.

Asynchronous Development

Giftedness affects all areas of life (Yermish, 2010). The *gifted* label inherently reflects asynchronous (i.e., uneven) development (Silverman, 2013). When their cognitive ability is far ahead of most age-peers', or when their talent development is astounding at a young age, gifted students understandably feel out of sync. When interests differ greatly from most age-peers', communication about interests is probably difficult.

Another area of asynchronous development is related to potentially great differences between level of cognitive development and level of social and/or emotional development. When gifted youth are told they are "immature," they may simply be asynchronous: brilliant intellectually, but socially just average, criticized by teachers who "expect more from someone so bright." When a close relative is seriously ill, or when someone dies, a gifted child may struggle emotionally— no matter how cognitively precocious. If verbally or physically bullied, a gifted child may put great cognitive effort into making sense of the experience and of the bully, but be traumatized nevertheless by even "just" one incident. Parents, teachers, and counselors may forget that a 10-going-on-40 child is, in spite of profound insights and great vocabulary, only 10, with the mind on overdrive, but only average or possibly below-average social and emotional development. Some gifted children and teens are inappropriately given adult-type responsibilities, or treated as an adult confidante, or deferred to for major family decisions. Anxiety may result, since they sense that they, not an adult, will be the "bottom line" in a crisis.

Perfectionism, Anxiety, and Concerns About the Future

Gifted children and teens probably have the ability to do many things well, but that does not preclude stress and anxiety when meeting challenges related to school work, school and community activities, public performance, and even chores at home. Perfectionism related to any of these areas is a common presenting issue when gifted kids come to counseling. Teachers see it as well. Though coaches and directors want excellence, they may become concerned when perfectionism precludes joy and satisfaction in accomplishment. Fortunately, Thomas, in the vignette, is invested positively in music, offering an opening for the counselor to discuss strengths and satisfaction in the midst of sadness.

Current debate in the gifted-education field about perfectionism involves viewing it on a continuum (Greenspon, Parker, & Schuler, 2000), with adaptive perfectionism on the positive end (i.e., reasonable goals, satisfying efforts and products, and working toward excellence) and maladaptive perfectionism on the negative end (i.e., unreasonable goals, difficulty "enjoying the trip," preoccupation with evaluation, anxiety, not being able to savor a good result, and negative impact on self, work, and relationships). Another perspective (Greenspon, 2016) is that *perfectionism* implies an undesirable impact on well-being, with fear of failure as the driving force.

A school counselor may meet with a gifted child or teen distressed by high expectations by self and/or others. The student may be preoccupied with evaluation, imperfect performance, and fears about the future, with well-being affected negatively. Individual counseling may be helpful; however, group counseling can also help to normalize concerns and develop strategies for coping with a persistent fear of failure, for example.

Even young gifted children can have great anxiety about the future. They may worry that they will not know which career is right for them, will not know how to be a parent, or will not know where they should live. They may or may not verbalize those fears. Unlike many of their age-peers, these children do not need to be pushed to think about the future, since they (and adults who are invested in them) already are quite concerned. A systematic career emphasis can be helpful for broadening gifted students' awareness of options. The emphasis need not be on career decisions, but on personal qualities and the importance of fit of career with personality, personal needs and preferences, and interests.

Existential Depression

Young gifted children may also seriously consider how world governments, or families, or learning, or intercultural relationships, or peer behavior *ought* to be. Gifted adolescents likely also ponder the real versus the ideal. However, both may be painfully aware of how far from the ideal the family or peer relationships they observe and experience are.

Through various media they are probably aware of violence near at hand and far away, hungry children and families without adequate shelter, and natural disasters. Cognitively sensitive gifted youth often have deep empathy for people and animals in distress, but may not be encouraged to express, or feel comfortable expressing, intense feelings. Cognitive and emotional responses may not be in sync when they ponder catastrophes, illness and death of people close to them, parental deployment or unemployment, parents' separation and divorce, sudden relocation, or conflict and violence at home. They may have questions about religion, and they may wonder how death is experienced. They may ruminate for days about something they witnessed on television or in the hallway or bus line at school. Their strong sense of justice and fairness when they observe cruelty, poverty, bullying, hunger, teacher favoritism or neglect, or capricious authority may lead to long, internal monologues. They may believe that no one could possibly understand how they feel.

In short, they may experience existential depression. They may lie awake at night, wondering if they will ever sleep again, and worrying that they will not be able to perform well in school if they are tired. Webb (2013), who has given considerable attention to this phenomenon, views it as a struggle of idealists to find meaning after realizing that the world is not as trustworthy and predictable as they once thought. The characteristics associated with giftedness, already discussed here, together with the ability to grapple with complex questions, may contribute to this disillusionment.

An alert teacher should refer such children or teens to the school counselor. The ensuing conversation may be the first related to disillusionment that these students have ever had and may help them make sense of uncomfortable feelings. Feeling heard in a small group—and "normal," instead of "weird" and "crazy"— might connect a disillusioned student to school. Thomas's counselor could explore the phenomenon of existential depression with him, given his lassitude, family history, and perfectionism, for example. Helping him express and make sense of feelings, without being patronizing, might be helpful.

High Achievers

It is not uncommon for educators, administrators, peers, and even parents to be unaware of social and emotional concerns of gifted children and teens, particularly high achievers. After all, most students who perform well academically validate teachers' and parents' efforts. Motivation to achieve is often assumed to reflect good mental health, and achievement is associated with future success. School districts frequently require high academic achievement for participation in a gifted-education program. Programming, in turn, may be limited to "advanced academics"—that is, more content and at a faster pace than in the regular classroom.

When high achievers have social or emotional concerns, they might hesitate to tell parents or teachers who are invested in their success about their worries, fears, distress, or despair. They may not want to risk tarnishing their positive social image at school or at home, and they may fear disappointing their adult supporters, not meeting their own or others' high expectations, or jeopardizing future goals.

Yet school counselors need to understand that the sensitivity, intensity, asynchronous development, and anxiety associated with giftedness have implications for high achievers' well-being. Instead of being in awe of amazing academic, athletic, or artistic performance, wise counselors assume that, like anyone else, high achievers struggle with developmental challenges, life transitions, illness, concerns about close relatives, and possibly even the aftermath of traumatic experiences. High achievers and gifted youth, in general, are not exempt from difficult experiences. Even when meeting with high achievers about a schedule change or about letters of recommendation, school counselors can inquire about well-being, sense of self, challenges, and satisfactions. Counselors should also assume that high achievers may not have had essential guidance about career-planning. Educators and even parents may erroneously assume that high achievers need less attention in that regard than do others.

Academic Underachievers

Invested adults might also miss concerns like those affecting Thomas if they are preoccupied with his IQ and view him only judgmentally. School counselors probably meet with more underachievers, regardless of ability level, than with high academic achievers. Gifted underachievers may be referred for counseling because a teacher is aware of their high ability or because of behavior problems, anger, truancy, or excessive tardiness, any of which might reflect distress. However, educators should not assume that all underachievers behave inappropriately; have low achievement in all classes (Peterson & Colangelo, 1996), talent areas, and contexts; have low self-esteem (McCoach & Siegle, 2003); and do not want to learn (Peterson, 2002).

It is certainly possible that systemic factors at home, in the classroom, in the peer culture, or at a job are complexly contributing to low performance. Grief after loss, posttraumatic stress after personal or natural disasters, difficulty navigating changes in peer culture, developmental stuckness (e.g., related to identity, relationships, direction, or autonomy), or other challenges may play a role. A referral to a school counselor might lead to further assessment by a school or community psychologist. Ideally, these professionals know that characteristics associated with giftedness may exacerbate difficulties related to life transitions, problems with peers, sibling relationships, personal disappointment, or trauma. Impulsivity, hyperactivity, distractibility, anxiety, compulsivity, depression, bipolar arcs, social anxiety or deficits, anger, or aggression may warrant assistance, but they might remain under the diagnosis threshold.

Multipotentiality

It is not unusual for gifted children and adolescents to have many strong interests and talents. Any of those might realistically be viewed as a career direction. The concept of multipotentiality (Kerr & Soldano, 2003), which reflects such multiple strengths, can be useful when counseling—helping gifted students make sense of career indecision, anxiety about the future, and distress about having so many options. Coupled with systematic career-development programming, psychoeducational information can help to normalize indecision and encourage patience and career-development activities while waiting for clear direction to emerge. One camp in the gifted-education field does not take the concept seriously, based on research (Achter, Lubinski, & Benbow, 1996). However, clinicians do see distress related to having too many reasonable options and believing that most must be left behind.

Gifted children and teens may also feel stressed about not having a college major and direction in mind. Career guidance should begin in early elementary grades for any child, and school counselors are usually acquainted with scaffolded resources to accomplish that support. As young gifted children age, they need more information and assessment (Hebert & Kelly, 2006).

Being skilled and knowledgeable in a domain does not guarantee career satisfaction. Considering interests, needs, and values (Kerr & Ghrist-Priebe, 1988), for instance, may help gifted students narrow their choices and experience satisfaction at work as adults. Career paths that are set aside along the way may still become avocational pursuits.

When families include good professional models, adults may assume incorrectly that sufficient career development happens naturally, without intentional guidance. In reality, it may not. Providing affective curricula geared toward career development can help gifted youth of all ages feel some control over the complex educational process that prepares them for the future.

Hidden, Denied, and Controlled Emotions

One counseling concern may be related to gifted students using a nimble mind or verbal strengths to control awkward or uncomfortable situations, to get a concession from someone, or to avoid shame. The concern is if, in an effort to maintain control, they do not take risks, including displaying emotions or talking about their distress with people who can offer support or feedback. Some of Peterson's studies attended to family conflict (Peterson, 2002), bullying (Peterson & Ray, 2006a, 2006b) and other trauma (Peterson, 2012, 2014), and sexual orientation (Peterson & Rischar, 2000) as the sole or a partial focus. Anxiety, distress, depression, and suicidal ideation were typically rarely, if ever, discussed with teachers, and not telling parents was also common. In a study of depression (Jackson & Peterson, 2003), highly gifted adolescents feared that communicating their distress would have a negative effect on whomever they told. Reflecting their sense of differentness and poorness of fit, they also believed no one could understand.

Common characteristics notwithstanding, gifted kids are highly idiosyncratic, and generalizations about them should be made only cautiously. The teachers in a study of teacher language when nominating students for a program for high-ability students (Peterson & Margolin, 1997) tended to look for verbal assertiveness, potentially not considering shy, quiet students. Keirsey and Bates (1984) noted that introverted children hold back responses until they have been "rehearsed internally" (p. 101), with the level of their intelligence perhaps being underestimated. Introversion characterizes only a minority of the general population, and in a world geared toward extraversion, reticence can contribute to social isolation and awkwardness, which can in turn exacerbate a tendency to deny strong emotions or keep them in check. School counselors can validate and normalize shyness and introversion for quiet gifted students, adding that temperament varies from person to person, and shy individuals may be particularly knowledgeable because they are keen observers. In general, school counselors who are aware of gifted students' tendency to hide, deny, or control emotions should be alert to possible distress when someone self-refers or is referred by a teacher or other school staff for angry outbursts, withdrawal, changes in personality, or flat affect.

KEY CONCEPT

Gifted and Gay

In a study of 18 (6 females, 12 males) gay, lesbian, bisexual, and transgender (GLBT) gifted young adults (Peterson & Rischar, 2000), rare in the counseling field in using qualitative methods to explore sexual orientation and rare in the gifted-education field in focusing on sexual orientation, half of the participants had wondered about their orientation before leaving elementary school. However, it was not a great concern for them until puberty. Half became convinced of their orientation during grades 10 and 11.

For 44%, awareness was associated with the junior or senior high school years. Associated with their awareness was, for example, "ultra-hetero" or anti-gay behaviors, depression, intense investment in academic

(continued)

achievement and activities, a drive to succeed, feeling like an outcast, feeling "doubly different," stressful either–or thinking, quitting sports because of fear (55% of males), or fear of abandonment by family. Some participants referred to gaps in experiences related to romantic and sexual development; they had attempted to fill those gaps with activities.

Socially, high school was better than junior high, and relationships with best friends went unchanged for 53%, but school life was affected negatively for 59% and home life for 29%, largely because they believed they could not be "honest." Most (65%) felt danger—41% at school. Most (78%) were achievers, and the four underachievers became achievers in college. Most (78%) had counseling, mostly sustained, and mostly during high school. Of those, 79% believed it was helpful. Of all participants, 88% had experienced depression and 76% had been suicidal. Only 29% told parents about depression and only 31% about suicidal ideation, and none told teachers. However, 71% discussed depression and 85% discussed being suicidal with someone (e.g., friend, counselor).

Pertinent to characteristics commonly associated with giftedness (e.g., heightened sensitivity, intensity, OEs) were a sense of differentness, depression, harassment, lack of role models, fears related to safety, retrospective concern about why adults did not question their extreme investment in activities, and the timely miracle of feeling active support for GLBT students in college. Some male participants described a troubled father–son relationship. The concept of disenfranchised grief (i.e., grief not accepted or understood by others) is pertinent, since contemplation of an "unacceptable" sexual identity often involved anticipating loss of friends or family.

The study was conducted prior to positive media attention to and portrayals of lesbian, gay, bisexual, transgender, queer, intersex, questioning (LGBTQIQ) persons; "out" actors, athletes, and other celebrities; and clubs and groups supporting GLBT students in schools. Some concerns emerging in the study might therefore be different today. However, political, cultural, and religious perspectives likely continue to have a bearing on safety and mental health for these individuals, perhaps as much for gifted LGBTQIQ youth as for any others with a minority sexual orientation.

Potential Misdiagnosis

How sensitivity, intensity, anxiety, and OEs are manifested can sometimes appear to meet the criteria for psychiatric diagnosis. Psychomotor, sensual, emotional, and even intellectual OEs can resemble attention deficit disorder, including the variant with hyperactivity. Emotional OE, heightened sensitivity, and intensity can appear to reflect bipolar disorder. Intensity, perhaps in the form of debilitating perfectionism, might be misassessed as obsessive-compulsive disorder. A great imagination, with creative products and perhaps an imaginary world or friend, might be viewed as schizophrenia. A groundbreaking book by Webb et al. (2005) detailed how behaviors that reflect characteristics of giftedness can be misdiagnosed as pathology.

Conversely, some behaviors might be inappropriately dismissed as simply "odd gifted." Gifted children and teens can indeed have mental health disorders, and school counselors are probably the "point person" for making an informal assessment of students whose behaviors, expressive language, or emotions argued for a meeting. A referral to a psychologist for further assessment might be warranted. With a few hundred (at least) students as their responsibility, school counselors should not be expected to provide long-term therapy for a few, at the expense of prevention- and intervention-oriented work with *all* other students.

● ● ●

RESPONDING TO CONCERNS

In the following subsections, the focus is on four broad approaches that can be useful with gifted students at various age, ability, and achievement levels and with varying kinds of disability, family contexts, and cultural backgrounds. Chapter 9 offers additional guidance for school counselors when needing to address concerns of gifted children and adolescents.

A Developmental Lens

School counselors are inherently developmentalists, probably drawn to counseling because they hoped to help students develop emotionally, socially, and academically in positive ways. However, counselors may not consciously consider development, per se, when working with gifted students (Peterson, 2015). If they did, they might ask questions like the following:

Identity
- What have you learned this year about yourself?
- What do others appreciate about you?
- How might your classmates describe you?

Direction

- Where would you like to be in 15 years?
- Which kinds of careers have you thought about over the past 3 years?
- Which parts of your personality and skills might help you get and keep a job?

Relationships

- How are your relationships with peers different from when you were younger?
- Which kinds of relationships usually go well for you? Which kinds sometimes do not?
- How do you usually feel about, and respond to, someone in authority?

Autonomy

- How much do you take care of your own clothes and make decisions about them?
- How much are you responsible for the room you sleep in? For managing money? Preparing food? Managing a schedule of your activities?"

When school and other counselors look through a developmental lens when interacting with gifted students, they might sense that an underachiever is "developmentally stuck" in one or more areas of development—identity, direction, or autonomy, for instance. A high achiever might have foreclosed prematurely on a career path, perhaps even during elementary school, honoring family values without exploration and without choice, uncomfortable with uncertainty (Josselson, 1996). In general, gifted students might have silent or dramatic conflict with a parent or guardian about a career choice deemed inappropriate by the adult (Peterson, 2001). An underachiever may feel paralyzed by career indecision or external pressure to succeed.

In these or similar situations, a school counselor can nonjudgmentally normalize developmental challenges and stress, use interactive activities to help students develop expressive language to explore options, or organize a panel of successful community members who struggled to find direction and develop appropriate levels of autonomy during adolescence. Being alert to the possibility of depression for any gifted child or teen is important, regardless of referral source. Referring to development at least changes the language, brings fresh air into what feels stuck, implies that nothing stays the same, and suggests that "this is a stage I trust you'll get past, sooner or later."

Reframing

Sensitive gifted students may judge themselves harshly. Using reframing, beyond a momentary reframe during a counseling session, can not only surprise gifted children, but also help them see shameful, ineffective, or unproductive behavior in a different light. Bright students like cognitive play and probably appreciate a counselor who avoids the strident critical language other adults might use. High achievement might be viewed as a way to feel in control in the midst of a chaotic family life. Underachievement can be reframed as "having enough guts not to follow the family path," anger as an "alive" alternative to depression, problematic behavior as creativity, and being late to school as "being sure Mom gets to work on time." Any of these unexpected perspectives might generate important conversation.

Change–Loss–Grief

Gifted students, like any others, are constantly developing, with tempo varying from person to person. Developmental change happens gradually. In contrast, an event or situation at home, school, or work can represent unexpected, non-normative change. Even though they are intellectually or otherwise highly capable, gifted youth might not be able to sort out what precipitated uncomfortable emotions and what to do about them. A change–loss–grief framework can help them make sense of what they are feeling or how they are behaving.

Change means that something is different. It is not how it *was*. Change is not always negative, of course. However, whether change is related to a normal developmental transition like puberty or leaving for college, or an unexpected change like parental separation and/or divorce, there is likely a feeling of loss. Other examples of unexpected or unwelcome change are loss of friendship, rejection after a sustained relationship, family relocation, moving to a different school, parental unemployment, a parent going back to full-time work, an accident resulting in impairment, the death of someone close, or a sibling's substance abuse. With loss, there is likely some sadness over leaving something behind. Compassionately framing a change as loss might help a gifted student of any age make sense of feelings of sadness and grief.

* * *

CONCLUDING THOUGHTS AND RECOMMENDATIONS

Yermish (2010) referred to the "culture" of giftedness. In multicultural terms, knowledge, awareness, and skills related to culture (Sue, Arredondo, & McDavis, 1992) contribute to social ease, appropriate interaction, and understanding in an unfamiliar cultural context. The material included in this chapter can help school counselors engage gifted children and adolescents as a culture within the broader school culture, in dialogue and in activities, respectfully and comfortably and with genuine interest and curiosity about how they experience giftedness.

Thomas, introduced at the outset, offers an opportunity to apply the material in this chapter. He might benefit from a counselor's developmental perspective, provoking self-reflection about developmental tasks, developmental stuckness, and potential developmental contributors to difficulties in some classes. In addition, collaboratively assessing his progress in identity, autonomy, direction, and relationships might be effective.

Thomas also might appreciate a creative reframe of his underachievement—helping him see it in a less negative light than how his mother and some of his teachers view it. Reframing can be a reminder of personal agency. His low motivation in general and his lack of conscientiousness in homework might be reframed as saving his energy for when he has some direction and can channel it more efficiently. His lack of eye contact makes sense in terms of heightened sensory sensitivity, but it could also be reframed as a good way to focus on what others are saying. His excellence in music might be viewed as being careful about risk, since music skills, for him, are within his control. His sadness might be viewed as stepping out of the fray and keeping the world at arm's length while focusing on missing his dad and "the way it used to be." Someday he will likely no longer feel a need to do that, even though his father may still not be a major player in his life. Similarly, Thomas will probably, sooner or later, figure out how to get what he needs from "the system," which probably includes regular submission of homework. For both Thomas and his mother, psychoeducational information about development and characteristics associated with giftedness might help them make sense of his feelings and behaviors. Engaging him in dialogue is a first step.

● ● ●

REFERENCES

Achter, J. A., Lubinski, D., & Benbow, C. P. (1996). Multipotentiality among the intellectually gifted: It was never there and already it's vanishing. *Journal of Counseling Psychology, 43,* 65–76.

Dabrowski, K. (1967). *Personality-shaping through positive disintegration.* Boston, MA: Little, Brown.

Daniels, S., & Piechowski, M. M. (2009). *Living with intensity: Understanding the sensitivity, excitability and emotional development of gifted children, adolescents and adults.* Scottsdale, AZ: Great Potential Press.

Greenspon, T. S. (2016, November). Helping gifted students move beyond perfectionism. *Teaching for High Potential,* 10–12.

Greenspon, T. S., Parker, W. D., & Schuler, P. A. (2000). The authors' dialogue. *Journal of Secondary Gifted Education, 11,* 209–214.

Hebert, T., & Kelly, K. (2006). Identity and career development in gifted students. In F. A. Dixon & S. M. Moon (Eds.), *Handbook of secondary gifted education* (pp. 35–63). Waco, TX: Prufrock Press.

Hollingworth, L. S. (1926). *Gifted children: Their nature and nurture.* New York, NY: Macmillan.

Jackson, P. S., & Peterson, J. S. (2003). Depressive disorder in highly gifted adolescents. *Journal for Secondary Gifted Education, 14*(3), 175–186.

Josselson, R. (1996). *Revising herself.* New York, NY: Oxford University Press.

Keirsey, D., & Bates, M. (1984). *Please understand me: Character and temperament types.* Del Mar, CA: Prometheus Nemesis Book Company.

Kerr, B. A., & Ghrist-Priebe, S. L. (1988). Intervention for multipotentiality: Effects of a career counseling laboratory for gifted high school students. *Journal of Counseling & Development, 66,* 366–369.

Kerr, B. A., & Soldano, S. (2003). Career assessment with intellectually gifted students. *Journal of Career Assessment, 11,* 168–186.

McCoach, D. B., & Siegle, D. (2003). Factors that differentiate underachieving gifted students from high-achieving gifted students. *Gifted Child Quarterly, 47,* 144–154.

Mendaglio, S. (2007). Affective-cognitive therapy for counseling gifted individuals. In S. Mendaglio & J. S. Peterson (Eds.), *Models of counseling gifted children, adolescents, and young adults* (pp. 35–68). Waco, TX: Prufrock Press.

Peterson, J. S. (2001). Gifted and at risk: Four longitudinal case studies. *Roeper Review, 24,* 31–39.

Peterson, J. S. (2002). A longitudinal study of post-high-school development in gifted individuals at risk for poor educational outcomes. *Journal for Secondary Gifted Education, 14,* 6–18.

Peterson, J. S. (2012). The asset–burden paradox of giftedness: A 15-year phenomenological, longitudinal case study. *Roeper Review, 34,* 1–17. doi:10.1080/02783193.2-12.715336

Peterson, J. S. (2014). Giftedness, trauma, and development: A longitudinal case study. *Journal for the Education of the Gifted, 37,* 295–318.

Peterson, J. S. (2015). School counselors and gifted kids: Respecting both cognitive and affective. *Journal of Counseling & Development, 93,* 153–162.

Peterson, J. S., & Colangelo, N. (1996). Gifted achievers and underachievers: A comparison of patterns found in school files. *Journal of Counseling & Development, 74,* 399–407. doi:10.1002/j.1556-6676.1996.tb01886.x

Peterson, J. S., Duncan, N., & Canady, K. (2009). A longitudinal study of negative life events, stress, and school experiences of gifted youth. *Gifted Child Quarterly, 53,* 34–49. doi:10.1177/0016986208326553

Peterson, J. S., & Margolin, L. (1997). Naming gifted children: An example of unintended "reproduction." *Journal for the Education of the Gifted, 21,* 82–100.

Peterson, J. S., & Moon, S. M. (2008). Counseling the gifted. In S. I. Pfeiffer (Ed.), *The handbook of giftedness in children: Psychoeducational theory, research and best practices* (pp. 223–245). New York, NY: Springer-Verlag.

Peterson, J. S., & Ray, K. E. (2006a). Bullying among the gifted: The subjective experience. *Gifted Child Quarterly, 50,* 252–269.

Peterson, J. S., & Ray, K. E. (2006b). Bullying and the gifted: Victims, perpetrators, prevalence, and effects. *Gifted Child Quarterly, 50*, 148–168. doi:10.1177/001698620605000206

Peterson, J. S., & Rischar, H. (2000). Gifted and gay: A study of the adolescent experience. *Gifted Child Quarterly, 44*, 149–164. doi:10.1177/001698620004400404

Piechowski, M. M. (1999). Overexcitabilities. In M. A. Runco & S. R. Pritzker (Eds.), *Encyclopedia of creativity* (Vol. 2, pp. 325–334). San Diego, CA: Academic Press.

Probst, B., & Piechowski, M. (2012). Overexcitabilities and temperament. In T. L. Cross & J. R. Cross (Eds.), *Handbook for counselors serving students with gifts and talents* (pp. 53–73). Waco, TX: Prufrock Press.

Silverman, L. K. (2013). Asynchronous development: Theoretical bases and current applications. In C. S. Neville, M. M. Piechowski, & S. S. Tolan (Eds.), *Off the charts: Asynchrony and the gifted child* (pp. 18–47). Unionville, NY: Royal Fireworks Press.

Sue, D. W., Arredondo, P., & McDavis, R. J. (1992). Multicultural counseling competencies: A call to the profession. *Journal of Counseling & Development, 70*, 477–486.

Webb, J. R. (2013). *Searching for meaning: Idealism, bright minds, disillusionment, and hope.* Tucson, AZ: Great Potential Press.

Webb, J. R., Amend, E. R., Webb, N. E., Goerss, J., Beljan, P., & Olenchak, F. R. (2005). *Misdiagnosis and dual diagnosis of gifted children and adults: ADHD, bipolar, OCD, Asperger's, depression, and other disorders.* Scottsdale, AZ: Great Potential Press.

Yermish, A. (2010). *Cheetahs on the couch: Issues affecting the therapeutic working alliance with clients who are cognitively gifted* (Doctoral dissertation). Retrieved from http://www.davincilearning.org/sketchbook/yermish_2010_gifted_clients_in_therapy.pdf

4

Diverse Gifted Students: Intersectionality of Cultures

RENAE D. MAYES, SADOHL GOLDSMITH JONES,
AND ERIK M. HINES

Michael is a 12-year-old Black male in the seventh grade in a remote rural farm community. He recently relocated to this community from a large metropolitan area, where he was a sixth-grader in a culturally diverse elementary school. He is the oldest of three children with parents who have become pillars in the community despite being new there. Identified as gifted in his previous elementary school, Michael took science and math classes in higher grade levels by single-subject acceleration. He had to work much harder in his language arts classes, but he loved his school and was liked by his peers and teachers.

While Michael's new school is culturally diverse, the school and community norms for students are different. The emphasis is on community fellowship, service, and helping one's family. Little is said about college; instead, jobs in agriculture and manufacturing are emphasized. Michael has been invited several times to participate in the 4H club. Upon arriving at his new school, despite providing his previous years' school records, he is placed in the traditional seventh-grade classes. He complains to his parents that his math and sciences courses are a repeat of information from his previous school. Michael is also encountering difficulties in his language arts classes, which require more traditional essay-writing than his last school did.

In a six-week progress report, Michael's teachers noted that he seems unengaged and withdrawn in class. His parents believe he has become apathetic about school, and they are worried he might lose his love of math and science. In addition, Michael's language arts homework frequently leads to anger and frustration at home.

Michael's parents have requested meetings with his teachers, with the school counselor, Brenda, also attending. Prior to the meeting, she evaluates Michael's cumulative file. Based on his grades, standardized test scores, and teacher comments, she determines that he is extremely bright and very talented in math and science, but has challenges in language arts and social sciences. His teachers' comments include "Handwriting continues to be a challenge, but he is working very hard," "Michael is a very hard worker, but writing paragraphs or persuasive essays requires much more effort," "He is quick at multiple-choice questions and short-answer questions are okay," "His reading comprehension is fantastic, but writing brings out frustrations," and "I realized Michael was much more at ease with oral book reports than written. His love of learning really shines through when he gets to talk about what he knows, in all subjects. He even manages to get his peers interested."

Brenda makes a phone call to the school counselor at Michael's former middle school and the elementary school he attended. She hears wonderful things about Michael, as well as about his challenges with written work. Many of his former language-arts teachers allowed Michael to demonstrate his mastery of content and skills orally or via multiple choice or computerized testing. The middle school counselor reported that he and Michael's parents had discussed talking to their school psychologist about more testing for Michael because they were concerned about the increased requirements for writing in middle school. But that conversation did not lead to changes before the end of the school year, when Michael's family moved.

Gifted education is typically viewed as a way to provide exceptionally bright students with advanced educational opportunities. Students in gifted education are estimated to represent about 6% of the student population (National Association for Gifted Children [NAGC], n.d.). Because gifted education is not regulated at the federal level, states and local education agencies define *giftedness* in their own terms and provide resources to implement appropriate educational opportunities (NAGC, 2015). Information and resources are then passed down to individual schools, which are charged with identifying students and implementing gifted education.

Processes related to identifying children and adolescents for gifted education and to implementing services for them have received a range of criticism. Much of the criticism concerning identification points to the lack of culturally appropriate identification tools, which historically has led to marginalized students (e.g., Black, Latino/a, and Native American students; students with special needs; students from low-income backgrounds) being underrepresented in gifted education (Ford, 2014; Mayes & Moore, 2016; Stambaugh & Ford, 2015). Further, once students are identified, services offered are inappropriate, too often representing a cultural mismatch between students and educators (Ford, 2014; Mayes & Moore, 2016) and a mismatch between areas of student giftedness and gifted services provided (e.g., being artistically gifted in a school where gifted services are provided in English/language arts and mathematics only). There may also be a mismatch between cultural values and receptivity to gifted education, as well as between the cultural values of dominant-culture educators and culturally different students (Peterson, 1999). Educators, including school counselors, may have misperceptions about giftedness that affect key relationships and services that students need to reach their potential (Colangelo & Wood, 2015; Peterson, 2013, 2015).

Related to these challenges, it is important to understand that school counselors can be collaborative supporters, ensuring the positive, holistic academic, personal/social, and career development of culturally diverse gifted students. This chapter explores the case of Michael, a twice-exceptional Black male in a rural community. Discussed will be the concept of intersectionality of identities and ways school counselors can work with students like Michael as advocates, counselors, consultants, and collaborators.

• • •

THE INTERSECTIONALITY OF MICHAEL'S IDENTITIES

Before looking at approaches, school counselors should first consider how the intersectionality of a student's identities may shape that student's world view and experiences. Intersectionality (Crenshaw, 1989, 1991) is a framework used to understand how inequality, power, and politics manifest based on a person's several identities. This framework allows deeper understanding of the complexities of discrimination and oppression that marginalized groups experience when they have two or more identities. It encourages a multidimensional examination of identity categories (e.g., race, gender, and ability status) to understand how individuals are treated and how they experience their environment (Crenshaw, 1989, 1991). In the case of Michael, the intersecting identities are ability status, culture, gender, and geography, all of which collectively come together and influence his experiences in his new school. These identities are outlined in this section in further detail. Some aspects of this discussion can be generalized to other culturally diverse or twice-exceptional groups.

Ability Status (Giftedness and Disabilities)

Michael's academic abilities vary across subjects. For example, his giftedness in math and science makes rigorous coursework in those areas a good fit for his strengths. Challenge appropriate for his abilities in other classes is also important for engaging him (Assouline, Nicpon, & Huber, 2006; Siegle & McCoach, 2005). In addition, gifted students can be resourceful and imaginative, allowing them to be creative in problem-solving and coursework (Hoh, 2008; Lovecky, 1994).

However, gifted students may struggle with perfectionism, which may make risk-taking, particularly in academic and social situations, challenging (Peterson, 2015). They may avoid activities or new learning opportunities because they fear they will not meet their own or others' high expectations. They may focus heavily on producing perfect products and view shortcomings and mistakes as shameful (cf. Greenspon, 2014).

Further, Michael has concerns in language arts and social studies classes, where writing is difficult for him. His struggles with writing may indicate a learning disability (e.g., dysgraphia), which may require additional support from school staff. Students like Michael, "who have outstanding gifts or talents and are capable of high performance, but who also have a disability that affects some aspect of learning," are identified as *twice-exceptional* (National Education Association, 2006, p. 1)—that is, as because of both their high cognitive abilities or talents and their disability. Michael's situation is not uncommon. Foley-Nicpon and Assouline (2015) suggested that "typically, twice-exceptional students exhibit exemplary verbal and nonverbal reasoning abilities and reading and math achievement but have less well-developed writing, working memory, and processing speed skills; adaptive skills, social skills, and behavioral control are often considered underdeveloped" (p. 204).

With the onset of disability, students often struggle with coming to terms with it and with the stigma that surrounds disabilities (Lavani, 2015). Stigma may have a negative impact on self-esteem and confidence in their ability to be successful. Students with disabilities may become easily frustrated with their learning experiences and may lack the ability to advocate for support for their specific needs and experiences (Lavani, 2015).

As Michael is forming his own academic identity, it is certainly shaped by both his giftedness and his special needs. Many twice-exceptional students struggle to come to terms with their giftedness, disability, and racial identities (Mayes & Moore, 2016). This challenge is influenced by personality and a desire to reach high goals in spite of disability. Students like Michael also must combat negative messages of racial inferiority as well as stigma around having a disability. Left unresolved, as could happen with Michael, these challenges may lead to loneliness and low self-concept while coping with the various identities (Mayes & Moore, 2016). However, students who are twice-exceptional can be successful if they have appropriate resources at school, including accommodations with high expectations and intentional support to develop healthy identities.

Culture

Culture matters. According to Ford-Harris, Schuerger, and Harris (1991), "Gifted Black students encounter more barriers to identity development than do Whites.

In addition, they may experience more psychological and emotional problems than do Black students not identified as gifted" (p. 577). Ford-Harris et al. (1991) noted that gifted Black students may struggle with the notion of high achievement, as it may be seen as a dominant-culture narrative that is not culturally relevant. Exum (1979) and Fordham (1988) wrote that students may experience conflict, isolation, and identity crisis. In addition, according to other researchers (Ford, 2014; Ford & Moore, 2013; Mayes & Moore 2016), gifted Black students may encounter rejection and purposely underachieve due to negative reactions to their high abilities. Moreover, Steele and Aronson (1995) suggested that stereotype threat may play a role in the underachievement of students of color, and of Black students in particular, with these students underperforming with academic tasks when race is emphasized, especially when compared to their White counterparts. In other words, if poor performance is expected from a particular racial or cultural group, that group tends to live up the expectation. Stereotype threat can also affect students psychologically, limiting their potential for academic success (Stone, 2002). For example, if a Black male is enrolled in an Advanced Placement biology course, and if his White peers and White teacher believe he is in the class because of quota rather than talent, his academic performance may be lower than his classmates' due to stereotype threat.

Gender

Gender can play a significant role in how students are serviced as well as in their treatment. For example, African American boys who present characteristics related to giftedness as well as disability may be referred more often for special education services rather than for programs for gifted and talented students. Moreover, these referrals can lead to relative overrepresentation of Black males in special education, higher expulsion rates, and a larger achievement gap between Black males and their female and ethnic/racial counterparts (Gregory, Skiba, & Noguera, 2010; Moore, Henfield, & Owens, 2008). School counselors are charged with ensuring equitable outcomes for *all* students. The aforementioned consequences can lead to the disenfranchisement of Black males as they progress through education.

Geography

The geographical context of a community has implications for the educational environment of which students are a part. African American students are more likely to be enrolled in urban schools (Aud et al., 2013). In fact, schools in urban environments have a great likelihood of primarily enrolling students of color and students from lower socioeconomic backgrounds. As such, these schools generally have limited access to resources within and outside of school, which in turn contributes to overcrowded schools, crumbling facilities, and fewer highly qualified and licensed teachers (Lee, 2005). While there may be extra educational opportunities, such as gifted education and Advanced Placement courses, it is likely that African American students are denied access to such opportunities and face deficit thinking concerning their abilities and culture (Ford & Moore, 2013)—that is, assumptions of inherent deficits, not strengths, in these areas.

Rural settings can mimic urban settings somewhat in regard to isolation and sheer lack of resources, including physical structures and relatively fewer highly qualified educators (Fishman, 2015). The lack of resources becomes more pronounced as the distance from metropolitan areas increases, ultimately limiting the opportunities students have to build skills necessary for positive academic, socioemotional, and career development. Issues related to diversity (e.g., race, class, and ability status) may be exacerbated in rural settings due to geographic isolation and distance from city centers (Mattingly & Schaefer, 2015). It is possible that a student with diverse identities is the only person, or one of only a few, with particular identities and experiences (e.g., gifted African American male with a disability). This rarity may also mean that few peers and educators can recognize and understand these experiences and offer support. In addition, rural districts, particularly those that are small or remote and serve primarily students from low socioeconomic families, are less likely to provide advanced learning opportunities, including Advanced Placement courses and programs for gifted students (Gagnon & Mattingly, 2016).

Regardless of geographic location, children who are from low socioeconomic backgrounds are at a higher risk for underachievement and are more likely to live in communities with poor living conditions, higher rates of crime, and limited access to proper health care (Gardner & Mayes, 2013). However, despite these challenges, students in these environments can be successful when educational stakeholders (e.g., parents, school counselors, teachers, administrators, and community members) work together to provide innovative, culturally responsive educational opportunities and supports to help students reach their potential.

* * *

THE ROLE OF THE SCHOOL COUNSELOR WITH CULTURALLY DIVERSE GIFTED STUDENTS

After careful consideration and understanding of intersectional identities, school counselors can begin their work toward helping students like Michael succeed. The American School Counselor Association (ASCA, 2013) calls for school counselors to be collaborative advocates who provide systemic and multilevel interventions tailored to the specific needs of gifted children and adolescents. In addition, ASCA (2015) requires school counselors to "demonstrate cultural responsiveness by collaborating with stakeholders to create a school and community climate that embraces cultural diversity and helps to promote the academic, career and social/emotional success for all students" (p. 20). Specifically, school counselors serve as advocates who take the lead in expanding and serving a diverse population in gifted programs. They also serve as consultants and collaborators who provide interventions and locate and generate supports for culturally diverse gifted students. In the case of Michael, the school counselor, Brenda, has several avenues to pursue to both nurture Michael's talents in math and science and ascertain his specific challenges in writing and language arts. She can move in these directions in her multiple roles of counselor, consultant, collaborator, and advocate. Brenda can also consult the NAGC (2011) position statement "Identifying and Serving Culturally and Linguistically Diverse Gifted Students," which provides not only suggestions for identification protocols but also recommendations for social and emotional support and family and community connections. The following discussion may apply, in part, to other culturally diverse students as well.

Counselor

The primary role of a school counselor is to provide individual, small-group, and large-group counseling to support students' academic, social/emotional, and career development. Chen-Hayes, Ockerman, and Mason (2014) suggested a systemic paradigm to help gifted Black students and their parents access resources so that the former can excel academically, adjust socially, and be comfortable with their identity.

Individual Counseling

School counselors can provide direct support to gifted students through individual counseling, focused perhaps on difficulties at home, school attendance, academic concerns, anxiety, or stress (ASCA, 2013). School counselors may find that working individually with gifted students leads to tailoring interventions for them that validate life experiences while also providing opportunities to build skills. Individual counseling can also help school counselors understand how cultural identity and background can affect students' experiences and needs in gifted education. For example, students of color and students from low-income families may hear negative messages and experience microaggressions from peers and teachers (Ford, 2014; Mayes, Harris, & Hines, 2016; Stambaugh & Ford, 2015). Ford-Harris et al. (1991) suggested that counselors help individual

Black gifted students find congruence between their academic identity and their cultural heritage. Those authors also recommended that counselors arrange for mentors and positive models knowledgeable about giftedness to interact with culturally diverse students to normalize their gifted identity. Brenda could engage and support Michael in these ways. Regarding gifted culturally diverse students with one or more disabilities, Harris, Mayes, Vega, and Hines (2016) underscored that school counselors need to be active on behalf of students during the individual educational plan (IEP) process, work closely with teachers to ensure that student accommodations are actually helping students with learning disabilities, and identify personal strengths and assets to help them succeed.

Group Counseling

School counselors may also provide direct support to gifted students through group counseling. Topics that group counseling might address include perfectionism, stress management, depression, underachievement, delinquency, and difficulty with peer relationships (ASCA, 2013; Wood, 2010). Mayes et al. (2016) recommended group counseling for twice-exceptional students to normalize their challenges, help them embrace their identities, and provide peer support. Moreover, these authors argued that the group process can help twice-exceptional students develop coping and self-advocacy skills both in the classroom and at home.

For example, students of color and students from low-income families may hear negative messages and experience microaggressions from peers and teachers (Ford, 2014; Mayes et al., 2016; Stambaugh & Ford, 2015), situations that can be discussed in a small group. Ford-Harris et al. (1991) encouraged counselors to use small-group work to help Black students improve self-esteem and feel comfortable at school. According to Jen's (2015) study, small-group discussion in groups of purposefully mixed culturally diverse and dominant-culture students can result in mutual benefits, such as awareness of shared developmental concerns, social skills, and cross-cultural social bridges.

Peterson (2013) suggested that school counselors use a group format with gifted students not only as a recruiting tool for gifted programs, but also to affirm and validate the experiences of these students related to giftedness. In a study (Peterson, 2013) of school counselors who used a small-group curriculum designed to support the personal/social and career development of gifted elementary school students from low-income backgrounds, two outcomes were identified. First, the school counselors developed a deeper understanding of giftedness through facilitating small-group discussion. For example, some had textbook knowledge of giftedness, but observing overexcitabilities, multiple intelligences, and other characteristics associated with giftedness gave the counselors a new understanding of gifted children, who, in turn, benefited from participation with intellectual peers. Second, in addition to expanding their understanding of specific needs, the counselors helped the children cope with anxiety and perfectionism and helped them develop trust, compassion, and social connections. In the groups, the gifted children were open about their experiences, worries, and difficulties with peer relationships (Peterson, 2013).

As school counselors work with students, it is important that school counselors use culturally appropriate interventions and supports that help students to develop positive gifted and cultural identities while challenging negative messages culturally diverse students may face in the classroom. Providing individual as well as group counseling can help in all of these areas. In addition to theses benefits, a series of small-group discussions (cf. Peterson, 2008) would provide Michael with an outlet to express himself as well as an opportunity to meet other gifted and talented students in the school.

Consultant

As consultants, school counselors seek guidance from other professionals to increase their knowledge, thereby increasing their ability to support students. A school counselor might first consult with the school psychologist and classroom teachers to gain a deeper understanding of Michael's strengths as well as his needs (see Chapters 6 and 10 of this volume). To follow up on his previous school counselor's expressed desire for additional testing, the school counselor can work with Michael's family and the school psychologist to see which kinds of additional testing might help to better understand Michael's strengths and needs. Then, as a team, the school counselor, school psychologists, and teachers can confer about how to address and accommodate Michael's possible disability while maintaining academic rigor and high expectations appropriate for his strengths. In addition, because Michael presents needs that may not be known at the current school, the school counselor might consult with educational administrators to determine available resources to support Michael and students with similar concerns. The school counselor can work with Michael's teacher to plan academic activities that fit his learning style. For example, the school counselor and the teacher can ensure that there is a mix of oral and written classwork to allow Michael to display his intellectual strengths. Moreover, school counselors are in a position to work with all school personnel, helping to bridge communication gaps among stakeholders so that gifted students' school success and well-being are priorities.

Collaborator

As a collaborator, the school counselor can focus on interpersonal communication with and among key stakeholders—Michael, his parents, the teachers, and the school psychologist, in this case. Collaborating with these individuals can help to ensure that Michael has a smooth transition into the new school district. In addition, the school counselor might collaborate with outside stakeholders like educational agencies or area university faculty members who may be able to offer guidance about working with gifted students with disabilities. This external collaboration would potentially increase the knowledge base for educators, Michael, and his family, who all undoubtedly want to understand both the strengths and challenges of twice-exceptionality in addition to strategies to address those challenges and enhance strengths.

Coordinator

School counselors can assist culturally diverse gifted students as coordinators, an integral role in support of achievement in the classroom. School counselors can coordinate direct student services to create individual, group, and classroom curricula to address the needs of this population (ASCA, 2012). These counselors can also work with the IEP team to ensure that co-curricular activities are part of student plans.

According to Epstein and Voorhis (2010), school counselors can take the lead in organizing partnerships to connect parents of gifted students with diverse backgrounds with resources essential to their children's success and welfare. Bryan (2005) recommended forming partnerships among and between schools, families, and communities to foster resilience among underserved students: "School–Family–Community Partnerships are collaborative initiatives or relationships among school personnel, parents, family members, community members, and representatives of community-based organizations such as businesses, churches, libraries, and social service agencies" (Bryan, 2005, p. 220). These stakeholders work together to improve academic outcomes for students (Epstein, 1995). Moreover, a school–family–community partnership can serve as a protective factor as students cope with circumstances that may impede their academic and emotional development (Bryan, 2005; Christenson & Sheriden, 2001).

Advocacy

A primary role for school counselors' involvement in gifted education is advocate for students. School counselors can be advocates during the process of identifying gifted culturally diverse students and then when services and programming for them are implemented. School counselors might also wonder if participation in gifted education is representative of the school population or how culturally diverse students fare once they are in gifted education (see also Chapter 12). The process of determining what the actual situation is may reveal areas where the school counselor can collaborate with educational stakeholders to bring about changes in gifted education that are important for culturally diverse students.

In particular, school counselors might use the Gifted Program Advocacy Model (G-PAM; Grantham, 2003; Grantham, Frasier, Roberts, & Bridges, 2005) to address these needs. G-PAM is a four-phase process model developed to address underrepresentation of various cultural groups in gifted education. The model, originally used for parent advocacy, lends itself well to forming a collaborative team, including school counselors and parents, to address identification issues in gifted education. Phase One of the model includes a needs assessment to understand (a) whole-school and gifted program enrollment patterns and demographics, (b) effectiveness of curriculum and dissemination of gifted program notices, (c) gifted program referral and screening procedures, (d) evaluation and placement procedures, and (e) student participation in gifted programming. Phase Two focuses on developing an advocacy plan. School counselors and the advocacy team collaborate with other educational stakeholders to define priorities, set goals, and create action plans to accomplish goals. Phase Three involves implementing the advocacy plan, during which school counselors, parents, and other educational stakeholders take both formal and informal actions outlined in the advocacy plan. In Phase Four, follow-up and evaluation determine the impact of their actions. In that final phase, school counselors and other school personnel examine the outcomes of their efforts to determine gains related to goals and priorities. This phase can illuminate where efforts were effective and reveal approaches or interventions that should be changed.

G-PAM: Phase One

Given Michael's current situation, Brenda might consider applying G-PAM with a team of stakeholders to understand how gifted education is implemented in the school. Brenda and the coordinators of both special education and gifted education can study data to determine identification and enrollment patterns in local schools, staying alert to how culturally diverse young men are placed into classes. The team may find that demographic percentages of participants in gifted education do not reflect percentages of the whole student population. It is quite likely that the population of students identified as gifted in Michael's school is primarily White and Asian students and students without disabilities (Foley-Nicpon, Allmon, Sieck, & Stinson, 2011; Ford, 2014; Mayes & Moore, 2016).

Further, the process of disseminating materials may need to be revised to create a more inclusive gifted program. In addition, if disseminating information and conducting assessments happens only at the beginning of the year, students who enroll later in the year or those who struggle during school and relocation transitions may miss the opportunity to participate in gifted education despite being qualified for it.

G-PAM: Phase Two

With this information and these concerns in mind, the team of Brenda, the school psychologist, the gifted-education coordinator, and the special-education coordinator can move into action-planning. This stage may involve working with the district liaison and their building administrators to research and review various formal and informal assessment tools. They might consult with schools that are implementing those screening procedures, and explore financial and training resources to support a change in the assessment process.

The team of four invested educators might establish intervals during the school year during which they disseminate program notices and information about gifted-education services to students and parents with the goal of increasing their access to those services. Because it is likely that students like Michael are missed, and essentially excluded, when students are assessed for eligibility for participation, the team might develop an advocacy plan that defines priorities, goals, and actions related to changing the current system of identification and services. The team may also consider ways to improve gifted-education outreach to parents.

When examining policies and practices related to disseminating information, Brenda, the school psychologist, the gifted-education coordinator, and the special-education coordinator may learn that Michael and his family were not provided information about gifted education and identification when he enrolled in the school midyear. Current referral and screening procedures did not require school personnel who registered him and placed him in classes to consider his previous gifted-education status or his grades. Thus Brenda's team may wish to revisit pertinent documentation, procedures, and policy related to evaluating students who enroll at various points during the school year. Specifically, the team should examine how educators review records and work with grade-level teachers to place gifted students in classes that might better address their needs *prior to* formal identification, evaluation, and placement (see Chapter 6 and the Key Concepts in this chapter for a discussion of best practices in identification).

G-PAM: Phase Three

When the team has finalized an action plan, they can move forward to implementation. They can initiate a process to change referral and screening procedures so that they are more comprehensive and culturally responsive than reliance on only one assessment to measure level of performance.

In the case of Michael, advocacy is needed for him as well as for his parents. Michael is clearly at risk for underachievement and even greater disengagement due to the lack of rigor in his current academic placement. Advocacy can take the form of reviewing Michael's records and working with the grade-level teachers to place him in a class within his grade level that provides more rigor while he waits for the gifted-identification evaluation and placement. Likewise, Brenda might help Michael's parents advocate for their son by providing them with information about the district culture, recommending ways to provide rigor at home with Michael's academic education, and suggesting other activities to improve Michael's engagement and help him with his transition. Offering guidance about how they can advocate effectively with school administrators, teachers, coaches, and directors can be helpful. The team can apply the same strategies to help other parents of culturally and economically diverse gifted youth advocate for their children.

G-PAM: Phase Four

Finally, for the teen to understand the impact of their actions, the fourth and final phase consists of follow-up and evaluation. In this phase, Brenda and additional stakeholders evaluate the outcomes of their efforts, determine gains related to goals and priorities, and consider whether and how changes contributed to the outcomes. Beyond indicating effectiveness, this phase can point to areas of advocacy that require a different approach or intervention. In addition, Brenda's team can utilize outcome data (e.g., student grades) and perception data (e.g., survey feedback) to determine how both students and parents are experiencing gifted education.

● ● ●

CONCLUDING THOUGHTS AND RECOMMENDATIONS

It is imperative for school counselors to create a school culture of inclusivity and cultural competency. School counselors can work with multiple stakeholders to ensure that twice-exceptional students have their academic needs addressed and are socially adjusted to the school culture. Specifically, school counselors can (a) facilitate workshops and information sessions for parents of gifted students with diverse backgrounds to inform them about the process of identifying gifted students and about social and emotional development; (b) train teachers in cultural competency and intersectionality to accurately identify giftedness in students of color and students with disabilities and to ensure an equitable process for placing them in gifted programs; (c) work with community leaders to identify extracurricular activities available outside of the school day that are conducive to enhancing the academic, personal, and career development of gifted students of diverse backgrounds; and (d) work with teachers and administrators to infuse culturally relevant pedagogy into the gifted curriculum to help students from diverse backgrounds with racial identity development.

Twice-exceptional students can realize their potential for success through the leadership and advocacy of school counselors, such as with interventions to promote gender equity for twice-exceptional students. For example, school counselors can review how girls and boys are evaluated so that both receive services that are strengths based and so that punitive responses (e.g., being labeled a problem), such as those that plague boys of color, are deterred. School counselors have expertise sufficient to create school–family–community partnerships (Bryan, 2005) and a resource network to assist twice-exceptional students with diverse backgrounds within and outside of the classroom. In general, school counselors can help parents identify community assets that build upon and reinforce achievement in cultural-minority and other diverse students during nonschool hours. Finally, school counselors can take the lead in paying attention to general needs related to development, to unique needs related to diversity, and to equitable outcomes that help to close achievement and knowledge gaps for twice-exceptional students and others who experience the intersection of multiple identities.

KEY CONCEPT

Identification of Twice-Exceptional Students

Tamra Stambaugh and Susannah Wood

Students who are diagnosed with attention deficit hyperactivity disorder (ADHD), are on the autism spectrum, or have another diagnosis are sometimes overlooked during identification for gifted programs (Baum & Owen, 2004; Foley-Nicpon et al., 2011). The National Education Association (2006) identified six areas of twice-exceptionality (in gifted education, the term typically refers to giftedness coexisting with one or more disabilities: physical, sensory, autism spectrum, learning, ADHD, and behavioral).

Characteristics of students with twice-exceptionalities differ, based on diagnoses and areas of strength and concern. If students are identified as gifted in addition to having a disability identified, the disability often

(continued)

has priority over the giftedness. Student strengths may be overlooked when determining needs and services. Instead, students need to be served in their area of talent first; then accommodations can be created for learning disabilities with an emphasis on students' strengths. Securing services for the giftedness exceptionality is difficult, but that attention is essential. There are federal mandates for serving students with disabilities, but not for serving gifted students.

Awareness of unique characteristics, coupled with a comprehensive identification profile that focuses less on a cut-score or full battery score and more on subtest battery scores, comparisons of higher-level thinking, and performance in a variety of settings and modalities, supports the likelihood of identifying talents in twice-exceptional students. Noteworthy here is that many twice-exceptional students learn to compensate for their limitations in a variety of ways and as such may show a moderate overall composite ability score that masks unique abilities (Baum & Owen, 2004; Foley-Nicpon et al., 2011; National Education Association, 2006). Using individual scores instead of a matrix is also supported (National Education Association, 2006).

School counselors may wish to consult Foley-Nicpon and Assouline's (2015) article, "Counseling Considerations for the Twice-Exceptional Client," in the *Journal of Counseling and Development*. These authors included a table entitled "Empirically based recommendations for counselors who work with twice-exceptional students," which presents ideas for school counselors and gifted-education educators involved in the identification and service of twice-exceptional students.

• • •

REFERENCES

American School Counselor Association. (2012). *The ASCA national model: A framework for school counseling programs* (3rd ed.). Alexandria, VA: Author.

American School Counselor Association. (2013). *The school counselor and gifted and talented student programs*. Alexandria VA: Author. Retrieved from https://www.schoolcounselor.org/asca/media/asca/PositionStatements/PS_Gifted.pdf

American School Counselor Association. (2015). *The school counselor and cultural diversity*. Alexandria, VA: Author. Retrieved from https://www.schoolcounselor .org/asca/media/asca/PositionStatements/PS_CulturalDiversity.pdf

Assouline, S. G., Nicpon, M., & Huber, D. H. (2006). The impact of vulnerabilities and strengths on the academic experiences of twice-exceptional students: A message to school counselors. *Professional School Counseling, 10*(1), 14–24.

Aud, S., Wilkinson-Flicker, S., Kristapovich, P., Rathbun, A., Wang, X., & Zhang, J. (2013). *The condition of education 2013* (NCES 2013-037). Washington, DC: U.S. Department of Education, National Center for Education Statistics. Retrieved from http://nces.ed.gov/pubsearch

Baum, S., & Owen, S. V. (2004). *To be gifted and learning disabled*. Mansfield, CT: Creative Learning Press.

Bryan, J. (2005). Fostering educational resilience and achievement in urban schools through school–family–community partnerships [Special issue]. *Professional School Counseling, 8*, 219–227.

Chen-Hayes, S., Ockerman, M. S., & Mason, E. C. M. (2014). *101 solutions for school counselors and leaders in challenging times*. Thousand Oaks, CA: Corwin/Sage.

Christenson, S. L., & Sheridan, S. M. (2001). *Schools and families: Creating essential connections for learning*. New York, NY: Guilford Press.

Colangelo, N., & Wood, S. M. (2015). Counseling the gifted: Past, present, and future directions. *Journal of Counseling and Development, 93*(2), 133–142. doi:10.1002/ j.1556-6676.2015.00189.x

Crenshaw, K. (1989). Demarginalizing the intersection of race and sex: A Black feminist's critique of antidiscrimination doctrine, feminist theory, and antiracist politics. *University of Chicago Legal Forum, 140*, 139–167.

Crenshaw, K. (1991). Mapping the margins: Intersectionality, identity politics, and violence against women of color. *Stanford Law Review, 43*, 1241–1299.

Epstein, J. L. (1995). School/family/community partnerships: Caring for the children we share. *Phi Delta Kappa, 76*(9), 701–712.

Epstein, J. L., & Voorhis, F. L. (2010). School counselors' roles in developing partnerships with families and communities for student success. *Professional School Counseling, 14*(1), 1–15.

Exum, H. A. (1979). Facilitating psychological and emotional development of gifted black students. In N. Colangelo & R. T. Zafrann (Eds.), *New voices in counseling the gifted* (pp. 312–320). Dubuque, IA: Kendall/Hunt.

Fishman, D. (2015). School reform for rural America. *Education Next, 15*, 9–15. Retrieved from http://educationnext.org/school-reform-rural-america

Foley-Nicpon, M., Allmon, A., Sieck, B., & Stinson, R. D. (2011). Empirical investigation of twice-exceptionality: Where have we been and where are we going? *Gifted Child Quarterly, 55*(11), 3–17.

Foley-Nicpon, M., & Assouline, S. G. (2015). Counseling considerations for the twice-exceptional client. *Journal of Counseling and Development, 93*, 202–211. doi:10.1008/j.1556-6676.2015.00196.x

Ford, D. Y. (2014). Segregation and the underrepresentation of Blacks and Hispanics in gifted education: Social inequality and deficit paradigms. *Roeper Review, 36*(3), 143–154. doi:10.1080/02783193.2014.919563

Ford, D. Y., & Moore, J. L., III. (2013). Understanding and reversing underachievement, low achievement, and achievement gaps among high-ability African American males in urban school contexts. *Urban Review, 45*(4), 399–415.

Ford-Harris, D. Y., Schuerger, J. M., & Harris, J. J., III. (1991). Meeting the psychological needs of Black students: A cultural perspective. *Journal of Counseling and Development, 69,* 577–580.

Fordham, S. (1988). Racelessness as a factor in Black students' school success: Pragmatic strategy or pyrrhic victory? *Harvard Educational Review, 58*(1), 54–85.

Gagnon, D. J., & Mattingly, M. J. (2016). Advanced placement and rural schools. *Journal of Advanced Academics, 27*(4), 266–284. doi:10.1177/1932202X16656390

Gardner, R., III, & Mayes, R. D. (2013). African American learners. *Preventing School Failure: Alternative Education for Children and Youth, 57*(1), 22–29.

Grantham, T. C. (2003). Increasing Black student enrollment in gifted programs: An exploration of the Pulaski County Special School District's advocacy efforts. *Gifted Child Quarterly, 47,* 46–65.

Grantham, T. C., Frasier, M. M., Roberts, A. C., & Bridges, E. M. (2005). Parent advocacy for culturally diverse gifted students. *Theory Into Practice, 44*(2), 138–147.

Greenspon, T. (2014). Is there an antidote to perfectionism? *Psychology in the Schools, 51*(9), 986–998.

Gregory, A., Skiba, R., & Noguera, P.A. (2010). The achievement gap and the discipline gap: Two sides of the same coin? *Educational Researcher, 39,* 59–68.

Harris, P. C., Mayes, R. D., Vega, D., & Hines, E. M. (2016). Reaching higher: College and career readiness for African American males with learning disabilities [Special issue]. *Journal of African American Males in Education, 7*(1), 52–69.

Hoh, P. S. (2008). Cognitive characteristics of the gifted. In J. A. Plucker & C. M. Callahan (Eds.), *Critical issues and practice in gifted education* (pp. 57–83). Waco, TX: Prufrock Press.

Jen, E. (2015). *Incorporating a small-group affective curriculum model into a diverse university-based summer residential enrichment program for gifted, creative, and talented youth.* Unpublished doctoral dissertation, Purdue University, Bloomington, IN.

Lavani, P. (2015). Disability, stigma and otherness: Perspectives of parents and teachers. *International Journal of Disability, Development, and Education, 62*(4), 379–393.

Lee, C. C. (2005). Urban school counseling: Context, characteristics, and competencies. *Professional School Counseling, 8*(3), 184–188.

Lovecky, D. V. (1994). Exceptionally gifted children: Different minds. *Roeper Review, 17,* 116–210. doi:10.1080/0278319940955363

Mattingly, H. J., & Schaefer, A. (2015). Education in rural America: Challenges and opportunities. In T. Stambaugh & S. Wood (Eds.), *Serving gifted students in rural settings: A framework for bridging gifted education in rural classrooms* (pp. 53–70). Waco, TX: Prufrock Press.

Mayes, R. D., Harris, P. C., & Hines, E. M. (2016). Meeting the academic and socio-emotional needs of twice exceptional African American students through group counseling. In J. L. Davis & J. L. Moore III (Eds.), *Gifted children of color around the world* (pp. 19–42). Charlotte, NC: Information Age Publishing.

Mayes, R. D., & Moore, J. L., III. (2016). The intersection of race, disability, and giftedness: Understanding the education needs of twice-exceptional, African American students. *Gifted Child Today, 39*(2), 98–104.

Moore, J. L., Henfield, M., & Owens, D. (2008). African American males in special education: Their attitudes and perceptions toward high school counselor and school counseling services. *American Behavioral Scientist, 51,* 907–927.

National Association for Gifted Children. (n.d.). Frequently asked questions. Retrieved from https://www.nagc.org/resources-publications/resources/ frequently-asked -questions-about-gifted-education

National Association for Gifted Children. (2011). *Identifying and serving culturally and linguistically diverse gifted students*. Washington, DC: Author.

National Association for Gifted Children. (2015). *State of gifted education*. Washington, DC: Author.

National Education Association. (2006). *The twice-exceptional dilemma*. Washington, DC: Author.

Peterson, J. S. (1999). Gifted–through whose cultural lens? An application of the post-positivistic mode of inquiry. *Journal for the Education of the Gifted, 22,* 354–383.

Peterson, J. S. (2008). *The essential guide to talking with gifted teens: Ready-to-use discussions about identity, stress, relationships, and more*. Minneapolis, MN: Free Spirit.

Peterson, J. S. (2013). School counselors' experiences with a summer group curriculum for high-potential children from low-income families: A qualitative study. *Professional School Counseling, 16*(3), 194–204.

Peterson, J. S. (2015). School counselors and gifted kids: Respecting both cognitive and affective. *Journal of Counseling and Development, 93*(2), 153–162.

Siegle, D., & McCoach, D. B. (2005). Making a difference: Motivating gifted students who are not achieving. *Teaching Exceptional Children, 38*(1), 22–27.

Stambaugh, T., & Ford, D. Y. (2015). Microaggressions, multiculturalism, and gifted individuals who are Black, Hispanic, or low income. *Journal of Counseling and Development, 93*(2)3, 192–201.

Steele, C. M., & Aronson, J. (1995). Stereotype threat and the intellectual test performance of African Americans. *Journal of Personality and Social Psychology, 69*(5), 797–811.

Stone, J. (2002). Battling doubt by avoiding practice: The effect of stereotype threat on self-handicapping in White athletes. *Personality and Social Psychology Bulletin, 28,* 1667–1678.

Wood, S. (2010). Best practices in counseling the gifted in schools: What's really happening? *Gifted Child Quarterly, 54*(1), 42–58. doi:10.1177/0016986209352681

Theories That Support Programs and Services in Schools

JEAN SUNDE PETERSON

An experienced, progressive superintendent is new to a large school district, and at her first meeting with all teachers, she describes ambitious goals, one of which is to reconceptualize and reorganize the program for gifted students. She wisely does not speak negatively of the present program; instead, she explains that an administrative transition is simply an opportunity to look at existing programs. Regarding gifted education, she wants to examine current thought in the field about giftedness, what residents in the district think about those perspectives, whether criteria used for identification of eligible students in the district match the programming offered, which programming models are available, which kinds of goals might be appropriate for local programming, which community resources might supplement and enhance programming, and whether the "whole" gifted child is adequately attended to.

The district she left had experienced individual and family tragedies and disturbing student behavior in recent years involving gifted scholars, gifted athletes, gifted musicians, gifted visual artists, gifted leaders, and gifted underachievers. She says she has already begun her own personal exploration of pertinent literature, and she wants the district to be proactive and strategic regarding preventing poor outcomes for gifted and talented students—at all school levels, beginning at the elementary level. She promises to organize a task force of representative classroom teachers, school counselors, gifted-education personnel, parents, and possibly students to study pertinent literature, explore various models, and make recommendations. She encourages individuals interested in being on the task force to contact her.

Ben, a middle school counselor, immediately expresses interest. He has been frustrated with not being able to connect adequately with some gifted students who have concerns—both high and low achievers. He was always a high achiever himself, but he has realized that gifted students are highly idiosyncratic, with many not fitting common stereotypes. He wants to understand them better and help them understand themselves better as well. He is glad the superintendent seems interested in their well-being, not just their academic performance.

Ben suspects there are many counseling needs in this population, but he has never heard a local or state counseling peer refer to these needs at professional meetings. He also has wondered about the identification process and the fit of his most complicated gifted counselees with the current programming. In fact, he has met with brilliant thinkers who have not been deemed eligible and assumes that learning disabilities affect the test scores used for screening. Last, since he has worked with a number of referred gifted underachievers, he has wondered which kind of program would engage them in school and academics—and even whether academic achievement should be the sole goal.

Ben believes that being on the task force, if he is selected, will be informative and helpful as he considers how to be more effective with this special population. In fact, he is selected. The superintendent is wise to include a counselor on the task force.

● ● ●
_____

DEFINITIONS AND DISTINCTIONS

The task force must first grapple with how *gifted*, the usual word on the programming ticket, should be defined—and even whether another term would be less controversial. Gagné (2012) noted that scholars' definitions "abound and often contradict one another," but generally distinguish between "*potential* versus *realization*, *aptitude* versus *achievement*, or *promise* versus *fulfillment*" (p. 4)—that is, between strong biological endowment and fully developed adult performance (Cross & Coleman, 2005). Gagné (2012) also distinguished between *giftedness* (e.g., natural aptitudes in the upper 10% among age peers, such as manual dexterity and analytical reasoning) and *talent* (competencies in the top 10%, such as in chess, football, music, writing, graphic art, or academics). Other scholars have wrestled with these distinctions as well.

Each of these terms is a construct—that is, it was, "constructed" at some point to represent something efficiently so that discussants could have some common understanding, similar to the function of diagnostic categories of psychopathology. The term *gifted*, therefore, is not the only possible term for extreme endowment or performance. It is not embraced universally, but perhaps any other descriptor would likewise not be thoroughly accepted.

Local control is highly valued in the United States, and therefore district coordinators and other local personnel have considerable responsibility in establishing policies and practices related to identification and programming (Peters, Matthews, McBee, & McCoach, 2014). In a survey of gifted-education policies in the United States (National Association for Gifted Children & Council of State Directors of Programs for the Gifted, 2015), among the 42 states responding, 37 had determined a formal definition, with intellectual abilities the most common area in it, followed by academics, performing and visual arts, creativity, and specific academic areas. State requirements included multiple criteria, IQ tests, achievement tests, any test on a menu of state-approved tests, and nominations, in descending order of frequency of mention. In 32 states, gifted-education services were mandated. The most commonly mentioned methods of delivery were cluster classrooms, resource rooms, regular classrooms, and self-contained classrooms. Pertinent to potential roles of school counselors, social and emotional development was essentially absent from the states' definitions.

The rest of this chapter presents theories driving identification of, and services for, gifted students. Included are various achievement-based conceptions of giftedness (Bland, 2012); several talent-development models, including Gagné's (2012) model; two Dabrowski (1970) theories; some perspectives about underachievement; and some interspersed thoughts about counseling gifted youth. Perspectives about giftedness, programming, and theories vary greatly from country to country, state to state, district to district, and even school to school. Views also often reflect where gifted-education teachers and coordinators received their foundational training. According to their new superintendent, Ben and his colleagues will be asked to put gifted education at arm's length as they ponder program direction. Being aware of theoretical foundations will help them think broadly and avoid having self-interest and personal experiences skew and narrow their perspectives.

* * *

THE ROLE OF CULTURAL VALUES

Findings from two studies exploring cultural bias during identification for program eligibility follow here. These findings underscore that there is no universal agreement about what giftedness "is."

A Study of Teachers' Nominating Language

One pertinent and still rare study (Peterson & Margolin, 1997) was focused on dominant-culture teachers' language in two culturally diverse middle schools. They were invited to nominate students for a hypothetical program for gifted students and asked to justify their nominations. This exploratory study was qualitative, not quantitative, with emerging themes from the teachers' language shedding light on ad hoc criteria arguing for inclusion or exclusion.

The teachers were asked only one open-ended question: Who would you nominate for a program for gifted kids (implied: at the grade levels you teach)? The study was driven by curiosity about biases that might affect identification, particularly when teachers are asked to refer students who might have been missed when group-administered tests are used to screen for eligibility. Students whose scores are above a designated cut-off score are often then studied further.

The unexpected main finding was that the themes reflected what the teachers valued and what fit their cultural experience and self-interest. *Giftedness* was represented by 42 elements or "definitions," including good behavior, verbal facility and assertiveness, a strong work ethic, family status, and social skills—the five major themes in the teachers' language. Intelligence, per se, was mentioned much less often. Achievement, motivation, perfection, dependability, leadership, competitiveness, demonstrating knowledge, and organization were other themes.

Yet when the teachers gathered in pairs or small groups to participate in the study by sharing their views, no one asked for a definition and no one questioned anyone else's views. They seemed to assume agreement about *giftedness*. However, positive attributes became negative if viewed as immoderate (e.g., "excellent student" versus "just working hard"; "demonstrating talent" versus "center of attention"; "quickness" versus "not taking time to go over things," "thorough" versus "overconscientious," "sense of humor" versus "likes to show off").

School counselors may also make assumptions about giftedness, based on personal experiences with gifted students, experiences of friends and family, and skeptical media messages. All of these can skew perceptions of highly able and creative individuals. Levy and Plucker (2008) noted that when "working with gifted and talented clients, it is crucial for counselors to develop an awareness of their assumptions, values, biases, and beliefs about giftedness and the gifted in general, as well as their assumptions about giftedness in culturally diverse children."

A Similar Study of Minority Culture

A second study (Peterson, 1999) explored a similar question in five minority-culture communities: Latino, African American, recent Southeast Asian immigrant, American Indian, and low-income White. Arts as expression, not as achievement, was the main theme for Latinos, followed by humility and community service. For African Americans, it was selfless contribution, followed by making art "out of nothing," concern for family, wisdom, and ability to inspire. For Southeast Asians, it was education as adaptation. Caring for family and asceticism were next. American Indians would not nominate anyone, since they did "not believe in standing out." For low-income White participants, the main theme was helping others, followed by manual dexterity, creativity, overcoming adversity, and nonbookish learning. Shared themes among the five minority-culture participants were related to helping, teaching the young, creativity and versatility, practical learning, and overcoming adversity.

Students Who Are Missed

A dominant-culture teacher might not think of minority-culture students when asked to refer anyone who might have been missed during screening. Teachers might also miss unassertive students, students with low English] proficiency, students with behavioral concerns, students whose parents do not advocate for services or have a regular presence at school events, and students who do not give eye contact and demonstrate eager learning. These bright students might then never participate in gifted-education programs. Dominant-culture teachers may not be aware of what cultural-minority students value and may not know that some cultures do not value the behaviors teachers look for (e.g., assertively demonstrating knowledge, being competitive).

The underachievement of high-ability children and teens who do not fit common *gifted* stereotypes or do not demonstrate qualities deemed by teachers to reflect giftedness is also often missed completely or ignored. In contrast, Thomas, in the Chapter 3 vignette, and his teachers, are from the dominant culture. Most likely, his exceptional intellectual strengths were recognized early and confirmed by tests. He and his teachers have similar cultural values, and his low classroom achievement in middle school frustrated them—and him. It still does in high school.

Teachers' showing interest in and encouraging expression of gifts valued in minority cultures, without being patronizing, might help students feel that they "matter" (A. L. Dixon & Tucker, 2008). School counselors can keep cultural values in mind when engaging bright minority-culture students or students from low-income families and when asked for referrals. Counselors can also advocate for programming that celebrates creativity, for example. Programs should fit and address needs. Too often, gifted children and teens are expected to fit a narrow program curriculum and narrow perspectives about giftedness, needs, and services. Counselors can also engage parents from underrepresented populations in events that offer guidance about current and postsecondary education and celebrate strengths and accomplishments.

. . .
_____

CONCEPTIONS OF GIFTEDNESS

Models and Theories Emphasizing Achievement

Probably few adults in the general public, and educators as well, would question equating giftedness with school achievement. Yet conceptions of giftedness based on ability or intelligence, regardless of achievement, also are part of the gifted-education literature. The former focuses on external, rather than internal, manifestations, usually with an emphasis on how academic achievement influences adult achievement, career choice, and productivity—later. Reflecting this perspective, the emphasis on eminence (Subotnik, Olszewski-Kubilius, & Worrell, 2011) implies that giftedness in adulthood requires eminent production. Silverman (2013) lamented that "the current Zeitgeist—endorsed by the press, popular writers, and national organizations advocating for this [gifted] population" (p. 18)—is focused on the external, on specific domains, and on hard work and motivation, not on developmental differences, such as advanced abstract reasoning and emotional intensity.

Tolan (2013) acknowledged that the tension between those espousing identification and services based on external aspects and those focused on the internal world (i.e., doing versus being, achievement versus development, product-centered versus child-centered) when considering special needs led to a meeting of what became known as the Columbus Group (1991). That group subsequently called attention to the complex differentness of highly and profoundly gifted children's developmental trajectory, beginning at birth—normal for those individuals, but "out of sync with expectations, norms, and averages" (Tolan, 2013, p. 14). Members of the Columbus Group noted complexities and risks associated with passion for learning, questioning, humor, isolation, and confusion about differentness. The group also challenged the talent-development perspective for appearing to view attention to psychosocial concerns as having no purpose other than to ensure success—that is, achievement. They emphasized that professionals need to understand gifted children's atypical, asynchronous development, and their complex subjective experience of it, if they are to help these children cope effectively with a world in which they likely have a poor fit.

Giftedness affects all aspects of life (Silverman, 2013; Yermish, 2010), and the intensity associated with it affects how a gifted child interacts with the world (cf. Daniels & Piechowski, 2009). Roeper (2013), a major force in the focus on the whole gifted child, argued that depth of awareness, view of the world, and structure of the self are all untypically complex, and therefore a child cannot be "partially gifted"—gifted in some areas and not in others.

Grant and Piechowski (1999) argued that achievement-based views suggest that "the most important aspect of being gifted is the ability to turn gifts into recognizable and valued accomplishments" (p. 8), a perspective that takes the focus away from the internal experiences of the child. In fact, according to a position paper entitled "Redefining Giftedness for a New Century: Shifting the Paradigm" (National Association for Gifted Children [NAGC], 2014), giftedness is ultimately manifested primarily in achievement and high levels of motivation, suggesting that achievement *will* occur if the individual is gifted. Such differing views continue to generate dialogue in the field.

Gagné

Gagné's (2004, 2012) Differentiated Model of Giftedness and Talent (DMGT) offers breadth and comprehensiveness regarding giftedness, talent, and talent development. In the DMGT, the transformation of gifts into talents is viewed in developmental terms. However, the model does not explain *how* talents emerge. Possible contributing factors such as emotional maturity, wisdom, or social sensitivity, for example, are not addressed in the model because, according to its creator, each of these has causal factors. Instead, the model presents potential contributors to the process of moving gifts into skills—that is, talents. Gagné argued that high levels of talent require high levels of giftedness, but he also noted that remarkable gifts are not always transformed into talents. In contrast, with dedicated effort and contextual support, individuals with strong, but unremarkable, natural abilities can be successful academically. Gagné's (2007) hierarchy of levels of ability, different from standard-deviation–based categories, is useful when considering program components and advocating for services:

5. Extremely gifted (1:100,000; IQ > 165)
4. Exceptionally gifted (1:10,000; IQ > 155)
3. Highly gifted (1:1000; IQ > 145)
2. Moderately gifted (1:100; IQ > 135)
1. Mildly gifted (IQ > 120)

According to Gagné's model (2012), four components influence talent development. *Giftedness* (intellectual, creative, social, perceptual, muscular, and motor control domains) is a component cluster of natural abilities that develop through maturation and use. Giftedness is most easily recognized in young children because formal learning has not yet moved them toward talents. Ease and speed of learning reflect natural ability. *Intrapersonal catalysts* (e.g., physical traits, mental characteristics, and goal management in the form of awareness, motivation, and volition) help individuals with lofty goals to overcome obstacles, tedium, and setbacks (Gagné, 2010). *Environmental catalysts* (e.g., milieu, significant individuals) and provisions (e.g., services, enrichment, and pedagogy) are social, psychological, and educational.

When the DMGT began, *chance* was in the environmental catalysts component. Because of eager, early support for it, *chance* is now viewed separately, representing elements in life that an individual does not control (e.g., genetic endowment, parents, and parenting).

Important points for counselors to consider are that giftedness is not static, and that gifted students continue to develop. These individuals are affected by factors beyond their control—not only available resources, but also characteristics associated with their level of ability.

KEY CONCEPT

Developmental Roots

Development is at the core of counselor-education curriculum. Licensure and accreditation assume knowledge of human development across the life span. Counselors-in-training become familiar with various developmental theories and write self-reflective papers accordingly. A systems course probably illuminates the complex effects of individual family members' development on the family. Other courses focus on the impact of disability, culture, gender, sexual orientation, economic status, and life events on the course of development. Clinical supervisors probably refer routinely to supervisees' intertwined personal and professional development.

However, just as school counselors may forget to put service delivery at arm's length, consider how to stop focusing mostly on students in crisis, and pay attention to all assigned students, it is easy to forget the continual emphasis on development in their training. School counselors witness developmental progress and stuckness daily, but may not consider those in developmental terms. Their work might benefit from considering the development of identity, relationships, direction, autonomy, and sense of competence *first* when meeting with a student or parent(s), or both together. All are developing, and that ongoing process may be at the heart of the internal and external conflict presented.

Asking where each individual is in various areas of development, and exploring the responses further, might lead to a rare and informative conversation for all involved. Perhaps parents are feeling a gradual loss of control as early adolescents become more and more influenced by peers and differentiated from and within the family. A child's

(continued)

experiences with bullies or other peer relationships may be provoking a parent to relive memories of distress at the same age. A parent's accepting an offer to relocate for a higher salary may have generated an unsettling ripple effect for the children. Anxiety in all family members is not unusual during complex individual and family development. As each experiences developmental transitions, all others react accordingly.

An emphasis on development can be particularly helpful with gifted students and their parents, since it appeals to cognitive strengths. Their rapid-processing brains are sensitive to stimuli not just at school but also at home. Gifted children and teens absorb tension in the family, like any other child, but probably more so. Their strong sense of justice and fairness, their intense empathy, their ability to see how the world *should* be, and their heightened sensitivity can contribute to high distress amid family or peer-relational upheaval. They may worry about their own or others' mental health. Dabrowski's theories of overexcitabilities (OEs) and positive disintegration apply here—especially the latter, which views personal struggle as essential to achieving high levels of personality development. Introducing those concepts to gifted individuals of any age may help them to feel purpose in current distress.

Bourque (2006), based on her developmental study of female underachievers, encouraged researchers to study developmental asynchrony, the malleability of personality, critical periods when change is possible, whether gains in one area of development affect other areas, interventions to address developmental gaps, and the possibility that the therapeutic relationship can meet core developmental needs. One of her findings was that the girls had distanced themselves from invested adults (particularly from their mothers) during a time when connection could be crucial to their well-being. In this regard, school counselors should consider that what they are doing, and how they are being, may in fact be helping to fill a developmental, relational gap for gifted children and teens.

Talent Development

Moon's (2006) talent-development model embraces not just academic development, but also personal, arts, social, and sports development. Each of these types has a chapter devoted to it in an edited book (F. A. Dixon & Moon, 2006) about secondary gifted education. Teachers have the responsibility to design appropriate experiences for developing talents. For all of those areas, the emphasis is on challenging learning experiences, opportunities to develop self-confidence and self-regulation, and family and peer support.

Renzulli

Renzulli's (2005) three-ring conception of giftedness (i.e., above-average intelligence, creativity, and task commitment) is represented by a Venn diagram, with the overlapping area indicating gifted *behaviors*. This model is achievement oriented in its emphasis on motivation and production. Identification generally involves casting a wide net, with the goal of recognizing and clustering a broad pool of students with "potential giftedness," including those without socioeconomic advantages. The implication is that someone is gifted when potential becomes production. The *Schoolwide Enrichment Model (SEM)* is widely used as a framework for programs.

Total Cluster Grouping

Total School Cluster Grouping (TSCG; Gentry & Mann, 2009; Peters et al., 2014) also serves a broad range of students and has been increasingly adopted in the education of gifted children. It is a whole-school approach, particularly geared toward the elementary level, because secondary-level schools tend to have some degree of leveled learning already in place, based on achievement.

In this model, standard deviation—a measure of variability—on one or more standardized assessments is used to form clusters of students with less variability in achievement than is usually found in regular classrooms. Variability still exists, but teachers can more easily differentiate curriculum and instruction, including for advanced students. Evaluation occurs at least annually, and possibly more frequently, allowing students to move in and out of five clusters according to need: high-achieving, above-average achieving, average achieving, low-average achieving, and low-achieving. Teacher recommendations are important for placement, changing placement, and differentiation. Other distinguishing features are that local norms are used, and placement is based on current achievement levels.

Betts

The Autonomous Learner Model (ALM; Betts & Kercher, 1999) addresses emotional, social, and cognitive needs of gifted learners. Of potential interest to school counselors are learner-directed group discussions on various topics and member-selected activities. Autonomous Learner is the last type of six categories of gifted and talented youth often used to guide services (Betts & Neihart,

1988), following Successful (e.g., navigating the system successfully, but may underachieve later), Challenging (e.g., frustrated, struggling with authority, may have high-risk behavior), Underground (i.e., insecurely and anxiously hiding gifts and talents), Dropouts (e.g., angry, focused on outside interests, typically identified late), and Double-labeled (e.g., gifted; disability; using humor to cope with feeling ignored or criticized).

Models and Theories Emphasizing Affective Development

Dabrowski

Dabrowski's (1970; Dabrowski & Piechowski, 1977) complex theory of positive disintegration (TPD) has had considerable impact on the social and emotional arenas of the gifted-education field for several decades, especially on clinicians specializing in giftedness and on scholars exploring the subjective internal world of gifted youth. As a psychiatrist and psychologist in Poland, Dabrowski formulated the theory after he perceived an association between giftedness and multilevel development in his clients. The concept of overexcitability (OE) is basic to the theory and has had some research attention (e.g., Mendaglio & Tillier, 2006; Tieso, 2007). Though TPD and OE have probably not influenced identification and programming directly, they are important for explaining feelings and behaviors of gifted children and teens.

In TPD (Dabrowski, 1970; Mendaglio, 2008), a theory of moral and emotional development, very few people reach Level 5, characterized by integrity, compassion, a lack of inner conflict, and altruism after overcoming great and extended distress. Self-mastery is associated with Level 4, with a commitment to a life of integrity. Level 3 reflects a new awareness of the possibility of living without anger, doubt, and reactivity, and instead with an intact moral compass. Levels 1 and 2 are about "normal people," with self-interest and awareness of others' judgments, respectively, without a sense of self-mastery.

Positive disintegration can occur when someone experiences great suffering, finds that old coping strategies are not effective, and slides into psychic disintegration, with the possibility of devolving into psychosis. However, gifted individuals may have the capacity for positive, rather than negative, disintegration—that is, moving toward the higher levels of personality development. Peterson (2012, 2014) found, in a 15-year longitudinal study of a gifted female survivor of multiple traumas, that not only was giftedness equally an asset and a burden as she struggled dangerously with posttraumatic distress, but her experiences also epitomized positive disintegration. TPD can be useful, and sometimes life-altering, when children and teens with extreme ability and extremely negative life circumstances meet with a counselor knowledgeable about it. This theory can be applied to help those with high distress make sense of their responses and have hope that they will not only survive, but also experience enhanced development as a result of their struggle.

Intellectual, emotional, imaginational, psychomotor, and sensual psychic OEs are often referred to with words such as *intensified, accelerated,* and *heightened* (Mendaglio & Tillier, 2006). When teachers, counselors, and parents observe emotional expression or behaviors that can be so described, there may be opportunities to help gifted youth make sense of themselves by acquainting them with TPD and OE. OE can be both positive (e.g., striving for understanding, creativity, openness, invention, fantasy, heightened emotional responses) and negative (e.g., extremes of feeling, inhibition, strong affective memory, anxiety, depressive modes, nervousness, tics, inner tension). Sensual and emotional OEs appeared to drive the young woman in Peterson's (2012, 2014) study forward, helping her survive, until intellectual OE gave her enough feelings of safety and control to allow emotions. Becoming aware of TPD in early adulthood helped her find meaning in her intense struggles. She could acknowledge the resulting resilience, wisdom, and leadership.

Silverman

One pillar of Silverman's (2013) perspectives is the concept of asynchronous development, which is a core concept of her edited book (Silverman, 1993) on counseling gifted youth as well as in her clinical work. Asynchronous development is inherent in the *gifted* label, since giftedness means having aptitude or performance in the top percentiles on a bell curve of some trait or behavior, reflecting significant differences from placement elsewhere on the curve. The term can refer to the difference between mental and chronological age as well—that is, IQ. Asynchrony can also refer to a marked difference between cognitive and social or emotional development, sometimes resulting in highly able children or teens being perceived as immature (Alsop, 2003), even though they are like most age-peers socially or emotionally. When they try to apply their cognitive strengths to gain control in chaotic situations, they may feel emotionally out of control (Jackson & Peterson, 2003). When tragedies occur, either close or far away, they might understand moral, political, or natural-disaster aspects of the events, yet not be emotionally developed enough to cope with the aftermath. Asynchronous development is important for anyone involved in the education of gifted youth to keep in mind, but particularly counselors, who can help these children and teens make sense of themselves by offering pertinent psychoeducational information and opportunities to interact with gifted peers about it.

Colangelo

In Colangelo's (2003) strengths-based, developmental approach to counseling gifted youth, a counselor creates a therapeutic environment conductive to educational growth, but the approach is not intended to be therapy. Educational goals are the focus, and social and emotional development supports those goals. Gifted students do not need to be determined to be at risk; this approach is appropriate for all gifted students.

Webb

The first author of the seminal *Guiding the Gifted Child* (Webb, Meckstroth, & Tolan, 1982) established a still-thriving program in which individuals are trained to facilitate discussion groups focused on parenting gifted youth (Webb, Gore, Amend, & DeVries, 2007). More recently, he and several colleagues (Webb et al., 2005) published another seminal book on the misdiagnosis of characteristics of giftedness (e.g., intensity, OE, sensitivity to environmental stimuli) as pathology (e.g., deficient attention, hyperactivity, bipolar disorder, oppositional defiance). Also pertinent here are Webb's (2013) theoretical perspectives related to existential depression in gifted children and teens, who become disillusioned when their view of the world is tarnished by what they experience personally or observe in the media, for example. Knowledgeable counselors can apply these perspectives when counseling gifted youth and when creating affective curriculum collaboratively with gifted-education personnel.

Peterson

The Peterson Proactive Developmental Attention (PPDA) model (Peterson & Jen, in press; see also Chapter 7) is based on the belief that gifted children and teens, like any age peers, do not typically engage in conversations about feelings and behaviors with references to development. *Proactive* attention is especially important for gifted students because they are often able to hide distress well (Peterson, 2001a; Peterson & Rischar, 2000). *Developmental* attention is focused on developmental tasks and challenges. The PPDA model is a framework that can be applied in individual and group counseling and in affective curriculum in classrooms. It can be useful and effective across cultures and ethnicities, socioeconomic circumstances, achievement levels, personality types, and school social groups, since all gifted children and teens are still developing and may believe that no one can understand them. Though this model assumes that well-being affects motivation and the ability to focus on academics, it does not put disproportionate emphasis on performance or products.

• • •

UNDERACHIEVERS: WHERE ARE THEY IN THE PICTURE?

One of Ben's concerns is how and where his currently underachieving gifted students fit into the confusing mix of theories. It is important to meet gifted underachievers where they are, not where educators and parents think they ought to be, and not be preoccupied with the future. Underachievers need to be identified and involved in programming, regardless of achievement level. Being with intellectual peers might validate their ability when they are losing faith in it and might help them survive depression, abuse, neglect, chaos, peer conflict, or disillusionment (Peterson, 2001b; see also Webb, 2013). They may be as intellectually gifted as their high-achieving peers, may be grappling with developmental challenges sensitively and even dangerously, and may eventually change in a positive direction (Peterson, 2000, 2001a, 2001b, 2002).

Unfortunately, identification and programming based strictly on achievement do not usually generate services for gifted underachievers, as Ben knows well, although some programs might keep the door open with annual reassessment. Rigid, rigorous programming may not appeal to underachievers or may require more focus than is possible at a particular time. Peterson's several studies of underachievers, cited earlier, led her to conclude that underachievement is largely developmental, involving struggles related to identity, direction, relationships, autonomy, and emotional differentiation. The incidence of positive change before leaving high school or during college or graduate school argues that programming should accommodate gifted underachievers with components that appeal to their intellect and talents, keep them interacting with intellectual peers and with school, and embrace them in the present (Peterson, 2009).

• • •

CONCLUDING THOUGHTS AND RECOMMENDATIONS

Perhaps more than they and even the students realize, school counselors can have significant impact on how gifted children and teens experience school. Service and support might take the form of helping them understand and cope with complicated feelings and behaviors, advocating for a child whose parents are challenging a rigid cut-off score for eligibility with no consideration of measurement error, or helping a teen self-advocate for enrollment in an advanced class, for example. In each situation, the process of following up with the student, program personnel, policy-making teachers, or parents is similar to actions on behalf of any other student.

When optimally prepared to deal with complex and potentially political situations involving gifted students, school counselors are aware of characteristics associated with giftedness, which may have some bearing on presenting problems. In addition, they are knowledgeable about district philosophy about gifted-education services. They are also aware of policies and practices related to teacher and parent referrals for gifted-education programming. Finally, they are aware of at least some theories and perspectives that drive identification for programs and services.

The vignette about Ben offers a context for several recommendations. Gifted-education program leaders should include school counselors in the process of assessing needs and determining direction. Both during the process of identifying gifted children and adolescents and when conceptualizing programs, school counselors can gain crucial awareness through interaction with gifted-education teachers, and the latter can gain from counselors' expertise in social and emotional development and alertness to needs and concerns. Counselors should request to attend gifted-education conferences now and then, not only to gain knowledge to help them advocate for gifted students who do not fit stereotypical profiles, but also to increase their understanding that common theories of giftedness may limit attention to stressors that affect both high and low academic achievers. In general, school counselors should observe critically and pay attention to whether school demographics, the identification process, program philosophy, and program components fit together appropriately at all school levels.

Ben's viewing gifted students as an "extreme," complex population, warranting special services to address critical needs, is a good start. By being involved in gifted-education processes, counselors can increase their knowledge, awareness, and appreciation of the *culture* of giftedness (Levy & Plucker, 2008; Yermish, 2010), helping them engage in it comfortably, skillfully, and effectively.

*   *   *

REFERENCES

Alsop, G. (2003). Asynchrony: Intuitively valid and theoretically reliable. *Roeper Review*, *25*, 118–127.

Betts, G. T., & Kercher, J. K. (1999). *Autonomous learner model: Optimizing ability*. Greeley, CO: ALPS Publishing.

Betts, G. T., & Neihart, M. (1988). Profiles of the gifted and talented. *Gifted Child Quarterly*, *32*(2), 248–253.

Bland, L. C. (2012). Achievement-based conceptions of giftedness. In T. L. Cross & J. R. Cross (Eds.), *Handbook for counselors serving students with gifts and talents* (pp. 21–38). Waco, TX: Prufrock Press.

Bourque, J. V. (2006). *Academically underachieving and achieving adolescent girls: Quantitative and qualitative differences in self-efficacy, planning, and developmental asynchrony*. Unpublished dissertation, York University, Toronto, ON.

Colangelo, N. (2003). Counseling gifted students. In N. Colangelo & G. A. Davis (Eds.), *Handbook of gifted education* (3rd ed., pp. 373–387). Boston, MA: Allyn & Bacon.

Columbus Group. (1991). Unpublished transcript of the meeting of the Columbus Group, Columbus, OH.

Cross, T. L., & Coleman, L. J. (2005). School-based conception of giftedness. In R. J. Sternberg & J. E. Davidson (Eds.), *Conceptions of giftedness* (2nd ed., pp. 52–63). Cambridge, UK: Cambridge University Press.

Dabrowski, K. (1970). *Mental growth through positive disintegration.* London, UK: Gryf.

Dabrowski, K., & Piechowski, M. M. (1977). *Theory of levels of emotional development* (Vol. 1: Multilevelness and positive disintegration). Oceanside, NY: Dabor Science Publications.

Daniels, S., & Piechowski, M. M. (Eds.). (2009). *Living with intensity: Understanding the sensitivity, excitability, and emotional development of gifted children, adolescents, and adults.* Scottsdale, AZ: Great Potential Press.

Dixon, A. L., & Tucker, C. (2008). Every student matters: Enhancing strengths-based school counseling through the application of mattering. *Professional School Counseling, 12*, 123–126.

Dixon, F. A., & Moon, S. M. (Eds.). (2006). *The handbook of secondary gifted education.* Waco, TX: Prufrock Press.

Gagné, F. (2004). Transforming gifts into talents: The DMGT as a developmental theory. *High Ability Studies, 15*, 119–147.

Gagné, F. (2007). Ten commandments for academic talent development. *Gifted Child Quarterly, 51*, 93–118. doi:10.1177/0016986206296660

Gagné, F. (2010). Motivation within the DMGT 2.0 framework. *High Ability Studies, 21*, 81–99.

Gagné, F. (2012). Differentiated model of giftedness and talent. In T. L. Cross & J. R. Cross (Eds.), *Handbook for counselors serving students with gifts & talents* (pp. 3–20). Waco, TX: Prufrock Press.

Gentry, M., & Mann, R. L. (2009). *Total school cluster grouping and differentiation: A comprehensive, research-based plan for raising student achievement and improving teacher practices.* Waco, TX: Prufrock Press.

Grant, B., & Piechowski, M. M. (1999). Theories and the good: Toward a child-centered gifted education. *Gifted Child Quarterly, 43*, 4–12.

Jackson, P. S., & Peterson, J. S. (2003). Depressive disorder in highly gifted adolescents. *Journal for Secondary Gifted Education, 14*(3), 175–186.

Levy, J. L., & Plucker, J. A. (2008). A multicultural competence model for counseling gifted and talented children. *Journal of School Counseling, 6*(4). Retrieved from http://www.jsc.montana.edu/articles/v6n4.pdf

Mendaglio, S. (2008). Dabrowski's theory of positive disintegration: A personality theory for the 21st century. In S. Mendaglio (Ed.), *Dabrowski's theory of positive disintegration* (pp. 13–40). Scottsdale, AZ: Great Potential Press.

Mendaglio, S., & Tillier, W. (2006). Dabrowski's theory of positive disintegration and giftedness: Overexcitability research findings. *Journal for the Education of the Gifted, 30*, 68–87.

Moon, S. M. (2006). Talent development in adolescence: An overview. In F. A. Dixon & S. M. Moon (Eds.), *The handbook of secondary gifted education* (pp. 198–201). Waco, TX: Prufrock Press.

National Association for Gifted Children. (2014). *Redefining giftedness for a new century: Shifting the paradigm*. Retrieved from https://www.nagc.org/about -nagc-position- statements-white-papers on September 1, 2016.

National Association for Gifted Children, & Council of State Directors of Programs for the Gifted. (2015). *State of the states in gifted education: 2014–2015*. Washington, DC: Author.

Peters, S. J., Matthews, M. S., McBee, M. T., & McCoach, D. B. (2014). *Beyond gifted education: Designing and implementing advanced academic programs*. Waco, TX: Prufrock Press.

Peterson, J. S. (1999). Gifted—through whose cultural lens? An application of the postpositivistic mode of inquiry. *Journal for the Education of the Gifted, 22*, 354–383.

Peterson, J. S. (2000). A follow-up study of one group of achievers and underachievers four years after high school graduation. *Roeper Review, 22*, 217–224.

Peterson, J. S. (2001a). Gifted and at risk: Four longitudinal case studies. *Roeper Review, 24*, 31–39.

Peterson, J. S. (2001b). Successful adults who were once adolescent underachievers. *Gifted Child Quarterly, 45*, 236–249.

Peterson, J. S. (2002). A longitudinal study of post-high-school development in gifted individuals at risk for poor educational outcomes. *Journal for Secondary Gifted Education, 14*, 6–18.

Peterson, J. S. (2009). Focusing on where they are: A clinical perspective. In J. VanTassel-Baska, T. R. Cross, & R. Olenchak (Eds.), *Social-emotional curriculum with gifted and talented students* (pp. 193–226). Waco, TX: National Association for Gifted Children/Prufrock Press.

Peterson, J. S. (2012). The asset–burden paradox of giftedness: A 15-year phenomenological, longitudinal case study. *Roeper Review, 34*, 1–17. doi:10.1080/02783193 .2012.715336

Peterson, J. S. (2014). Giftedness, trauma, and development: A longitudinal case study. *Journal for the Education of the Gifted, 37*, 295–318.

Peterson, J. S., & Jen, E. (in press). The Peterson Proactive Developmental Attention (PPDA) model: Nurturing the whole gifted child. *Journal for the Education of the Gifted*.

Peterson, J. S., & Margolin, L. (1997). Naming gifted children: An example of unintended "reproduction." *Journal for the Education of the Gifted, 21*, 82–100.

Peterson, J. S., & Rischar, H. (2000). Gifted and gay: A study of the adolescent experience. *Gifted Child Quarterly, 44*, 149–164.

Renzulli, J. (2005). The three-ring conception of giftedness: A developmental model for promoting creative productivity. In R. J. Sternberg & J. E. Davidson (Eds.), *Conceptions of giftedness* (pp. 246–279). Cambridge, UK: Cambridge University Press.

Roeper, A. (2013). Asynchrony and sensitivity. In C. S. Neville, M. M. Piechowski, & S. S. Tolan (Eds.), *Off the charts: Asynchrony and the gifted child* (pp. 146–157). Unionville, NY: Royal Fireworks Press.

Silverman, L. K. (Ed.). (1993). *Counseling the gifted and talented*. Denver, CO: Love.

Silverman, L. K. (2013). Asynchronous development: Theoretical bases and current applications. In C. S. Neville, M. M. Piechowski, & S. S. Tolan (Eds.), *Off the charts: Asynchrony and the gifted child* (pp. 18–47). Unionville, NY: Royal Fireworks Press.

Subotnik, R. F., Olszewski-Kubilius, P., & Worrell, F. C. (2011). Rethinking giftedness and gifted education: A proposed direction forward based on psychological science. *Psychological Science in the Public Interest, 12,* 3–54.

Tieso, C. L. (2007). Patterns of overexcitabilities in identified gifted students and their parents: A hierarchical model. *Gifted Child Quarterly, 51,* 11–22.

Tolan, S. S. (2013). Hollingworth, Dabrowski, Gandhi, Columbus, and some others: The history of the Columbus Group. In C. S. Neville, M. M. Piechowski, & S. S. Tolan (Eds.), *Off the charts: Asynchrony and the gifted child* (pp. 9–17). Unionville, NY: Royal Fireworks Press.

Webb, J. T. (2013). *Searching for meaning: Idealism, bright minds, disillusionment, and hope.* Tucson, AZ: Great Potential Press.

Webb, J. T., Amend, E. R., Webb, N. E., Goerss, J., Beljan, P., & Olenchak, F. R. (2005). *Misdiagnosis and dual diagnoses of gifted children and adults: ADHD, bipolar, OCD, Asperger's, depression, and other disorders.* Scottsdale, AZ: Great Potential Press.

Webb, J. T., Gore, J. L., Amend, E. R., & DeVries, A. R. (2007). *A parent's guide to gifted children.* Tucson, AZ: Great Potential Press.

Webb, J. T., Meckstroth, E. A., & Tolan, S. S. (1982). *Guiding the gifted child: A practical source for parents and teachers.* Dayton: Ohio Psychology Press.

Yermish, A. (2010). *Cheetahs on the couch: Issues affecting the therapeutic working alliance with clients who are cognitively gifted.* Available at ProQuest Dissertations and Theses Database (UMI NO. 3415722).

...

Identifying Gifted and Talented Learners in Schools: Common Practices and Best Practices

TAMRA STAMBAUGH AND SUSANNAH M. WOOD

Ben, the middle school counselor from Chapter 5, continues to work with the district's task force. There, he also meets Julie the district's coordinator of gifted and talented services. Based on the superintendent's concerns, Julie wants to re-imagine the district's identification and programming for gifted youth. Ben's experiences have given Julie new insights into potential roles of school counselors when working with high-ability learners and their parents. Julie was particularly drawn to Ben's discussions of talking with parents about why their students were not identified. Ben's frustrations with the gifted services have also included the pervasive mythology that the program is a "cookie" program used as a reward for "good" students with "good" behavior and even better grades—a myth that disenfranchises diverse populations in the school district, including underachieving students, and doesn't accurately identity those students who may need services. Historically, because the district has implemented identification procedures in third grade, Julie has contacted several of the elementary school counselors in her district to get their perspectives. She is surprised by the range of their knowledge about identification and the degree of the school counselors' involvement in this process. While Ben has informed her that all practicing school counselors have training in testing and assessment, not all have connected this with identification practices for gifted learners—until they meet with their first parent.

Few practicing school counselors have formal training focused on working with gifted students as a special population (Peterson & Wachter, 2010). However, school counselors from Council for Accreditation of Counseling and Related

Educational Programs (CACREP)–accredited school counseling preparation programs have essential knowledge and skills to interpret a wide range of tests, assessments, and other types of student appraisal (CACREP, 2015). School counselors also frequently utilize behavioral, personality, and career inventories and suicide assessments and interpret scores from an array of educational measures, including the ACT and the SAT, to support students' mental, social, and academic well-being. They may also get to know students and see their academic strengths in ways that are not possible in a general classroom setting. Therefore, they can have a role when students are evaluated for eligibility for gifted-education programming. The process of identification is multifaceted, involving multiple stakeholders and data sources. Some school counselors are active in the process, while others are confused about where they might fit in it. According to a pertinent American School Counselor Association (ASCA) position statement (2013, p. 28), school counselors are to provide consultation, when appropriate, during identification of gifted and talented students. Applying multiple criteria to that process is recommended and often required in school districts, related, for example, to intellectual ability; academic performance; visual and performing arts; practical arts; creative thinking; leadership; parent, teacher, or peer nomination; or expert evaluation (National Association for Gifted Children [NAGC] & Council of State Directors for Programs of the Gifted, 2015). Although school counselors may be involved in analyzing data from various sources about areas of strength, they are not responsible for coordinating, administering, and/or collecting any of the assessments used during the selection process. School counselors can serve as members of the identification team to discuss students' strengths, needs for gifted education programming, and social and emotional concerns that may hinder identifying unique gifts.

The school counselors' role in the identification process should be clearly articulated and should include whether or not he or she will be the person to contact parents to discuss students' needs and services. School counselors, school psychologists, and gifted-education colleagues may be asked to interpret or explain test scores, discuss why a student was not deemed eligible for a gifted-education program, and potentially act as a "buffer" when these discussions become heated or confusing (Chandler, 2012, p. 564).

To provide these services to teachers and parents, school counselors must first be knowledgeable about theories that drive identification of high-ability youth (Chapter 5) and about best practices for identifying them. This chapter presents an overview of what school counselors need to know about identification to provide effective consultation for parents and teachers and to be helpful allies to educators of gifted children and teens in their districts. Five key principles and best practices for effective identification are examined first, followed by discussion of these implications for school counselors.

• • •
_____

WHAT IS KNOWN ABOUT IDENTIFYING GIFTED STUDENTS?

For a talent to be developed, it must first be recognized and nurtured. Because there is no perfect identification system or one assessment that will find every student, school counselors and educators must be talent scouts (ASCA, 2013), constantly on the lookout for emerging talents, including those that may have been overlooked or overshadowed by behavioral issues, twice-exceptionalities, lack of access, financial barriers, constricting definitions of *gifted*, or cultural differences and norms that may not coincide with prevailing notions of talent in the district. They also can advocate for changing poorly implemented identification protocols or ill-conceived policies. Most individuals involved in the field of gifted education are probably acutely aware of inequitable identification of students who are Hispanic, are African American, speak a second language, or are from low-income families. Calls for action include using less biased measures (Naglieri & Ford, 2003), changing testing systems to ensure more equity (Lohman, 2005a; Worrell & Erwin, 2011), and working toward more equitable practices at state and national levels (NAGC, 2008, 2011).

Historically, identification of gifted, talented, and other high-ability students has involved significant challenges. First, as discussed in Chapter 5, conflicting conceptualizations of giftedness have led to no central definition of *giftedness*: "Although there is a federal definition of giftedness in the No Child Left Behind Act (P.L. 107-110 [Title IX, Part A, Definition 22] [2002]; 20 USC 7801[22] [2004]), states have the authority to determine their own definition to guide identification and programming options" (NAGC & Council of State Directors for Programs of the Gifted, 2015, p. 27). Differing state definitions drive which constructs are utilized and which tests are employed, as well as whether there should be threshold cut-off scores or more fluid approaches in the process of identification (Erwin & Worrell, 2011; Lohman, 2005a, 2006; Pfeiffer, 2002). In a recent survey, 37 of the 39 states responding had a state definition of *gifted* and *talented*, including intellectually gifted, creativity, visual/performing arts, academically gifted, and/or specific academic areas, for example. Few states mentioned of culturally diverse, twice-exceptional, rural students, or English language learners in their definitions (NAGC & Council of State Directors for Programs of the Gifted, 2015).

Another difficulty is the lack of a federal mandate for gifted education in the United States, which leaves states to create their own policies and definitions and to determine whether services for gifted students will be funded or given priority:

> In the absence of a federal mandate, gifted education programming decisions are made at the state level, or more often by local school districts. A few states could be said to be leaders in the gifted education field, based on one or more of the following: funding, identification practices, oversight and reporting,

supportive policies, and teacher preparation. However, a far greater number of states provide little, if any funding to local schools, leaving both funding and service delivery issues to local school districts. (NAGC, n.d.)

Because of the absence of a federal mandate for gifted education, most funding for programming and services for gifted children and teens is determined by the states. The Jacob Javits Gifted and Talented Students Education Act (Javits Act), which has been the only federal funding source for gifted education, was initially authorized in 1998 as a part of the Elementary and Secondary Act. Javits funding supports programming research (specifically the National Research and Development Center for the Education of Gifted and Talented Children and Youth), interventions, and strategies, with a focus on identifying and serving gifted students from marginalized populations (e.g., twice-exceptional students, English language learners). The Javits Act was unfunded from 2011 to 2013, but was refunded in 2014 by Congress as the reauthorization of the Every Student Succeeds Act. Limited funding for identification, services, and competitive research grants is determined each legislative fiscal year, and allotment is often subject to competing educational priorities. Thus, when federal funds or mandates for identification and services are not appropriated, the burden for financing all gifted programming falls to the states, rendering gifted education largely "local" in its articulation.

According to the 2014 to 2015 *State of the State Report* (NAGC & Council of State Directors of Programs for the Gifted, 2015, p. 11), "[although] decentralization allows for states to respond to the specific needs of their population, it results in a wide disparity in services across and within states. In states that did provide direction, there was often a lack of specificity, leaving it to the local education agencies to determine best practices." Since gifted education is indeed "local," various students may or may not be identified, depending on what a school district deems to constitute giftedness or what states or districts can afford to serve adequately or choose to emphasize. Some states have a "top down" structure, in which the state department puts forth mandates or provides a series of options to school districts for identification, including specific criteria and procedures. Other states grant more autonomy to local districts in regard to criteria used. Therefore, students might be identified as gifted in one district or state, but not in another. For example, some states may identify only those with exceptional general intellectual ability while others identify specific areas of exceptional academic strength such as math, reading, social studies, and/or science. Other states may also mandate identification of creativity, leadership, and visual-performing arts. Some may identify 3% of their population; others may identify the top 5% to 10%. Still others may identify potential for performance or identify only documented performance and motivation (Pfeiffer, 2002).

Counselors are probably aware of these differences but may not be aware of how states and districts identify gifted students and how these decisions affect program implementation. Depending on a state's definition and policies, there will likely be a need to recognize the talents of students in areas that are not within state policy. For example, if a state recognizes high ability but does not recognize individual, subject-specific talent domains as then some students who would benefit greatly from services could be overlooked.

• • •

WHAT DO SCHOOL COUNSELORS NEED TO KNOW ABOUT IDENTIFYING TALENT?

Because few teachers, counselors, psychologists, and administrators are required to take formal training courses in gifted education, myths and misconceptions about giftedness can interfere with appropriate identification of talent. Educators, through lack of pertinent knowledge and awareness, may not recognize exceptional strengths if not demonstrated in familiar ways (Peterson, 1999). Table 6.1 illustrates both common misconceptions about identification and guiding principles

TABLE 6.1

COMMON MISCONCEPTIONS AND GUIDING PRINCIPLES FOR IDENTIFICATION OF GIFTED STUDENTS

Common Misconceptions	Guiding Principles for Best Practice in Identification
1. One assessment tool can accurately capture all types of ability.	1. Multiple assessments and qualified teams are necessary for equitable identification.
2. Gifted students will automatically emerge whether you look for them or not.	2. Whole-grade screening happens early and often. All individuals in the school district are talent scouts.
3. Gifted students perform well in all subjects/areas.	3. While students may (or may not) have the ability/interest to perform well in multiple subject areas, they are likely to display their giftedness in specific academic domains. They may also have dual exceptionalities that suppress performance in certain subjects.
4. A one-size-fits-all approach to identification results in finding talent in all populations.	4. Context, experience, program goals, and school/individual values affect whether students are identified.
5. A one-size-fits-all approach to gifted services results in meeting the needs of the students identified as gifted.	5. Services provided should match the talents identified.

for best practice. Five key principles for practice are offered here as guidelines for moving toward an effective system for identifying gifted students and are discussed at greater length in the following sections. If these are not reflected in a systemic protocol, then school counselors can follow protocols for reassessing students, work with students to find outlets to showcase strengths, and advocate for an appropriate identification protocol.

Principle 1: Multiple Measures and Qualified Teams are Necessary for Equitable Identification.

Multiple measures are to be utilized as part of a multidimensional approach to identifying students (Erwin & Worrell, 2011; Lohman, 2005a; Pfeiffer, 2002; Stambaugh, 2007). Students should not be excluded, on the basis of one assessment, from consideration for services. A strong identification system includes multiple assessments, both quantitative and qualitative. Ability and achievement are typically measured by nationally normed, standardized quantitative assessments such as ability or IQ tests and achievement tests. These may be administered in a group setting or individually. Qualitative measurement involves behavioral checklists, teacher recommendations, student interviews, academic performance, classroom participation, portfolios of student work, and/or auditions.

Results of standardized quantitative assessments may be examined by subtest category as well as overall indices. Simply looking at a full-scale ability score without considering possible discrepancies in subtest scores, for example, or testing for only nonverbal or verbal ability while ignoring other areas of strength does not provide adequate information to determine the level and types of services a student might need (Lohman, 2005b). Similarly, students with advanced spatial ability may be missed without the administration of assessments sensitive to meeting their needs (Lubinski, 2010). In other situations, students who have severe test anxiety or have not been exposed to advanced levels of learning, but learn quickly and with abstraction after exposure, may not score as high on some quantitative assessments but demonstrate a strong qualitative profile through advanced performance and motivation in areas of strength. They should not be excluded from consideration solely because of their quantitative scores (See reference section for the NAGC position statement on the Wechsler Intelligence Scale for Children, Fourth Edition (WISC-IV).

After various data are collected, a school team should examine all available data to determine what a child needs and the best placement for developing strengths. At that point, individual subtest scores, experience, qualitative performance, and other data are discussed to provide a holistic portrait of potential and needs. Gaps and deficits may be noted in a profile; however, the purpose of identification is to identify and promote student strengths and not to remediate weakness. Exclusion from the identification process or services simply because a student does not produce homework, has sloppy handwriting, is distracted in class, has difficulty coping with frustration or ignores basic skill-type work, for example, is not appropriate. Instead, those behaviors may suggest need for services. Moreover, discrepancies in assessment profiles may indicate that a student is twice-exceptional or lacks access to advanced content. Therefore, an identification team needs to include individuals who know how to read student profiles, interpret assessments, and articulate the unique needs and characteristics of gifted students.

Principle 2: Whole-Grade Screening Happens Early and Often. All Individuals in the School District are Talent Scouts.

Because few educators and school counselors receive training related to gifted students, relying on teacher, counselor or parent recommendation as the primary means of identification is likely to exclude many students from the talent pool, especially those who are members of minority cultures and ethnicities (McBee, 2006, 2010) or from low income backgrounds (McBee, 2006; Plucker, Hardesty, & Burroughs, 2013; Stambaugh, 2007). According to the 2014 to 2015 State of the States report (NAGC & Council of State Directors for Programs of the Gifted, 2015), while districts may use multiple measures to identify gifted students, these measures are used only after a referral. This timing is problematic when families are unaware not only of the identification process, but also of how they might advocate for their child within it and when. In addition, negative behaviors because students are not challenged academically may discourage some teachers from referring students initially or in the future. Therefore, universal assessments or screening tools administered to all students should be part of a standardized protocol, at a minimum, for each grade-level cluster (i.e., primary grades, intermediate grades, middle school, and high school). The screening protocol should cast a wide net and include liberal cut-off scores and qualitative assessments. When all individuals in the school are scouts looking for strengths, and all students have similar opportunity to showcase their potential through whole grade access to the same level of testing, students are less likely to be overlooked. Gifted students who are quiet, refuse to do mundane work when content is already known, or who display their talents in nontraditional ways need scouts so their strengths can be recognized.

Principle 3: While Students May (or May Not) Have The Ability/ Interest to Perform Well in Multiple Subject Areas, They are Likely to Display Their Talents in Specific Academic Domains. Valid and Reliable Assessments are Essential.

Collectively, gifted students vary widely in shape, size, ethnicity, income level, ability level, and interests. Assessments must be reliable and valid for this complex school population (Lohman, 2005a; Pfeiffer, 2002). While group tests are relatively easy to administer, some gifted students' knowledge extends beyond what a group test designed for a specific grade level measures, precluding an accurate measure of their capabilities. Extended norms for individual assessments (Silverman, 2013) and local norms or out-of-level group assessments (Lohman, 2005a) allow a better understanding of what children are capable of as well as which students need more intensive services to develop their advanced strengths within the context of their local school. Similarly, district- or state-created checklists, benchmark assessments, or other local district sources may lack validity or reliability for accurately identifying gifted individuals if these have not been normed for that population. For example, if referral checklist says "uses a large vocabulary," what constitutes such a vocabulary for those who are not English proficient versus those who have traveled internationally? It is important to know if a measure has technical adequacy data available and if specific scales were normed or designed specifically for a particular population (Peters & Gentry, 2010).

Another issue related to reliability and validity of assessments includes their intended purposes. If students have quantitative strengths but are administered only a verbal assessment during screening, their strengths may be missed. The same is true for administering only a nonverbal assessment in hopes of finding populations underrepresented in gifted education (Lohman, 2005b). When they assess only one construct (e.g., verbal, nonverbal), evaluators miss as many students as are found (Lohman, 2005b; Pfeiffer, 2002).

Valid and reliable assessments are then used to determine which areas of strength need further development and acceleration beyond the typical classroom environment. Although students may have a high IQ, their talents are likely to be demonstrated in a specific content domain. High ability is manifest in a specific content area (Subotnik, Olszewski-Kubilius, & Worrell, 2011). Therefore, the examination of full profile to determine the motivation, interest, performance, and strengths of a student is imperative to determine which content domain(s) require accelerated and enriched learning opportunities beyond what the classroom provides.

Principle 4: Context, Experience, Program Goals, and School/Individual Values Affect Whether Students Are Identified.

The aforementioned principles support equitable identification for all students; however, additional considerations for special populations are also important, especially for those typically underrepresented, such as low-income, culturally diverse, or twice-exceptional (e.g., giftedness coinciding with learning disability, attention deficit hyperactivity disorder [ADHD], autism spectrum, or behavioral issues) students. A few suggestions for supporting identification and talent development of students from underrepresented groups follow.

Encourage Early-Access Programs That Promote Thinking Skills and Habits of a Scholar

Many young-scholar programs have been instituted, such as the Fairfax Young Scholar Model in Fairfax County, Virginia. These programs provide early teaching of thinking skills to all students. Educators then become talent scouts, watching for students who show enormous growth or thrive when exposed to more advanced reasoning, critical-thinking, and problem-solving opportunities. Underrepresented students are more likely to be formally identified through typical identification systems when they have had opportunities to access advanced curriculum and instruction with scaffolding, and their teachers are aware of various ways in which some students may show their talents (Horn, 2015). This is especially pertinent when multidimensional assessments (i.e., quantitative and qualitative) are used—not just test scores. Other programs, such as the Jack Kent Cooke Young Scholars initiative, provide paths to college access by supporting high-ability, low-income students from middle school through high school with mentors, advanced academics, and guidance for developing scholarly habits. According to data from the Cooke initiative, students involved in an early college identification program are more likely than others are more likely than those who are not involved to attend and complete college and to apply to elite universities (Giancola & Davidson, 2015).

Understand the Context and Demographics of the Local School and District

It is common to hear from many who work in low-income schools either that "we don't have any truly gifted students here" or that "everyone in the school is gifted in some way." Using local norms and a combination of qualitative and quantitative measures, schools may choose to provide services to students in their top percentiles in core content areas or in areas of strength in the local population, regardless of whether they meet core state requirements or mandated cut-off scores. Lohman (2005a) explained that, just because assessment results are correlated, the assessments do not necessarily measure the same constructs.

Lohman (2005a) also argued that because the normed sample of a typical school rarely follows the national normed sample, local normative samples, in conjunction with other measures, including performance, are a better indicator of talent potential than the former. Using local norms within a building can support talent development of the school's most able students regardless of their assessment scores. If the majority of students are performing below grade level and a few are performing slightly above grade level but may not be formally identified by state policies (e.g., if relying heavily upon cut-off scores), they may still be considered for services as part of a talent identification model. It is unlikely that their needs will be met in the general classroom if the focus there is on remediation.

Previous federal definitions of giftedness have suggested that giftedness be considered within a student's particular context and domain of strength as well. The National Excellence report (Ross & United States, 1993) defined gifted students as follows:

> children and youth with outstanding potential for performing at remarkably high levels of accomplishment when compared with others of the age, experience, or environment. These children and youth exhibit high performance capability in intellectual, creative, and/or artistic areas, possess an unusual leadership capacity, or excel in specific academic fields. They require services or activities not ordinarily provided by the school. Outstanding talents are present in children and youth from all cultural groups, across all economic strata, and in all areas of human endeavor. (p. 5)

Understand the Unique Characteristics of Various Populations and Their Scoring Profile

Some studies have found that students in low-income families show uneven profiles similar to students with dual diagnoses, who are culturally diverse, or who lack exposure to advanced content or specific content disciplines (Olszewski-Kubilious & Clarenbach, 2012). VanTassel-Baska, Feng, Swanson, Queck, and Chandler (2009), in a qualitative study of the impact of identification and programming on low-income students, found that students who were White and low income were more likely to be identified as gifted through nontraditional assessments such as performance tasks in verbal domains, and these students were reportedly more creative than their age-peers in their approaches to schoolwork. Almost half of the participants were thought to have learning disabilities as well because they lacked motivation, organizational skills, and time-management skills, according to their parents and teachers, although no diagnoses had been made. In the same study, low-income African American student profiles were also examined. Profile patterns were similar to those of the White low-income students although the African American students seemed to have more interest in dance, music, and the arts outside of school. In addition, members of this group were adamant about not spending all of their school time in the gifted class, as they also wanted time with peers in the general classroom and did not want to brag about their giftedness or stand out (VanTassel-Baska et al., 2009). Parents of this group were also more supportive of their children. Similar to the VanTassel-Baska et al. (2009) findings, Ford (2011) noted a stronger emphasis in African American communities on building relationships, focusing on family, working in communal contexts, and thriving in more collaborative environments. In summary, an understanding of the context and unique characteristics of a given school's population and individual students within the school is important to consider during the identification process.

Encourage Participation in Extracurricular Opportunities During the Summer and After School

This guideline is pertinent to identification, since, like early access, extracurricular activities beyond the school day are opportunities for educators to identify talent, to support strength and interest areas not provided at school, for in-depth enhancement of talent, and for access to peers with similar abilities and content experts. Because school services may be limited or may not identify (or offer programming for) a broad array of talent areas, students need other options for talent identification and support.

Moreover, some students need access to challenging opportunities before talents emerge. U.S. regional talent search programs such as Northwestern University Midwest Academic Talent Search (NUMATS), Duke TIP (Talent Identification Program), Denver Rocky Mountain Talent Search, and Johns Hopkins Talent Search provide opportunities for students to take out-of-level (i.e., tests designed for students at higher grade levels) assessments, determine their strengths, and learn more about options for enrolling in accelerated programs outside of school. Studies focused on talent development consistently emphasize experiences in students' areas of strength (Bloom, 1985; Csikszentmihalyi, Rathunde, & Whalen, 1997). Moreover, the impact on career development of engagement or the "educational dose" gifted students experience through accelerated and enriched programs (e.g., competitions, academic clubs, dual credit options, opportunities for research, and accelerated classes) has been documented, especially in the STEM fields (Wai, Lubinksi, Benbow, & Steiger, 2010). These accelerated and enriching supplemental programs are particularly beneficial for high-achieving students from low-economic circumstances (Olszewski-Kubilius & Clarenbach, 2012; VanTassel-Baska & Stambaugh, 2007), especially when coupled with early identification, ongoing and consistent services (including preparatory as well as accelerated and enrichment opportunities), cultural enrichment, and parental education and support (Olszewski-Kubilius & Thomson, 2010).

Principle 5: Services Provided Should Match the Talents Identified.

This principle may seem to be a simple notion, but mismatches between talent areas and services provided can be an ongoing problem for gifted learners—especially in districts with limited funding, a narrow view of programming, or a lack of understanding of giftedness. A one-size-fits-all approach to addressing needs related to giftedness is often the norm. Regardless of how students are identified as eligible for participation, each is placed in a program designed for all gifted students, without attention to individual strengths or limitations.

To illustrate, consider that a student is provided entry based on high nonverbal scores, a work portfolio showing precocity in science, and scores from a motivation scale. She is subsequently placed in the one-size-fits-all pull-out program focused on language arts. This student may indeed be in a designated gifted program in her area of talent, but the school is not addressing her strengths or deepening her understanding or interest.

School teams should ensure that identification procedures and actual services match the strengths and talent area(s) of each student. Reaching this goal requires an awareness that strengths, abilities, and interests of gifted students vary. Thus, their abilities need to be differentially nurtured, according to their unique profile within domains of strength (Subotnik, Olszewski-Kubilius, & Worrell, 2011).

KEY CONCEPT

Identification and the Whole Student

School counselors have the advantage of having professional relationships with their students. These relationships can facilitate school counselor understanding of *typical behavioral characteristics of gifted students that may prevent gifted students from being identified.* Some

(continued)

behaviors might be attributed to unique family circumstances or the school environment. School counselors may find themselves in leadership and advocacy roles when supporting appropriate identification of talent.

Because of their unique training, school counselors focus on the whole student, not just test scores. Meeting individually with students for academic planning or personal/social concerns may help counselors find high-ability students who might otherwise be missed during traditional screening. Students may not be identified because of logistical challenges, such as incomplete cumulative files for highly mobile populations or flawed implementation of or lack of rigorous and evidence-supported policies for equitable identification.

Potential personal barriers to identification are twice-exceptionalties, income status, or second-language-learner status. School counselors can also be alert to characteristics that are not traditionally assessed and that can block identification (e.g., emotional sensitivity, moral intelligence, or intense passion for one or two areas being misconstrued as not being "well rounded"). Their having long-term relationships with students can also mean that school counselors are aware of concerns or struggles (e.g., grief and loss) that interfere with testing or interviews or observation protocols.

In essence, school counselors play an important role in identifying behaviors that indicate giftedness but may not be reflected in test scores and/or referrals. When they are aware of students who may not have been identified, school counselors may need to leverage relationships with their colleagues and their problem-solving and advocacy skills to secure appropriate services. These situations may ruffle feathers. Chapter 12 describes strategies school counselors can use to support identification of gifted students and appropriate services.

• • •

IMPLICATIONS FOR SCHOOL COUNSELORS

School counselors have many important roles in their everyday work, and because of their unique responsibilities, they are invaluable talent scouts.

Following are admonitions for school counselors related to identifying students with high potential.

- **Be a talent scout.** Acknowledge that there are likely to be more false negatives than false positives when committees or program coordinators attempt to identify giftedness. School counselors can help to lower the number of false negatives by being alert during classroom guidance lessons; hall supervision; interactions with staff, parents, and students; and child-study and 504 team meetings for students whose exceptional abilities may have been overlooked.
- **Consult and collaborate with a school psychologist and educators who are specifically trained to work with gifted and talented students.** School counselors should share their expertise as part of a team that works together to find and support those students whose academic needs are not being met in the classroom. School counselors, teachers of gifted students, and their school psychologist colleagues each have a different perspective to share regarding student academic, assessment, and social/emotional needs profiles. Each individual on the team has a unique lens for viewing the child. Together, they can ensure that all students have equal opportunities to show their talents and have equal access to screening to be eligible for services. All can address specific needs related to underachievement, twice exceptionality, racial diversity, income status, and nonconforming behaviors that block referrals for assessment during the identification process (Ward & Theodore, 2012).
- **Know the limitations of state and local identification policies.** School counselors are probably aware that districts and states have gifted-education policies related to assessment. Sometimes, implementing prescribed policies has unintended negative consequences. Poorly executed policies often do not match best practices for equitable assessment opportunities (e.g., a heavy reliance on teacher referral for identification instead of universal screening), or have definitions of giftedness that are single-faceted, limiting the percentage identified. In other instances local school districts may not have the resources to fully execute best practices, yet they have many students who need advanced-level services. Counselors who understand best practices and how state policies fit within best practices, including where the gaps in best practices are, are better equipped to advocate for their students.
- **Review past training on testing and assessment.** All graduate students in CACREP-accredited master's-level programs are required to have at least one class focused on educational and psychological

testing and assessment, often in addition to courses in mental health, psychopathology, and diagnostics. However, if school counselors are reluctant to become involved in the assessment aspects of identification, then professional development through conferences and/or consultation with school psychologists and university training personnel can be helpful. Organizing a workshop led by a local expert can benefit all school counselors in a district. School counselors and teachers need to be aware of the types of assessments being used so that they can apply the resulting data effectively and ask good questions when determining strengths and appropriate services. When school counselors are aware of what a test measures, whether that test is appropriate for their school population, and how the assessments and system-wide approaches support or inhibit talent identification, they are likely to advocate appropriately for students who are in need of differentiated approaches to help them learn and develop.

- **Involve parents as partners; educate them about identification processes and benefits of talent development at home and at school**. Because of their training, school counselors can act as a support for students and families during the identification process through advocacy, consultation about extenuating circumstances, and discussions about how to make the most of student strengths based on their testing profiles. They can also support the development of non-cognitive factors that influence talent such as self concept, mindset, and persistence (see Subotnik, Olszewski-Kubilius, & Worrell, 2011). In addition, when necessary, they can help families with awareness, with next steps, and with how to support a talent trajectory, navigate the identification process, and secure appropriate services. Many states have appeal processes, regulations for requesting assessments, or other policies that are mandated. Of course, discussions can move beyond process to investigating college and career paths, exploring student–parent relationships, and answering questions about common concerns such as perfectionism, intensity, and socialization.

- **Advocate for talent identification and outlets for pursuing interests beyond the school day**. School counselors are uniquely situated to find resources that can supplement gifted students' education, including the talent searches mentioned earlier in this chapter, Saturday and summer programming via local universities, job shadowing, and mentoring. School counselors and educational teams might consider using community asset mapping to document these resources and opportunities. School counselors should become familiar with universities and agencies that can help with student scholarships or accelerated programming opportunities with mentors or content experts such as talent search organizations or programs: Purdue University's Diversity Initiatives for Gifted Students (DIGS) through its Gifted Education Resource Institute (GERI), Vanderbilt University's Programs for Talented Youth (PTY), or the Jack Kent Cooke Foundation's low-income, high achievers programs. Research suggests increased growth in social–emotional and academic achievement gains when they participate in accelerated academic programs beyond the school day (Kim, 2015).

• • •

CONCLUDING THOUGHTS AND RECOMMENDATIONS

Julie now has several different ideas of how she and Ben can provide professional development focused on identification. These opportunities will be good refreshers for all district educators who are involved in gifted education including school counselors. Julie also wants to increase the skills the gifted educators need to have in order to help families and students better understand themselves better and be able to navigate school processes in a way that supports students' talents. Ben and Julie both realize that school counselors and gifted-education professionals need to improve their talent scouting. Ben may go on to ask his fellow school counselors to examine the demographic data for their gifted-education classes while Julie and her teams revised identification protocols to include more diverse criteria for identification. In addition, working together Julie and Ben can develop relationships with talent programs that can support gifted students beyond what their district can provide.

• • •

REFERENCES

American School Counselor Association. (2013). *The school counselor and gifted and talented programs*. Alexandria, VA: Author.

Bloom, B. (1985). *Developing talent in young people*. New York, NY: Ballantine/Random House.

Council for Accreditation of Counseling and Related Educational Programs. (2015). *2016 CACREP standards*. Alexandria, VA: Author.

Csikszentmihalyi, M., Rathunde, K., & Whalen, S. (1997). *Talented teenagers: The roots of success and failure*. New York, NY: Cambridge University Press.

Erwin, J. O., & Worrell, F. C. (2011). Assessment practices and the underrepresentation of minority students in gifted and talented education. *Journal of Psychoeducational Assessment, 30*, 74–87. doi:10.1177/0734282911428197

Ford, D. Y. (2011). *Multicultural gifted education: Rationale, models, strategies, and resources* (2nd ed.). Waco, TX: Prufrock Press.

Giancola, J., & Davidson, E. (2015). *Breaking down walls: Increasing access to four-year colleges for high-achieving community college students.* Lansdowne, VA: Jack Kent Cooke Foundation.

Horn, C. V. (2015). Young scholars: A talent development model for finding and nurturing potential in underserved populations. *Gifted Child Today, 38,* 19–31.

Kim, M. (2016) A meta-analysis of the effects of enrichment programs on gifted students. *Gifted Child Quarterly, 60*(2), 102–116. doi:10.1177/0016986216630607

Lohman, D. F. (2005a). An aptitude perspective on talent: Implications for identification of academically gifted minority students. *Journal for the Education of the Gifted, 8,* 333–360. doi:10.4219/jeg-2005-341

Lohman, D. F. (2005b). The role of nonverbal ability tests in identifying academically gifted students: An aptitude perspective. *Gifted Child Quarterly, 49*(2), 111–138.

Lohman, D. F. (2006). *Identifying academically talented minority students* (Research Monograph RM05216). Storrs: The National Research Center on the Gifted and Talented, University of Connecticut.

Lubinski, D. (2010). Spatial ability and STEM: A sleeping giant for talent identification and development. *Personality* and *Individual Differences, 49,* 344–351.

McBee, M. T. (2006). A descriptive analysis of referral sources for gifted identification screening by race and socioeconomic status. *Journal of Secondary Gifted Education, 17,* 103–111.

McBee, M. T. (2010). Examining the probability of identification for gifted programs for students in Georgia elementary schools: A multilevel path analysis study. *Gifted Child Quarterly, 54,* 283–297.

Naglieri, J. A., & Ford, D. Y. (2003). Addressing underrepresentation of gifted minority children using the Naglieri Nonverbal Ability Test (NNAT). *Gifted Child Quarterly, 47,* 155–160.

National Association for Gifted Children. (n.d.). Gifted education in the U.S. Retrieved from https://www.nagc.org/resources-publications/resources/gifted-education-us

National Association for Gifted Children. (2008). *Position statement: The role of assessments in the identification of gifted students.* Retrieved from: https://www.nagc .org/sites/default/files/Position%20Statement/Assessment%20Position%20 Statement.pdf

National Association for Gifted Children. (2010). *Position statement: Use of the WISC-IV for gifted identification.* Retrieved from http://www.nagc.org/sites/default/ files/Position%20Statement/Use%20of%20WISC-IV%20%28rev%203 -2010%29. pdf

National Association for Gifted Children. (2011). *Position statement: Identifying and serving culturally and linguistically diverse gifted students.* Retrieved from http://www .nagc.org/sites/default/files/Position%20Statement/Identifying%20and%20 Serving%20Culturally%20and%20Linguistically.pdf

National Association for Gifted Children & Council of State Directors for Programs of the Gifted. (2015). 2014–2015 state of the states in gifted education. Retrieved from https://www.nagc.org/sites/default/files/key%20reports/2014-2015%20 State%20of%20the%20States%20(final).pdf

Olszewski-Kublius, P., & Clarenbach, J. (2012). *Unlocking emergent talent: Supporting high achievement of low-incoming, high-ability students.* Washington, DC: National Association for Gifted Children.

Olszewski-Kubilius, P., & Thomson, D. (2010). Gifted programming for poor or minority urban students: Issues and lessons learned. *Gifted Child Today, 33*(4), 58–64.

Peters, S. J., & Gentry, M. (2010). Multigroup construct validity evidence of the HOPE scale: Instrumentation to identify low-income elementary students for gifted programs. *Gifted Child Quarterly, 54*(4), 298–313. doi:10.1177/0016986210378332

Peterson, J. S. (1999). Gifted—through whose cultural lens? An application of the post-positivistic mode of inquiry. *Journal for the Education of the Gifted, 22,* 354–383.

Peterson, J. S., & Wachter, C. A. (2010). Understanding and responding to concerns related to giftedness: A study of CACREP-accredited programs. *Journal for Education of the Gifted, 33,* 311–336.

Pfeiffer, S. I. (2002). Identifying gifted and talented students: Recurring issues and promising solutions. *Journal of Applied School Psychology, 1,* 31–50.

Plucker, J. A., Hardesty, J., & Burroughs, N. (2013). *Talent on the sidelines: Excellence gaps and America's persistent talent underclass.* Storrs: Center for Education Policy Analysis, University of Connecticut. Retrieved from http://cepa.uconn .edu/mindthegap

Ross, P. O. C., & U.S. Department of Education. (1993). *National excellence: A case for developing America's talent.* Washington, DC: Office of Educational Research and Improvement, U.S. Department of Education. Retrieved from https://www .ocps.net/cs/ese/programs/gifted/Documents/National%20Excellence_% 20A%20Case%20for%20Developing%20America's%20Talent_%20 Introduction.pdf

Silverman, L. (2013). *Giftedness 101.* New York, NY: Springer Publishing.

Stambaugh, T. (2007). Next steps: An impetus for future directions in research, policy and practice for low-incoming promising learners. In J. VanTassle-Baska & T. Stambaugh (Eds.), *Overlooked gems: A national perspective on low-incoming promising learners: Proceedings from the National Leadership Conference on Low-Income Promising Learners* (pp. 83–90). Washington, DC: National Association for Gifted Children.

Subotnik, R. F., Olszewski-Kubilius, P., & Worrell, F. C. (2011). Rethinking giftedness and gifted education: A proposed direction forward based on psychological science. *Psychological Science in the Public Interest, 12*(1), 3–54.

VanTassel-Baska, J., Feng, A. X., Swanson, J. D., Queck, C., & Chandler, K. (2009). Academic and affective profiles of low-income, minority and twice-exceptional gifted learners: The role of gifted program membership in enhancing self. *Journal of Advanced Academics, 20*(4), 702–739.

VanTassel-Baska, J., & Stambaugh, T. (2007). *Overlooked gems: A national perspective on low-incoming promising learners: Proceedings from the National Leadership Conference on Low-Income Promising Learners*. Washington, DC: National Association for Gifted Children.

Wai, J., Lubinski, D., Benbow, C. P., & Steiger, J. H. (2010). Accomplishment in science, technology, engineering, and mathematics (STEM) and its relation to STEM educational dose: A 25-year longitudinal study. *Journal of Educational Psychology*, *102*, 860–871.

Ward, S., & Theodore, L. A. (2012). Role of the school psychologist working with the school counselor. In T. L. Cross & J. R. Cross (Eds.), *Handbook for counselors serving students with gifts and talents: Development, relationships, school issues, and counseling needs/interventions* (pp. 569–582). Waco, TX: Prufrock Press.

Worrell, F. C., & Erwin, J. O. (2011). Best practices for identifying gifted students for gifted and talented education programs. *Journal of Applied School Psychology*, *27*, 319–340. doi:10.1080/15377903.2011.615817

Working With Classrooms and Small Groups

JEAN SUNDE PETERSON

In a rural school district, Abby is responsible for creating and delivering gifted-education programming across all school levels. She wants to develop a comprehensive K–12 affective curriculum for it. Though the majority of students are from middle-class families, others come from families that are struggling economically due to unemployment, military deployment, parental incarceration, single parenting, and addictions. Teachers and administrators are concerned about student well-being. Bullying has been a school concern, and the community has been shocked by three student suicides among the "best and brightest" over the past 2 years. Abby believes that attention to the social and emotional development of gifted students during all school years might make a difference. She wants to collaborate with Jack, the one K–12 school counselor, in possibly cofacilitating two proactive small discussion groups of gifted students. She wants to observe his listening and responding skills and share information with him about giftedness. In the past, Jack has not thought of organizing small groups for gifted students, but agrees to the collaboration. He says they should conduct a needs assessment among students identified as gifted and organize a group of high achievers around a common concern, such as bullying or bereavement—an approach he used in the past with the general population. Abby has something different in mind, but is hesitant to advocate for her view, since group work is in Jack's "territory." After she learns some skills from Jack, she wants all identified students to have a small-group experience at some point. She also understands that programming should address needs of more than just high achievers, including highly intelligent academic underachievers, who currently are not viewed as eligible for it.Abby needs to have a clear rationale for both the group format and mixing achievers and underachievers in the groups before she talks with the counselor again.

Small group counseling and classroom guidance have traditionally been the purview of the school counselor. As suggested in earlier chapters here, gifted students encounter the same types of life stressors (e.g., grief, illness, parental divorce) that their nongifted peers experience, but experience them differently because of unique traits. They may have additional stressors because of high expectations from others and from themselves (see Chapter 3 for additional information). However, little has been written about how small groups and classroom guidance can address academic, career, and personal–social needs of gifted students. Semistructured, developmental, prevention-oriented groups can be positive, memorable, high-impact experiences for high-ability learners (Peterson, Betts, & Bradley, 2009) and an efficient use of counselor time, since several students are seen simultaneously (Peterson & Servaty-Seib, 2008). In addition, gifted students can benefit when teachers and counselors collaborate to incorporate affective components into the core curriculum and into differentiated classroom instruction (Wood & Lane, 2017). This chapter explores ways Jack and Abby can accomplish such benefits, including how to develop small groups, facilitation skills, and affective curriculum.

• • •

GUIDANCE FOR HIGH-ABILITY LEARNERS

Classroom Guidance

Guided by the American School Counselor Association

When developing classroom guidance curricula addressing academic, personal/social, and career needs of K–12 students, professional school counselors can consult the American School Counselor Association Model (ASCA, 2012), which has been revised several times since 2003. Recently, ASCA (2014) produced the *ASCA Mindsets & Behaviors for Student Success: K-12 College- and Career-Readiness Standards for Every Student.* The mindsets and behaviors are organized into academic, personal/social, and career domains, with standards within categories and competencies detailing knowledge, skills, and attitudes necessary for academic success, college- and career-readiness, and social/emotional development. The categories consist of Mindset Standards (e.g., personal attitudes or self-perceptions related to academics) and Behavior Standards (e.g., learning strategies, self-management skills, and social skills). Learning strategies include critical thinking, a life skill applicable beyond academics.

Abby wants to support gifted students with social and emotional concerns and improve their career- and college-readiness, but is not as familiar with the ASCA Model and *Mindsets* as Jack is. However, during her preparation in gifted education, Abby was exposed to other curriculum-development models, such as the Integrated Curriculum Model (ICM; VanTassel-Baska, 2012). Individual components include self-assessment of temperament, interests, achievement, beliefs, life themes, and meaning; a talent development plan; bibliotherapy via biographies and issues-based fiction; and emotional intelligence. VanTassel-Baska, Cross, and Olenchak (2009) argued for programs, throughout the school years, that are proactive, deliberate, planned, focused on developmental changes, responsive to changing needs, and catalytic for student productivity. Jack and Abby might also find the Peterson Proactive Developmental Attention (PPDA) model (Peterson & Jen, in press) useful for integrating affective components into the classroom and advocating for small-group discussion.

Counselor and Teacher Collaboration

Both the ICM (VanTassel-Baska, 2012) and the PPDA (Peterson & Jen, in press) models offer guidance for incorporating affective components into the classroom curriculum—for gifted students in regular classrooms, in pull-out or self-contained classrooms, or in advanced or "honors" classes. Abby and Jack might work toward incorporating social and emotional components into language arts (e.g., discussion of emotions, developmental challenges, resilience, or coping in connection with literature; an essay about stress; persuasive writing or speaking about self-harm), social studies (e.g., a skit about family emotional life during the settlement of the prairie; a dialogue between adolescents in the weeks just before the Civil War), the arts (e.g., portraying emotions visually; portraying relationships in minimalistic ways; expressing feelings in response to music), mathematics (e.g., discussing emotional responses to a new math level or new way of thinking), and family science (a creative graph showing family members in various developmental transitions, simultaneously). Perhaps gifted students could be released during portions of a class period once a week for discussion related to social and emotional aspects of a historical event, a need for human services, or a moment in a novel or children's book. Guided viewing of film (Hébert & Hammond, 2006) and bibliotherapy (Hébert, 2000) are two other possibilities for attending to affective development.

Counselor and teacher could also utilize a challenging, creative, cross-disciplinary, multiday activity related to cyber- and other bullying (Wood & Lane, 2017). Assignment options include online investigation of blogs, safety issues and safeguards, mental health sites, and school, district, and state policies; interviews with community stakeholders; email contact with college admissions personnel about social-media policies and whether online "footprints" are considered; website creation; debates about punishment; and criteria for healthy friendships. A tic-tac-toe graphic guides the activity; having three products up, down, or diagonally "wins."

Affective Programming

An affective component in a gifted-education program should focus on prevention and development—concepts familiar during school-counselor preparation, but perhaps not obvious in practice. Too often, intervention for pressing concerns is the priority. The same tendency can occur in gifted education and in school counselors' response to gifted students in their case load.

The Proactive Aspect

Proactive suggests anticipating, addressing, and even preventing challenges before problems emerge (i.e., primary prevention), rather than waiting until distress demands reaction and intervention (i.e., secondary or tertiary prevention). Abby wants to be proactive. According to Capuzzi and Gross (2004), "all young people have the potential for at-riskness" (p. 14). In their view, primary prevention can take the form of discussion groups, psychoeducation, and activities intended to foster expressive language and self-awareness. Secondary prevention refers to early intervention (e.g., support groups) for problems that already exist, with the goal of preventing them from worsening. Tertiary prevention is intended to avoid impairment after crises are resolved, perhaps with aftercare in the form of informal monitoring or individual or group counseling at school. Too often, especially in middle and high schools, primary prevention takes a backseat to intervention for serious concerns and crises.

Primary prevention can be helpful even when students have serious emotional or behavioral concerns, since challenges related to developmental tasks continue. They can benefit from preemptive attention not directly connected with their presenting problems. Relative homogeneity of ability level (e.g., simply identified as gifted) is important for trust in small-group discussion with high-ability students, since they may be struggling with not feeling understood by less able peers. However, for groups of gifted students, mixing cultural backgrounds, levels of socioeconomic status, personalities, levels of social adeptness, levels of achievement, and even bullies and targets can foster respect, compassion, and connection. They may not otherwise talk about "growing up" even with their best friends. Not just invested adults, but gifted children and teens themselves, may talk mostly about academics and activities—and performance. They may therefore lack expressive language and can benefit from a weekly opportunity to talk about nonacademic life.

The Developmental Aspect

All school-age gifted youth are developing—figuring out who they are, where they are going, how to move toward culturally appropriate autonomy, how to manage social relationships, how to resolve conflict, how to develop competence, and who they are as sexual beings. Attending to development proactively in small-group discussion or with affective curriculum in the classroom can help gifted youth acknowledge developmental tasks, normalize challenges, reduce anxiety, recognize changes, make sense of feelings and behaviors, and develop coping skills. In small groups, with highly able peers and an informed and trustworthy adult, they can discuss stress, life balance, decision making, social challenges, and pressures related to high expectations. Both shy and garrulous group members can interact and gain from one another in that social context. In addition, psychoeducational information about development, stress, depression, anxiety, trauma, disordered eating, hyperactivity, problems with sleeping, personal transitions, and self-harming behavior, for instance, can be presented to individual small groups or to combinations of groups by school counselors or community mental health professionals. Gifted students might otherwise have little or no opportunity to learn and self-reflect about development and any of these areas of potential concern.

KEY CONCEPT

A Proactive, Developmental Model

The PPDA (Peterson & Jen, in press) emphasizes challenges related to growing up. This model can be a framework for several program components for gifted youth, who may otherwise have little opportunity to examine their social and emotional development. *Proactive* attention is deemed important especially because gifted youth tend not to tell adults about their distress (Peterson, 2003; see also Chapter 3). *Developmental* attention is focused on developmental tasks (e.g., identity, direction, autonomy, relationships). Affective curriculum, including focused, but flexible, small-group discussion (Peterson, 2008), helps gifted children and teens talk about and normalize developmental struggles, develop expressive language for current and future relationships, connect socially, discover common ground, and make sense of disturbing feelings and behaviors.

The PPDA assumes that gifted youth, whether high or low achieving and in good or poor mental health, are among the "all students" whom school counselors are to serve (ASCA, 2012). They are all developing, but may *experience* development differently, collectively, from others (Peterson, 2016), and may believe that no one can understand them. The PPDA model can connect them meaningfully—ideally in age-stratified groupings, which increase the likelihood of shared developmental concerns.

(continued)

A gifted-education teacher and a school counselor might cofacilitate group discussion, learning skills and gaining knowledge from one another and together learning about the complex internal world of gifted students. If teachers recognize that semistructured, topic-oriented discussion helps them avoid an inappropriate therapy mode, they may eventually be able to apply the skills modeled by the counselor independently (cf. Peterson & Lorimer, 2011, 2012).

Though the PPDA assumes that well-being can affect motivation and ability to focus, the model does not emphasize performance or products. Instead, it focuses on meeting children and teens "where they are" (Peterson, 2009). Talking about social and emotional development tends not to be competitive. No one "wins" or "loses." Arrogance does not fit (Peterson, 1990).

Peterson and Lorimer (2011, 2012) studied the whole-school implementation of a small-group curriculum based on *The Essential Guide to Talking With Gifted Teens* (Peterson, 2008) with 220 gifted early teens in grades 5–8. Teacher-facilitators and students both gained confidence in talking about social and emotional concerns and observed a positive impact on school climate.

In another PPDA study, Peterson (2013) examined the perceptions of seven school counselors at a summer program for K–4 gifted children. After brief training about giftedness, they facilitated small-group discussions with children supported by scholarships. They said they recognized characteristics associated with giftedness, saw economic differences disappear during classroom interaction, and realized they could have important roles with gifted children.

Jen (2015) examined the PPDA-based small-group component (Peterson, 2008) of a residential summer program for gifted adolescents (grades 5–6, 7–8, and 9–12) from nine countries and five American Indian tribes. She studied curriculum, campers, philosophy, training, and young-adult facilitators. Campers learned that developmental challenges exist across cultures, and social connections in the groups were sustained during other activities.

● ● ●

FORMING SMALL GROUPS OF GIFTED LEARNERS

Information about establishing small groups for gifted learners may not be readily available. This section describes how Jack and Abby might establish groups, gain the support of their peers, and even extend the content and process of the groups into other areas of school life.

Determining Group Membership

In a multifaceted high school program conceptualized by Peterson (1990, 2003, 2016), 140 high school students were identified as gifted, and almost all were involved in at least one aspect of the program. One-third were underachievers, many of whom were identified by perusing student files to find who might have been missed earlier (e.g., because of relocation, family chaos, or poor academic performance) or had chosen to stop participating in middle school. The program was organized with both high and low achievers in mind. Several options were intellectually or esthetically stimulating, and many Advanced Placement courses were available, but "academic challenge" and competitive performance were not the prime concerns. Instead, the goal was to broaden worldview and understanding—beyond the regular curriculum. Participants in various program components interacted over shared interests, ameliorating isolation, and lack of connectedness for some. Regular classes were not missed, since before- and after-school times and two lunch hours were available. Athletes occupied with sports programs after school could attend noon activities.

The most popular program component was the weekly discussions about growing up. All gifted students could participate. Supporting this offering was the reality that gifted youth tend to hide their distress (Jackson & Peterson, 2003; Peterson & Ray, 2006; Peterson & Rischar, 2000). Grouped by grade level, the participants found common ground socially and emotionally. For 30 weeks per year, after 3 weeks of logistical preparation, 80–100 students participated. The groups were not intended to "fix behavior." They were also not organized around a common issue. Instead, the groups were presented to students, teachers, administrators, and parents as being focused on development and self-care, with social interaction serving as practice for employment, relationships, parenting, and friendship. The groups were a chance to connect with other gifted students and receive pertinent psychoeducational information now and then. The groups were also a safe place to talk about the burdens of high capability (Peterson, 2012).

Being able to interact with intellectual peers might help gifted children and teens survive a poor fit in a school. In fact, discussion about social and emotional development, with content coming from group members, can level social hierarchies, underscore the universality of challenges, and even address bullying. "Not being known" was a vulnerability in Peterson and Ray's (2006) study of bullying. Group interaction brings each member into respectful, meaningful contact with several others, maybe enough for each to feel connected to school.

Logistics

If staffing is inadequate, if identified children/teens per grade level are small in number, and if teachers resist pull-out and differentiation, weekly small groups over lunch or elsewhere may serve the most gifted kids most efficiently and effectively. Just as important, groups can mix race, ethnicity, culture, socioeconomic status, achievement level, life experiences, and attitude. Students are curious about each other and usually appreciate connection. Abby might consider organizing small-group discussion first, ideally with one group per grade level, or a group with students at two grade levels, depending on number identified. Other options might develop as she learns of students' interests and talents.

In the program just discussed, the double lunch period, in which each hour was comprised of lunch and a study hall, allowed 50 minutes for discussion. With the reminder slip in hand, received early in the day via the homeroom teacher, group members could leave class a few minutes early to go through the "cold line" and bring food to the group room (a conference room). Each day, 16–20 gifted students in two groups, with mixed achievement levels, had substantive discussion. The optimal number for trust was eight students. When the program was replicated in a middle school, six to seven seemed best. At the elementary level, three children in grades 1 and 2, four in grades 3 and 4, and five to six in grades 5 and 6 function well, with everyone having a chance to talk in the shorter meetings. Hands-on activities are helpful for children and early teens; five minutes with sentence stems or another brief paper-and-pencil activity at the outset can orient older groups to serious discussion.

Rationale

For Proactive Group Work

Developing expressive language is a worthy goal for these groups. However, other rationales can include listening and responding skills; discovering shared concerns; increasing self-awareness; breaking down stereotypes; reducing the stigma of "counseling"; developing coping skills; giving and receiving feedback; learning how to recognize and deal with anger, stress, anxiety, fear, and perfectionism; asking for help; appreciating peers and teachers; and developing empathy and compassion.

For Some Structure

Prevention-oriented groups are rare outside of schools (Peterson & Servaty-Seib, 2008). Prevention is not simply "hanging out." It is difficult to justify logistical effort and asking for teachers' and administrators' cooperation without presenting a "map." Having a well-organized affective curriculum, with a predictable format, and making the groups focused, but flexible, also helps to put parents and adult school personnel at ease. Having a brief paper activity allows shy students to read a response during a "go-around," an opportunity to contribute. Having a focus provides an excuse to steer a group back to the topic when a member dominates or narrates extensively. Having an activity gives restless members something to keep hands busy. Without some structure, especially when participation is voluntary, students who become irritated when someone is "always dramatic" or "always getting attention" may opt out.

Having adequate facilitation skills, a meaningful topic to focus on, and a few open-ended questions in mind can help to make meetings unusual and engaging. However, being flexible allows unexpected directions to emerge and even supports a focus on a local tragedy for an entire meeting. When members become accustomed to the topic-focused format, they are likely to expect a new topic the next week. Telling students the topic beforehand is usually not helpful ("Let's let it be a surprise"), since potentially generative topics may not initially sound appealing.

When parents or teachers ask, suspiciously, what the groups do, the facilitator can simply list recent topics and indicate that the discussion is substantive and focused on development, allaying concerns that teacher-bashing or family secrets are the focus. Facilitators who adhere to confidentiality guidelines can assure parents that they (and appropriate authorities, if warranted) will be told if their child is deemed at risk of being harmed or of harming someone else, since mandatory reporting applies. Otherwise, privacy will be respected. Wise facilitators emphasize confidentiality and caveats as a group begins—and along the way, if needed. Even though confidentiality cannot be guaranteed in a group, since more than the facilitator are involved with each member, students in a group are admonished to honor it so that trust can be established.

Determining Content

Making Sense of Self

Counselors and teachers who work with affective curriculum can help gifted kids make sense of feelings and behaviors. For that purpose, when these professionals are knowledgeable about giftedness, they can share pertinent psychoeducational information, including about developmental tasks, characteristics associated with giftedness, overexcitabilities, and the theory of positive disintegration (see Chapter 9).

Development

With students of any age, information about development can be related to identity, direction, relationships, and autonomy, and, at the secondary level, to emotional differentiation within and from family. Bowen (1978) explained that "emotional differentiation is, in part, being able to maintain a nonanxious presence in the face of anxious others. . . . [and] taking maximum responsibility for one's own emotional being and destiny rather than blaming others or the context" (Friedman, 1991, p. 141). Characteristics associated with giftedness may make such differentiation especially difficult when adults are highly invested. Abby and Jack could create or find age-appropriate curricula, with development-related themes, for their wide range of grade levels. Free Spirit Publishing, for example, is focused not only on social and emotional concerns, but also on self-help for, and counseling issues of, gifted children and teens.

High-ability individuals may have a pronounced period of active exploration of identity (Erikson, 1968), trying out a new social image, clothing style, interests, or peer relationships as they move toward culturally appropriate autonomy. However, a school counselor might consider that gifted kids can be imprisoned by social image as much as anyone else, afraid to take risks with it. Their identity may also be wrapped up in being "the best," leaving them emotionally vulnerable when their sense of competence feels precarious with new challenges. In addition, a champion athlete may experience grief if an injury precludes participation. Chronic tendonitis might halt a promising career with a stringed instrument. Brain damage from an accident can interfere with learning. A joker might be sad when friends do not take him seriously when he has a concern. Using a developmental lens during individual counseling can put identity into perspective—as an explanation of sadness, for instance. A group facilitator can have these perspectives in mind, too, but need not interject them if group members explore identity spontaneously. Trusting that a group will "go where it needs to go" with a topic is wise. One good open-ended question may generate a long and productive discussion.

Preoccupation With Performance

Schools are inherently competitive, with performance constantly measured. Comments to gifted children and teens by adult school personnel, including school counselors, are often related to performance (Peterson, 2009), with high achievers complimented for academic or talent excellence, and underachievers met with a furrowed brow. Gifted students, even low achievers, may focus mostly on performance-related benchmarks. Perhaps few adults ask how they are feeling about life, how they are reacting to what they hear or read in the media, how it feels to be getting ready for middle school or high school or leaving home for college, or how they are dealing with an accident or the death of someone close.

Any gifted student, regardless of performance level, is likely to feel unsettled during one or more periods of development or in difficult family circumstances. During an 11-year study of negative life events (Peterson, Duncan, & Canady, 2009), gifted students' parents annually completed a checklist. Midway in the study, when participating parent units numbered 105, 94 deaths in the immediate or extended family, 77 serious illnesses in the family, 13 new or chronic serious illnesses in the student, 13 major changes in family constellation, 10 scary accidents, 7 major health changes, and 6 deaths of friends had been reported. Parental incarceration, mental illness, family financial reversal, and incest were among other categories checked less often or written in. Teachers may not be aware of these life events. Successful students probably appear to be "doing fine." As discussed elsewhere in this book, gifted students often hesitate to ask for help.

Career- and College-Readiness

Marcia (1993) discussed premature foreclosure status related to career path, perhaps due to anxiety over multiple options or deference to opinions of invested adults. To nurture career development, psychoeducational information may come from community speakers and panels, who can model positive career changes and application of college majors in unexpected ways. According to Peterson's (2000a) follow-up study, 4 years after high school, being unsure of direction even in college is not uncommon. Nearly one-third of the gifted participants were unsure of career direction, and only 42% were very sure. High school achievement was only modestly related to sureness of career direction. Small groups can attend to career development and anticipate social and emotional challenges of university life. Anxious gifted youth with many realistic options can also consider personality, interests, wishes, and educational requirements without pressure to "decide" (cf. Hébert & Kelly, 2006).

Content From the Students

Except for infrequent psychoeducational information (e.g., depression, eating disorders, self-harm, giftedness), the content of Peterson's (2003) groups came from the students, related to the topic for the day (e.g., stress, influencers, identity, strengths and limitations, mood swings, worry, anger, anxiety, sadness, sensitivity, change and loss, competition, small talk, compliments, best advice, satisfaction, maturity, perfectionism, encouragers and discouragers, dealing with authority, fears about the future). The most generative topics eventually became various "talk with teens" books (e.g., Peterson, 2008).

Giving proactive developmental attention to the "whole" gifted student may not only be crucial to well-being, but may also help all participants prepare for marriage and partnership, parenting, career, and roommate and other relationships. That attention will likely contribute to self-awareness, understanding of others, ability to relax and find balance, and ability to connect with peers more than just superficially. Bringing gifted students together may help them feel connected to school, less alone, more understood, less "different," and less "crazy."

Extending Programming: Connecting Groups and Classrooms

As their collaboration progresses and students show gains from small groups, Jack and Abby may wish to extend group topics into classrooms, even school-wide. In the program described earlier, lecturers and volunteers integrated and elaborated on some topics.

Lectures

Weekly after-school lectures or panels by local experts (e.g., futuristic specialty medical practice, world religions, law, visual art, mental health, unusual applications of science and other majors), with 30–80 students attending regularly, were popular. Some teachers gave extra credit for pertinent topics—and attended themselves. The lectures were open to anyone, and some students who had missed the cut-off for gifted-program eligibility during early school years came regularly, as did several underachievers. Teachers' viewing the program-sponsored lectures as a service to the school helped to gain their cooperation for other options.

Volunteers and Speakers

In addition, local volunteers taught noon-hour philosophy and classical music appreciation classes as well as after-school mime and dance classes. Poetry-writers met before or after school (Peterson, 1996). Some students studied Chinese and Arabic after school with local volunteers, and students interested in teaching foreign languages taught basics at nearby elementary schools. Some taught or took sign language. Field trips to see engineers at work were arranged. The art and gifted-education teachers collaborated to engage gifted artists with the local art community, and student art was routinely displayed at school. Any student in the program could arrange, on a one-time basis, to shadow a professional for a full day.

Student Panels

To address transitions related to leaving home, a panel of first-year college students, home for Thanksgiving, might discuss social and emotional challenges of college (Peterson, 2000b). Discussion about vulnerability to demagogues, cults, and even charismatic talent mentors can be important for highly intelligent young adults (cf. Deikman, 1994). Asking a group whether they would like to "be told what to think" or would like to stop worrying about the future may generate substantive interaction. The topic of resilience (Peterson, 2012) in the midst of adversity is also likely to be productive and affirm strengths.

These varied elements reflect proactive attention to personal development and well-being and bringing gifted students together around shared interests. Friendships forged through these activities begin informally and genuinely. Whether or not they continue, students likely gain confidence through knowing that mind-mates do exist and that social connection is possible. Even in small, rural communities, some of these components are possible. Abby might canvas parents to learn about available expertise and encourage them to help her develop a list of resources within easy driving distance. If most students are bused to school, a creative lunch schedule once a month might make outside expertise available for broadening the vision.

● ● ●

PREPARING GROUP FACILITATORS

Basic Counseling Skills, Tenets, and Ethics

Listening Skills

Peterson (2003, 2016) described basic listening and responding skills teachers and other noncounselors need for effective work with affective curriculum. School counselors might share some of their expertise with teachers and administrators. Listener–responder pairs, practicing one skill at a time after brief instruction and rationale, can develop rudimentary skills in less than an hour: (a) nonverbals and monosyllabic encouragers, (b) recognizing and reflecting feelings, (c) checking for accuracy, (d) paraphrasing and summarizing, and (e) using open-ended questions. Jack might instead work individually with Abby, switching speaker and listener roles after two minutes per skill, or invite interested teachers to join them for a mini-workshop before or after school, with a similar format.

Basic Counseling Tenets

In those activities, Jack can emphasize a nonjudgmental attitude (because negatively critical judgment is not conducive to growth), a focus on strengths (because everyone has strengths, but may not hear about them from people who matter), resisting the urge to self-disclose (because it is difficult to reestablish a focus on the student), avoiding "a rush to fix" (because advice-giving is disempowering, and struggle can foster growth), recognizing the importance of feeling heard (likely more important than "being fixed"), and the importance of a one-down, nonexpert posture ("not knowing"; inviting the speaker to "teach" the listener). Not focusing on deficiencies, fostering autonomy, and listening actively are additional counseling tenets that counselors are steeped in and teachers can benefit from (Peterson, 2009).

Ethics

Guided by his code of ethics (American Counseling Association, 2014), Jack should also discuss ethics, particularly regarding confidentiality. The facilitator of small-group discussion can promise respect for privacy of student and family, but cannot guarantee that others in the group will be trustworthy. Jack can tell Abby or the teachers what he routinely says to students and parents about confidentiality, and why he has to be careful in his communication with teachers about students. Teachers who interact with students on social and emotional topics should adhere to similar constraints. Jack can also talk about the dangers inherent in teacher voyeurism. When adults with responsibilities for the welfare of children and teens are titillated by gossip, dramatic revelations, or "family dirty linen," they should not facilitate small-group or large-group discussion focused on social and emotional development. Less intimate activities carry less risk.

In addition to privacy concerns, Jack should encourage Abby to avoid calling the groups "counseling groups": When teachers lack formal training as counselors, but refer to themselves as counselors providing counseling, they assume liability. Because of this risk, school counselors often carry liability insurance independently. The groups are best described as "discussion groups," and it should be clear to school adults, students, and parents alike that the purpose is not therapy (cf. Colangelo, 2003). Classroom affective curriculum should likewise not be seen as counseling. Unfortunately, *counseling* is a term often used loosely to refer to many kinds of advice-giving and consultation. In schools, especially given the vulnerability of children, teens, and families, this term should be reserved for the services provided by school and mental health counselors.

Teachers' Adjustments

A school counselor who trains teachers to deliver affective curriculum, regardless of format, can keep in mind that nonacademic discussion means less control of content and more ambiguity. Group work may be an adjustment for Abby because she is probably accustomed to being in control and *not* discussing social and emotional concerns. The kind of group work emphasized here is not geared toward pathology, crises, or problem solving. Nevertheless, teachers may initially have fears about not knowing what to say, have a strong impulse to give advice instead of allowing the students to problem solve, and be uncomfortable with tears or unsettling information. With practice, skills typically improve. With experience, teachers become alert to, and comfortable with, the possibility of depression, suicidal ideation, posttraumatic distress, disordered eating, and substance misuse. They also become increasingly adept at recognizing strengths, scaling ("On a 1–10 scale, with 10 being great, how was your group today?"), "being taught" by the group, and staying open-ended with questions.

The school counselors in the Peterson (2013) study and the teachers in the Peterson and Lorimer (2011) study gained knowledge and awareness related to giftedness. Small-group facilitators probably benefit as much as the group members do—just differently.

• • •

CONCLUDING THOUGHTS AND RECOMMENDATIONS

School counselors can collaborate with gifted-education teachers to provide crucial program support for students identified as gifted and those who are highly capable, but are overlooked or deemed ineligible because they do not behave in ways viewed as demonstrating giftedness. Even during conversations about recent or upcoming relocation, course selection, letters of recommendation, or college-entrance essays, counselors should be alert for concerns in high-stress high achievers, staying aware that their own stereotypical thinking that these students are at low risk for mental health concerns can easily preclude attention. Distress in gifted underachievers may or may not be more obvious, but these students, too, warrant open-ended questions about their well-being when there are similar opportunities to inquire.

As the developmental specialists in schools, counselors should share some of their expertise with educator colleagues, thereby spreading the responsibility for monitoring the well-being of students, and increasing the possibility that concerns can be addressed. Counselors can help teachers develop basic listening skills so that affective curriculum in any of several forms is delivered skillfully and ethically. With even rudimentary skills and guidelines about privacy in hand, teachers are likely to be less anxious when asking about a gifted student's well-being, not fearing what they might hear and knowing that school counselors are available for follow-up and referral if necessary.

Counselors and teachers will likely gain awareness of needs and concerns when facilitating nonacademic, nongraded curriculum components geared toward nonacademic development—a positive gain. All students involved, ideally regardless of social behavior and level of academic performance, can have abilities validated and concerns received nonjudgmentally. Developmental challenges can also be normalized when gifted students participate meaningfully, substantively, and noncompetitively with peers who can relate to them.

● ● ●

REFERENCES

American Counseling Association. (2014). *ACA Code of Ethics*. Alexandria, VA: Author.

American School Counselor Association. (2012). *The ASCA National Model: A framework for school counseling programs* (2nd ed.). Alexandria, VA: Author.

American School Counselor Association. (2014). *Mindsets and behaviors for student success: K–12 college- and career readiness for every student*. Alexandria, VA: Author.

Bowen, M. (1978). *Family therapy in clinical practice*. New York, NY: Aronson.

Capuzzi, D., & Gross, D. R. (2004). *Youth at risk: A prevention resource for counselors, teachers, and parents* (4th ed.). Alexandria, VA, American Counseling Association, Upper Saddle River, NJ: Pearson/Merrill/Prentice Hall.

Colangelo, N. (2003). Counseling gifted students. In N. Colangelo & G. A. Davis (Eds.), *Handbook of gifted education* (3rd ed., pp. 373–387). Boston, MA: Allyn & Bacon.

Deikman, A. (1994). *The wrong way home: Uncovering the patterns of cult behavior in American society*. Boston, MA: Beacon Press.

Erikson, E. H. (1968). *Youth and crisis*. New York, NY: W. W. Norton.

Friedman, E. H. (1991). Bowen theory and therapy. In A. S. Gurman & D. P. Kniskern (Eds.), *Handbook of family therapy* (Vol. II, pp. 134–170). New York, NY: Brunner/Mazel.

Hébert, T. P. (2000). Helping high ability students overcome math anxiety through bibliotherapy. *Journal of Secondary Gifted Education, 8*, 164–178.

Hébert, T. P., & Hammond, D. R. (2006). Guided viewing of film with gifted students: Resources for educators and counselors. *Gifted Child Today, 29*, 14–27.

Hébert, T. P., & Kelly, K. R. (2006). Identity and career development in gifted students. In F. A. Dixon & S. M. Moon (Eds.), *The handbook of secondary gifted education* (pp. 35–64). Waco, TX: Prufrock Press.

Jackson, P. S., & Peterson, J. S. (2003). Depressive disorder in highly gifted adolescents. *Journal for Secondary Gifted Education. 14*(3), 175–186.

Jen, E. (2015). *Incorporating a small-group affective curriculum model into a diverse university-based summer residential enrichment program for gifted, creative, and talented youth*. Unpublished doctoral dissertation, Purdue University, West Lafayette, IN.

Marcia, J. E. (1993). The status of the statuses: Research review. In J. E. Marcia, A. S. Waterman, D. R. Matteson, S. L. Archer, & J. L. Orlofsky (Eds.), *Ego identity: A handbook for psychosocial research* (pp. 22–410), New York, NY: Springer-Verlag.

Peterson, J. S. (1990). Noon-hour discussion groups: Dealing with the burdens of capability. *Gifted Child Today, 13*(4), 17–22.

Peterson, J. S. (1996). The breakfast club: Poetry and pancakes. *Gifted Child Today Magazine, 19*(4), 16–19, 49.

Peterson, J. S. (2000a). A follow-up study of one group of achievers and underachievers four years after high school graduation. *Roeper Review, 22*, 217–224.

Peterson, J. S. (2000b). Preparing for college—beyond the "getting-in" part. *Gifted Child Today, 23*(2), 36–41.

Peterson, J. S. (2003). An argument for proactive attention to affective concerns of gifted adolescents. *Journal for Secondary Gifted Education, 14*, 62–71.

Peterson, J. S. (2008). *The essential guide to talking with gifted teens: Ready-to-use discussions about identity, stress, relationships, and more.* Minneapolis, MN: Free Spirit.

Peterson, J. S. (2009). Focusing on where they are: A clinical perspective. In J. VanTassel-Baska, T. R. Cross, & R. Olenchak (Eds.), *Social–emotional curriculum with gifted and talented students* (pp. 193–226). Waco, TX: Prufrock Press.

Peterson, J. S. (2012). The asset–burden paradox of giftedness: A 15-year phenomenological, longitudinal case study. *Roeper Review, 34*, 1–17.

Peterson, J. S. (2013). School counselors' experiences with children from low-income families and other gifted children in a summer program. *Professional School Counseling, 16*, 194–204.

Peterson, J. S. (2016). Affective curriculum: Proactively addressing the challenges of growing up. In K. R. Stephens & F. A. Karnes (Eds.), *Best practices for curriculum design in gifted education.* (pp. 307–330). Waco, TX: Prufrock Press.

Peterson, J. S., Betts, G., & Bradley, T. (2009). Discussion groups as a component of affective curriculum for gifted students. In J. VanTassel-Baska, T. R. Cross, & R. Olenchak (Eds.), *Social–emotional curriculum with gifted and talented students* (pp. 289–320). Waco, TX: National Association for Gifted Children/Prufrock Press.

Peterson, J. S., Duncan, N., & Canady, K. (2009). A longitudinal study of negative life events, stress, and school experiences of gifted youth. *Gifted Child Quarterly, 53*, 34–49.

Peterson, J. S., & Jen, E. (in press). The Peterson Proactive Developmental Attention (PPDA) model: Nurturing the whole gifted child. *Journal for the Education of the Gifted.*

Peterson, J. S., & Lorimer, M. R. (2011). Student response to a small-group affective curriculum in a school for gifted children. *Gifted Child Quarterly, 55*, 167–180.

Peterson, J. S., & Lorimer, M. R. (2012). Small-group affective curriculum for gifted students: A longitudinal study of teacher-facilitators. *Roeper Review, 34*, 158–169.

Peterson, J. S., & Ray, K. E. (2006). Bullying among the gifted: The subjective experience. *Gifted Child Quarterly, 50*, 252–269.

Peterson, J. S., & Rischar, H. (2000). Gifted and gay: A study of the adolescent experience. *Gifted Child Quarterly, 44*, 149–164.

Peterson, J. S., & Servaty-Seib, H. (2008). Focused, but flexible: A developmental approach to small-group work in schools. In H. L. K. Coleman & C. Yeh (Eds.), *Handbook of school counseling* (pp. 409–429). Mahwah, NJ: Lawrence Erlbaum.

VanTassel-Baska, J. (2012). The integrated curriculum model. In C.M. Callahan & H.L. Hertberg-Davis (Eds.), *Fundamentals of gifted education: Considering multiple perspectives* (pp. 315–325). New York, NY: Routledge.

VanTassel-Baska, J., Cross, T. R., & Olenchak, F. R. (Eds.) (2009). *Social–emotional curriculum with gifted and talented students.* Waco, TX: Prufrock Press.

Wood, S. M., & Lane, E. M. D. (2017). Using the Integrated Curriculum Model to address social, emotional, and career needs of advanced learners. In J. VanTassel-Baska & C. W. Little (Eds.), *Content-based curriculum for high-ability learners* (3rd ed., pp. 523–542). Waco, TX: Prufrock Press.

Academic Advising and Career Planning for Gifted and Talented Students

MICHELLE MURATORI AND CAROL KLOSE SMITH

As best friends in a small Midwestern town, Jon and Stephen, both extremely bright and inquisitive, often talked with each other about their dreams of jobs they would have as adults. Throughout childhood, made alive through imaginative play, their wide-ranging ideas about careers were inspired largely by television and movie characters. They were enthralled with the idea of "special powers" to save the universe, but soon realized that "superhero" wasn't a career. A few years later, they considered becoming crime scene investigators, lawyers, emergency room doctors, and, briefly, even astronauts. Jon and Stephen were inseparable and were regarded by the elementary school's Gifted and Talented (G/T) coordinator as the most academically advanced students in her memory. They loved to learn, had vivid imaginations, and inspired their classmates and each other to "dream big" about the future. They were big fish in a little pond (e.g., Marsh, 1987; Salchegger, 2016).

Then Jon's family relocated to an affluent suburban neighborhood on the West Coast after his father took a position in Silicon Valley. Jon, in middle school, had to adjust to a new set of expectations and found the adjustment quite challenging—in fact, far more so than he had imagined. Surrounded by a large group of intense and extremely driven students, who all seemed to aspire to top-tier universities, and struck by the harsh realization that he was no longer one of the very best students, Jon now felt as if he were a fish out of water. He was plagued with self-doubt about his abilities and future educational and career prospects. Compared to the other students, who had long positioned themselves to earn coveted spots in the local STEM-oriented magnet high school, Jon felt inadequately prepared to compete and felt his excitement for learning fading quickly. Once a confident and enthusiastic student, Jon was immobilized by his fear of making mistakes, especially in the presence of his new peers, and he began to retreat from others both at school and at home. He had difficulty dealing with even minor setbacks and grew to resent the students who seemed ambitious and competitive. Adopting a defensive posture, Jon downplayed the importance of thinking about future goals; in his own words, it was "stupid" to worry too much about college and career. Although he generally maintained respectable grades (mainly to make his parents happy and to keep their anxieties at bay), he refused to take the most challenging courses at school and stopped taking academic risks. Since he was getting mostly As and Bs and an occasional C on his report card, Jon's parents were not alarmed by the changes in his behavior and failed to notice that he had turned away from learning. His academic self-concept had taken a major hit.

In contrast to Jon, Stephen remained in the same small Midwestern school district for the remainder of his precollege years and continued to feel passionate—about everything! Stephen's parents encouraged him to indulge his intellectual curiosity and explore every subject that captured his interest. But Stephen had difficulty narrowing his interests for the sake of establishing career direction. When he was first exposed to chemistry, for instance, he quickly memorized the periodic table and spent many nights at the dinner table teaching his younger brother everything he had learned about each element. Later, when introduced to physics, he could hardly contain his excitement about quantum field theory, cosmic inflation, fluid dynamics, and a host of other topics. Of course, he also loved math and was eager to learn computer languages. Adept not only in STEM subjects, Stephen also excelled in and enjoyed writing, history, and politics. However, because the school district was small and lacked resources, he often learned advanced content on his own by reading books and searching the Internet. The local public high school he attended offered few Advanced Placement (AP) courses, and school officials believed they could not justify offering additional AP courses just for him. Without his friend Jon, he had no intellectual peer with whom he could share ideas and interact meaningfully. As his precollege years progressed, Stephen did not gain sufficient clarity about educational and career direction to focus his efforts on developing any particular interest to a high level outside of the classroom.

This chapter provides perspectives, approaches, and interventions that might be useful to school counselors as they provide career counseling and academic advising to students in middle or high school. Effective guidance can help gifted students meet challenges, develop college- and career-readiness, and reach for their dreams.

Although career development is an ongoing process over much of a person's lifetime, career exploration during precollege years tends to be particularly intense for many gifted students, especially if college is on the horizon and they need to choose a major field of study. School counselors have the training and knowledge necessary to connect academic planning and future career aspirations, and they are uniquely positioned to deliver effective career-oriented interventions to high-ability students. Since career counseling is one of the most requested services by gifted students and their parents (Yoo & Moon, 2006), school counselors need to be equipped with a basic understanding of the needs of this student population and an awareness of factors that may have an impact on talent development and career decisions.

Many educators assume that gifted students' strong reasoning abilities and interests enable them to grasp the process of career development intuitively, pursue any career path they wish, and achieve a fulfilling professional life (Muratori & Smith, 2015); however, this is often not the case. Although being gifted can make some aspects of career choice easier, giftedness also presents unique challenges (Sampson & Chason, 2008). Some gifted students grapple with issues related to early emergence of career interests (Matthews & Foster, 2005) and commit to a career path before they have been exposed to or have had sufficient time and opportunity to explore a range of options. While prematurely foreclosing on options can be problematic, the opposite phenomenon—that is, avoiding commitment to a path—can also be a formidable challenge for some gifted individuals. Experiencing what scholars have termed "overchoice syndrome" (Rysiew, Shore, & Carson, 1994; Rysiew, Shore, & Leeb, 1999) or "multipotentiality" (Greene, 2003), high-ability students who wrestle with persistent career indecision may experience delayed career development (Jung, 2012).

Personality traits such as perfectionism and extreme sensitivity or intensity (Park, Choi, Nam, & Lee, 2011; Sampson & Chason, 2008) as well as underachievement (Peterson, 2001, 2002) can also impede gifted students' talent development and career readiness. While excellence is a realistic and appropriate goal for academically talented students, some gifted youth may internalize unrealistically high expectations from parents and others (whether perceived or real). These expectations may place inordinate pressure on them to make full use of their gifts to contribute to society and attain a high level of academic and career success. Students may feel obligated "to select careers and colleges that others deem sufficiently challenging or esteemed, rather than ones based on their own personal strengths and interests" (Greene, 2006, p. 38). Students labeled *gifted* may also succumb to the false notion or "incorrect positive stereotype … that gifted children are 'naturals' and do not need to study or practice to reach higher levels of expertise and accomplishment" (Subotnik, Olszewski-Kubilius, & Worrell, 2011, p. 10). This erroneous belief about the role of effort can hinder high-ability students from reaching their potential (Dweck, 2006; Subotnik et al., 2011). Undoubtedly, these complicating factors may be a source of stress for academically talented students, and, if left unaddressed, can derail them from achieving success and fulfillment in their educational and career pursuits. Thus, effective career interventions with gifted individuals need to be proactive and intentional (Greene, 2006; Sampson & Chason, 2008).

School counselors and other professionals who interact with academically talented students should keep in mind that gifted students do not fit one particular profile. The very heterogeneity of this population of students on so many dimensions would make it reductionistic and inaccurate to suggest that most are like Jon or Stephen, and, therefore, should follow a prescribed path or benefit from the same intervention. Differentiating academic planning and career development for this population of students is important since their career development needs likely require individualization. Like students at any other ability levels, those with high ability are multidimensional human beings whose needs, personalities, motivation levels, interests, family backgrounds, parental expectations, cultures, lifestyle preferences, and values vary. In fact, their abilities also vary. For example, a student who has been identified with exceptional mathematical ability and relatively lower verbal reasoning abilities may not struggle with determining an educational or career path to the same extent as a student who has similarly high abilities across mathematical and verbal domains. The former student, whose talents lie predominantly in science and math, may find a path easier to identify than the student who has talent in both mathematical and verbal domains. When also taking into account personal characteristics, needs, and preferences, determining educational and career paths becomes exponentially more complicated for gifted students.

In addition, external factors such as resources, or the lack thereof, provided by a school may influence how much support an academically talented student receives to achieve college- and career-readiness. As most counselors and educators are aware, schools differ dramatically in the resources they can offer students, including access to advanced coursework, academic advising, and college counseling. In contrast to some private schools or even well-funded public schools that can provide extensive individualized attention and guidance as well as advanced opportunities for learning and talent development (e.g., access to a large selection of AP courses, International Baccalaureate programs, internships, and research experience), many schools are limited by budgets that are stretched to the limit, rendering services such as college counseling unavailable. Some students, including those with high ability, seek assistance with college and career planning outside of their schools, but hiring a college consultant may be a luxury that only the privileged and wealthy can afford.

The common myth that academically talented students intuitively find their own path toward a career that meets their needs, and surmount barriers on their own, can result in inequalities of opportunity and can deprive academically talented students of basic knowledge about careers (Green, 2006; Maxwell, 2007; Muratori & Smith, 2015). School counselors and other involved professionals must be careful not to fall into the trap of assuming that the brightest and most talented students can figure out a career path themselves simply because they demonstrate competence in academic pursuits (Moon, 2009; Peterson, 2009). In fact, being gifted often adds to the need for academic and career planning that requires discussion, especially for students who face additional barriers such as oppression and discrimination. As school counselors know, understanding the contextual variables of a student's experience is an important part of counseling. It is an important aspect of career development as well.

Students who identify with a minority population may experience being gifted in a different way than do those who identify with the majority culture. For example, a gifted African American student who excels in academics may be taunted as "acting White" (Ford, Grantham, & Whiting, 2008a), and a gifted Latina/o student may experience challenges such as feeling isolated from educators and classmates, the majority of whom may be White (Ford, Grantham, & Whiting, 2008b), when identified and provided with opportunities to excel. These students may be subjected to microaggressions on the basis of their cultural backgrounds, socioeconomic status, or giftedness, undermining their sense of well-being and leading to "avoidance of more difficult course work or careers—especially if stereotype threat is also at play" (Stambaugh & Ford, 2015, p. 193). These experiences, each of which carries explicit or implicit messages, are likely to influence students' thinking about which types of careers are appealing to them and affect how far they are willing to move from family to pursue further education. The students' perceptions and beliefs about educational paths and careers that are within reach may inhibit their career aspirations.

Discussing these potentially sensitive issues with students requires a strong working relationship with them if they are to explore the many nuances of academic and career decision making. For reasons noted earlier, all students in minority cultures may not believe the notion that they can be anything they wish to be with hard work and initiative. While encouragement, the instillation of hope, unconditional positive regard, empathy, and genuineness are all essential to cultivating strong counseling relationships, a more active approach is needed when working with individuals who have experienced oppression, discrimination, and a lack of support. Interventions such as academic planning, raising awareness of relevant services in both the school and the larger community, and assistance with arranging mentorships and other beneficial opportunities are likely to be necessary when providing career guidance to gifted students from marginalized groups.

In spite of their friendship and apparently comfortable social and economic circumstances, Jon and Stephen followed differing educational trajectories and each, uniquely, encountered challenges in middle school and high school that hindered them from maximizing their potential. Although Jon transferred to a well-resourced school district in Northern California that offered advanced coursework and plentiful opportunities for challenge, he experienced a crisis of confidence, which thwarted precollege exploration of interests and development of his talent. Stephen, though remaining enthusiastic about learning and more confident than Jon, struggled with a different type of challenge that some academically talented students encounter—that is, career indecision related to multipotentiality (e.g., Greene, 2003; Muratori & Smith, 2015). Since his school lacked funding and resources to support his talent, he was often left to his own devices to find challenge and intellectual stimulation.

● ● ●

A THEORY-INFORMED CAREER COUNSELING FRAMEWORK

With so much variability among gifted students as well as among the schools they attend, the resources to which they have access, and the conditions to which they are exposed, it may seem antithetical to provide a single blueprint for college and career guidance; however, we recommend that school counselors or others serving this population adopt a theory-informed career counseling framework (see Muratori & Smith, 2015). This approach draws from the work of Gottfredson (2005), who outlined four intervention categories, aligned with four developmental processes, which can help to reduce the risks linked to each developmental process and enhance academic and career development. As Gottfredson (2005) explained, "cognitive growth points to effective learning; self-creation, to adequate experience; circumscription, to self-insight; and compromise, to wise self-investment" (p. 86). The framework that we recommend reflects the broad Gottfredson intervention categories, but is tailored to address career development needs of gifted individuals. To illustrate how school counselors and helping professionals might use this framework with this population, we discuss the cases of Jon and Stephen and describe how we might intervene with these students during each of the developmental processes.

Intervention Category 1: Optimizing Learning

Gifted students who never encounter a significant academic challenge early in school may internalize the message that being gifted means that learning should be effortless. When they eventually do encounter academic challenges, as Jon did when he relocated to a new and more competitive school, the change can be quite disconcerting and unsettling; thus, *optimizing learning* through academic challenge must be an integral part of the career development process, and ideally it should begin early in a child's education. School counselors are advised to utilize academic intervention strategies that have been proven to engage high-ability students effectively in the learning process, such as (a) encouraging above-grade testing to assess a student's mathematical and verbal reasoning abilities and readiness for advanced content (e.g., Muratori & Brody, 2012) and (b) advocating for flexibility in curricular programming (e.g., supporting enrichment and academic acceleration in its numerous forms) and being open to individualizing a student's educational program (e.g., Watters, 2010).

The process of optimizing learning for a gifted child varies, depending on the child's developmental level and unique strengths, interests, and needs. High-ability elementary school students may benefit from exposure to a differentiated curriculum within the classroom, access to accelerated content in their talent domain (e.g., math or language arts), or even whole-grade advancement (i.e., grade skipping) if their abilities are advanced across subjects. Tools such as the *Iowa Acceleration Scale* (3rd ed.; Assouline, Colangelo, Lupkowski-Shoplik, Lipscomb, & Forstadt, 2009) can be used to determine whether whole-grade acceleration is an appropriate intervention for a particular student. As gifted students mature and enter middle school and later high school, they are likely to have access to a greater selection of course options and electives. Although some schools may resist adopting this view, especially when they have a large student body to serve, curricular flexibility and openness to acceleration are necessary to accommodate gifted students' strengths and challenges. To illustrate this perspective, an eighth-grader with exceptionally strong math-reasoning abilities who has accelerated his coursework in mathematics might be ready to study precalculus, yet may be adequately challenged in grade-level courses in other subject areas. A talented ninth-grader with high verbal and mathematical reasoning skills may be ready for advanced coursework in both the humanities and STEM courses. Both of these students are likely to complete the high school curriculum early in one or more content areas and may need to supplement their remaining high school coursework with part-time college courses either online or in person. School counselors are uniquely positioned to assist students with arranging their schedules to accommodate dual enrollment or part-time college enrollment.

Of course, decisions about grade placement and course selection should be guided by data; many able students find participation in an academic talent search to be useful in determining the level of their abilities. Academic talent search centers across the United States have had success with above-grade testing (e.g., giving standardized tests such as the SAT or ACT, designed

KEY CONCEPT

Acceleration

Susannah M. Wood

With acceleration, gifted students can move through traditional academic curriculum at a more rapid pace than is typical, in proportion to their abilities (National Association for Gifted Children [NAGC], n.d.; Southern & Jones, 2015). The term *acceleration* often provokes apprehension related to school and local politics, concerns about educational equity, and fears about negative social and emotional outcomes for accelerated students. The concern about harm is the negative argument cited most often.

Fifty years of acceleration research were analyzed for *A Nation Deceived: How Schools Hold Back America's Brightest Students* (Colangelo, Assouline, & Gross, 2004), and findings suggested that acceleration generally has positive benefits, including academic challenge, an increased likelihood of earning graduate degrees, and social acceptance. However, according to Cross, Anderson, and Mammadov (2015) in the follow-up compendium of research (*A Nation Empowered: Evidence Trumps the Excuses Holding Back America's Brightest Students*), an "omnibus" claim that acceleration is entirely positive should be avoided in favor of a more qualified statement. While only a few studies have found negative outcomes, they do exist, amid the preponderance of studies with mostly positive outcomes (Cross et al., 2015, p. 39). The mixed results may be due to lack of diversity among participants, varying research designs, and differing types of acceleration studied. Among the 20 types of acceleration are these: (a) early admission to kindergarten, (b) early graduation from high school or college, (c) grade skipping, (c) self-paced instruction, (d) subject-matter acceleration, (e) curriculum compacting, (f) telescoping curriculum, (g) extracurricular programs, (h) distance learning, (i) concurrent/dual enrollment, (j) AP courses, and (k) International Baccalaureate programs (Southern & Jones, 2015).

The National Association for Gifted Children (n.d.) lists several positive outcomes; however, the American School Counselor Association (ASCA) has no stance on acceleration and does not mention it in its 2013 position statement on the role and function

(continued)

of school counselors with gifted programs. School counselors receive little, if any, training in gifted education, including acceleration (Wood, Portman, Cigrand, & Colangelo, 2010; Peterson & Wachter Morris, 2010). Yet school counselors are often the first resources consulted by parents, teachers, and administrators about acceleration. School counselors may feel more comfortable recommending dual enrollment in high school and college, AP classes, or early college entrance than more radical options (e.g., grade-skipping, early kindergarten, or first-grade entrance; Wood et al., 2010). With grade-skipping, students are removed from familiar peers, a more visible departure from the school norm that is perhaps viewed as potentially more harmful to their social and emotional adjustment (Wood et al., 2010).

However, school counselors should consider whether *not* accelerating students might be more harmful academically and socially. School counselors approached about acceleration can refer to the *Iowa Acceleration Scale* (3rd ed.) and state policies. They should also consider best practices regarding student–learning fit, course and content sequencing, teacher training, district and school policy, and student readiness, as well as effective measurements of ability and need, student personality and interests, and available resources (Wood et al., 2010, p. 174). The resource section at the end of this text provides websites to help counselors, teachers, and parents determine if acceleration is appropriate for gifted students.

for 11th and 12th graders, to middle school students) to assess verbal and mathematical reasoning abilities of able students.

In the case of Stephen, who is living in a small community with limited resources, the school counselor may need to help him find a challenging curriculum and explore his many interests outside of school. A good starting point would be above-grade-level testing for him through a regional talent search center to assess his reasoning abilities, and subsequently using these data to guide course selection. Since Stephen is highly motivated academically, he may enjoy this experience. His test scores may make him eligible to enroll in online or summer courses through the talent search center or elsewhere, enabling him to accelerate and/or enrich his coursework. With qualifying math and verbal scores on the SAT, he could, for example, enroll in a self-paced online math course and finish a yearlong course in 3 to 6 months; take an online writing course and hone skills in crafting essays, poetry, or fiction; participate in an academic summer program; and explore areas not offered at school, such as probability and game theory, number theory, or astrophysics. It is worth noting that participating in a summer program would connect Stephen with intellectual peers in person. One potential barrier could be cost; however, if his parents could not afford these programs, they might qualify for need-based financial aid and receive a discounted price. They could also search for less expensive options.

Jon's situation is a bit more complicated. Although his school offers many rigorous courses and advanced electives, he has retreated from coursework that might provide meaningful challenge. That pattern has persisted, and he is now underachieving academically even though his grades may be too high to be considered problematic. Underachievement, in this context, is a discrepancy between expected and actual achievement (Figg, Rogers, McCormick, & Low, 2012); thus, while Jon is by no means earning failing grades, he is not performing as well as he had at his previous school.

Unfortunately, there is no magic bullet to reverse underachievement. However, counselors should keep several important considerations in mind when working therapeutically with Jon to address his underachievement. It is essential to establish a trusting relationship that creates a safe space for him to discuss his thoughts and feelings about the many changes in his life (both personal and academic) since relocating to the West Coast, potentially resulting in his feeling cared for (Rubenstein, Siegle, Reis, McCoach, & Burton, 2012). He also might benefit from an opportunity, with a nonjudgmental adult, to reflect on his apparent withdrawal from socializing with peers. If all-or-nothing thinking and perfectionistic strivings seem to be contributing to Jon's distress (e.g., to be successful means being the top student, and if that is impossible, it is best to stop trying), the counselor may consider cognitive behavioral strategies to address the faulty thinking. However, it is also possible that talking about changes and losses, and feeling heard, might nudge him toward reengaging in academics. Although Jon's issues may be rooted in self-doubt and may require a social/emotional intervention, a counselor should not lose sight of Jon's career development. Exploring his interests and aspirations might help to generate hope for the future (Emerich, 1992; Muratori & Smith, 2015).

Intervention Category 2: Optimizing Experience

One central goal of career counseling is to provide opportunities for students to discover and explore career options and pathways. Career interventions can expose students to a broad range of experiences and encourage them to sample some that are unfamiliar (Gottfredson, 2005; Muratori & Smith, 2015). These experiences, which may or may not be school based, can broaden the horizons of gifted youth and help them discover whether they have the foundational resources (e.g., temperament, personality traits) for certain interests and occupational paths.

Optimizing experience can be facilitated in several ways (Muratori & Smith, 2015). Initially, in elementary school, optimizing experience may involve exposing students to careers not represented in their communities. As a child matures and enters middle school and high school, linking interests and preferences to potential careers should become more focal and evolve into more targeted exploration through mentorships, internships, summer programs, independent study projects, community service, and extracurricular activities. Formal and informal programs and opportunities can help students determine whether they wish to continue to pursue an interest as a potential career, whether an interest will be embraced as a hobby or leisure activity rather than as a career path, or whether an interest is not quite as interesting as once thought and is dropped altogether.

Students of all ability levels should explore interests and potential careers during career counseling. However, gifted students are more likely to begin this process at a young age by expressing a need for interest exploration and career development sooner than expected (Matthews & Foster, 2005). To guard against early foreclosure, counselors should encourage gifted students to keep an open mind about career options and, at the same time, continue to develop their interests and talents through classroom experiences and supplemental opportunities.

Both Jon and Stephen are troubled with career indecision—but for different reasons. Whereas Jon's issue is related to his avoidance of preparing and planning for his future due to his adjustment difficulties (and possible depression, for which he should be screened), Stephen has expressed diffuse interests and claims to love everything he learns. Encouraging deeper exploration of his many interests through participation in academic summer programs and competitions may help him identify a career cluster. He may find, for instance, that while he enjoys discussing politics with friends and family members and reading history books for enjoyment, his true passion is in the STEM fields. Of course, he might not achieve clarity simply through involvement in pertinent activities, and instead may continue to flounder if everything he does seems equally exciting. Therefore, school counselors and other career development professionals can utilize interest inventories and other career assessment tools to help indecisive students like Stephen become unstuck. The most important point here is that strategies used to optimize experience, whether recommending internships, involvement in clubs or academic competitions and science fairs, or even job shadowing, can be useful for clarifying career direction. Even if students discover through these experiences what they *do not* want to do, that new awareness should be considered progress.

Intervention Category 3: Optimizing Self-Insight

Optimizing self-insight involves exploration of self (Gottfredson, 2005) and can be fostered through examining abilities, interests, personal goals, and values. While traditional trait-factor interest inventories can fail to differentiate interests for gifted students, a variety of vocational assessments can be quite useful for gaining clarity about values, personality preferences, and interests. Indeed, career assessments can help students of all ability levels to gain insight not only into which career fields may be a good match, but also into those that may not be such a good fit. The circumscription process, referring to the process of eliminating potential career paths, can be accomplished through the use of career assessments, extracurricular involvement, summer programs, and other experiences; it is an integral part of career decision making. However, that process may be frustrating for some students who are uncomfortable with ambiguity and are upset about not having clarity. An important caveat here is that career assessments should be accompanied by an opportunity to process and reflect. Career assessments given in isolation without the opportunity for interpretation, discussion, and reflection may create more confusion and even disinterest.

Given Jon's current state, a counselor working with him can reassure him that career decision making is a process. By actively engaging in the circumscription and compromise processes (i.e., letting go of preferred alternative pathways so as to focus on ones that are more accessible, albeit less compatible), Jon may find a few promising paths that have meaning, enable him to use his abilities, and fit his preferred lifestyle. Aware that Jon may be reluctant to commit to career exploration, his counselor can encourage him to explore career options and take advantage of opportunities and experiences that might help him gain clarity. Through processing the results of career assessments with his counselor, if he does take a battery of assessments, Jon may better understand his needs and preferences and feel more hopeful about his career prospects. He may already realize that choosing an educational and career path is not a simple matter. He can be reminded that even though he is now competing with high school peers for positions on academic teams and admission to selective colleges, there are a multitude of fine universities where he can distinguish himself.

Optimizing self-insight also entails evaluating perceptions of what it means to be gifted and of the impact of this label, especially as it pertains to gifted students' expectations of self and others' expectations of them in the career decision-making process (Muratori & Smith, 2015). After facing a setback upon relocating and experiencing a loss of identity, Jon has an opportunity, with his counselor, to develop a realistic appraisal of himself through examining how being identified as gifted when he was younger has influenced his expectations. If his school took away the label when he underachieved, he can be reassured that many schools include emphasis on natural endowment in their philosophy. Giftedness, therefore, does not "go away" during times of low academic performance.

Intervention Category 4: Optimizing Self-Investment

Creating a plan for moving toward goals and aspirations requires intention. *Optimizing self-investment* implies a sense of direction and motivation and diligence to move forward. The process of investing time, effort, and other resources in developing one's talent may involve participating in various activities, such as academic summer programs, academic competitions, advanced coursework, research opportunities, internships, service projects, and job shadowing. Pursuing opportunities may result in skill development and knowledge acquisition (Gottfredson, 2005). For instance, academically talented high school students who are interested in medical research as a potential career field may learn a great deal more about their suitability for it by participating in one or more of the following activities: engaging in advanced and enriching coursework through summer or online programs that exposes them to subjects that may not be available in the school curriculum (e.g., genetics, neuroscience); working with a mentor (e.g., a professor or advanced graduate student at a nearby university or a family friend who has expertise) on a research project or participating in a research internship in a laboratory; and/or submitting research projects to science fairs and participating in Science Olympiads. Investing in these kinds of activities can bring into sharper focus what a particular career actually entails and help students to further define educational and career goals.

One caveat is that barriers may prevent students from taking advantage of opportunities that might help them reach aspirational goals. Often the biggest hurdle is finding opportunities for underrepresented gifted students (e.g., students of color; lesbian, gay, bisexual, transgender, and queer [LGBTQ] students) and/or economically disadvantaged students. A counselor can, by working collaboratively, help students with significant barriers not only gain access, but also develop a greater sense of personal agency by finding opportunities that foster competence and confidence.

This process requires time and investment from the counselor, student, and family. Opportunities for a student to explore an interest area are essential for growth, and interests and career goals should be carefully and appropriately matched with them. The proliferation of and emphasis on STEM careers have created opportunities, both in and outside of school, for students to experience growth in those areas. However, for those students who are gifted in the arts or humanities, counselors may need to find connections outside of school for developing skills and direction or locate STEAM programs that have added the arts into various STEM initiatives. Especially when local schools have eliminated arts programs for budgetary reasons, promoting summer opportunities in the visual or performing arts (or in other areas with limited school offerings) is important. Successful experiences, whether in STEM fields, the arts, or humanities, can give students a sense of accomplishment and increased self-efficacy.

Since Stephen's community has limited educational resources, counselors can provide information about opportunities. An excellent online resource with an impressive list of links to opportunities is *Imagine*, which is also a print magazine that his parents might order (see the list of resources at the end of the book). As has been noted, Stephen's greatest challenge is narrowing his preferences and targeting a content area or career cluster to pursue. Learning about additional realistic options might make decision making an even more agonizing process for him, but opportunities to learn firsthand whether a direction is or is not a good fit are particularly important for someone like him.

For Jon, who has lost motivation and some self-efficacy regarding school performance, extracurricular and summer programs may be a way for him to reconnect with his intense curiosity and identify aspirations. An opportunity to see himself in an academic context outside of his current school may be vital to reversing underachievement. A counselor might help him and his parents find experiences that will engage, encourage, and motivate him. Ideally, the result of these activities will be that Jon develops self-knowledge and increases skills that contribute to his career development.

● ● ●

CONCLUDING THOUGHTS AND RECOMMENDATIONS

One of the most essential points for counselors working with academically talented students to remember is to approach academic advising and college and career interventions with flexibility and open-mindedness. A one-size-fits-all approach is usually not effective with high-ability students, just as it is unlikely to be effective with students with lower ability levels. As Gottfredson (2005) suggested, "one-size-fits-all instruction works no better in career education than in academic, health, or other kinds of education" (p. 90). School counselors can have a special function in their work with gifted students when helping them develop career readiness. With their training and empathy helping them be attuned to gifted students' need for educational and career guidance, school counselors can make it a priority to provide academic advising and career counseling to the ablest students just as much as to other students. Without the capable guidance of compassionate school counselors, students like Jon and Stephen might slip through the cracks of the educational system and fail to develop their abilities optimally—a loss not only for them, but potentially for society as well.

● ● ●

REFERENCES

American School Counselor Association. (2013). *The school counselor and gifted and talented programs*. Alexandria, VA: Author.

Assouline, S. G., Colangelo, N., Lupkowski-Shoplik, A., Lipscomb, J., & Forstadt, L. (2009). *The Iowa Acceleration Scale, 3rd edition: Manual*. Scottsdale, AZ: Great Potential Press.

Colangelo, N., Assouline, S., & Gross, M. (2004). Executive summary. In N. Colangelo, S. Assouline, & M. Gross (Eds.), *A nation deceived: How schools hold back America's brightest students* (Vol. 1, p. 53). Iowa City, IA: Connie Belin & Jacqueline N. Blank International Center for Gifted Education and Talent Development.

Cross, T., Anderson, L., & Mammadov, S. (2015). The academic, socialization, and psychological effects of acceleration: Research synthesis. In S. G. Assouline, N. Colangelo, J. VanTassel-Baska, & A. Lupowski-Shoplik (Eds.), *A nation empowered: Evidence trumps the excuses holding back America's brightest students* (pp. 31–42). Iowa City, IA: Connie Belin & Jacqueline N. Blank International Center for Gifted Education and Talent Development.

Dweck, C. S. (2006). *Mindset: The psychology of success*. New York, NY: Ballantine.

Emerich, L. J. (1992). Academic underachievement among the gifted: Students' perceptions of factors that reverse the pattern. *Gifted Child Quarterly, 36*, 140–146. doi:10.1177/001698629203600304

Figg, S. D., Rogers, K. B., McCormick, J., & Low, R. (2012). Differentiating low performance of the gifted learner: Achieving, underachieving, and selective consuming students. *Journal of Advanced Academics, 23*, 53–71. doi:10.1177/1932202X11430000

Ford, D. Y., Grantham, T. C., & Whiting, G. W. (2008a). Another look at the achievement gap: Learning from the experiences of gifted Black students. *Urban Education, 43*(2), 216–239. doi:10.1177/0042085907312344

Ford, D. Y., Grantham, T. C., & Whiting, G. W. (2008b). Culturally and linguistically diverse students in gifted education: Recruitment and retention issues. *Exceptional Children, 74*(3), 289–306.

Gottfredson, L. S. (2005). Applying Gottfredson's theory of circumscription and compromise in career guidance and counseling. In S. D. Brown & R. W. Lent (Eds.), *Career development and counseling: Putting theory and research to work* (pp. 71–100). Hoboken, NJ: Wiley.

Greene, M. J. (2003). Gifted adrift? Career counseling of the gifted and talented. *Roeper Review, 25*, 66–72. doi:10.1080/02783190309554201

Greene, M. J. (2006). Helping build lives: Career and life development of gifted and talented students. *Professional School Counseling, 10*(1), 34–42.

Jung, J. Y. (2012). Giftedness as a developmental construct that leads to eminence as adults: Ideas and implications from an occupational/career decision-making perspective. *Gifted Child Quarterly, 56*, 189–193. doi:10.1177/0016986212456072

Marsh, H. W. (1987). The big-fish–little-pond effect on academic self-concept. *Journal of Educational Psychology, 79*, 280–295. doi:10.1037/0022-0663.79.3.280

Matthews, D. J., & Foster, J. F. (2005). A dynamic scaffolding model of teacher development: The gifted education consultant as a catalyst for change. *Gifted Child Quarterly, 49*, 222–230. doi:10.1177/001698620504900304

Maxwell, M. (2007). Career counseling is personal counseling: A constructivist approach to nurturing the development of gifted female adolescents. *Career Development Quarterly, 55*, 206–224. doi:10.1002/j.2161-0045.2007.tb00078.x

Moon, S. M. (2009). Myth 15: High-ability students don't face problems and challenges. *Gifted Child Quarterly, 53*(4), 474–476.

Muratori, M. C., & Brody, L. (2012). Schools and talent search centers: Meeting the needs of academically talented students. *Parenting for High Potential, 1*(6), 16–19.

Muratori, M. C., & Smith, C. K. (2015). Guiding the talent and career development of the gifted individual. *Journal of Counseling & Development, 93*(2), 173–182. doi:10.1002/j.1556-6676.2015.00193.x

National Association for Gifted Children. (n.d.). Acceleration. Retrieved from https://www.nagc.org/resources-publications/gifted-education-practices/acceleration

Park, H., Choi, B. Y., Nam, S. K., & Lee, S. M. (2011). The role of career stress in the relationship between maladaptive perfectionism and career attitude maturity in South Korean undergraduates. *Journal of Employment Counseling, 48*(1), 27–36. doi:10.1002/j.2161-1920.2011.tb00108.x

Peterson, J. S. (2001). Successful adults who were once adolescent underachievers. *Gifted Child Quarterly, 45*, 236–250. doi:10.1177/001698620104500402

Peterson, J. S. (2002). A longitudinal study of post–high-school development in gifted individuals at risk for poor educational outcomes. *Journal for Secondary Gifted Education, 14*, 6–18. doi:10.4219/jsge-2002-384

Peterson, J. S. (2009). Myth 17: Gifted and talented individuals do not have unique social and emotional needs. *Gifted Child Quarterly, 53*, 280–282. doi:10.1177/0016986209346946

Peterson, J. S., & Wachter Morris, C. (2010). Preparing school counselors to address concerns related to giftedness: A study of accredited counselor preparation programs. *Journal for the Education of the Gifted, 33*, 311–366.

Rubenstein, L. D., Siegle, D., Reis, S. M., McCoach, D. B., & Burton, M. G. (2012). A complex quest: The development and research of underachievement interventions for gifted students. *Psychology in the Schools, 49*, 678–694. doi:10.1002/pits.21620

Rysiew, K. J., Shore, B. M., & Carson, A. D. (1994). Multipotentiality and overchoice syndrome: Clarifying common usage. *Gifted and Talented International, 9*(2), 41–46.

Rysiew, K. J., Shore, B. M., & Leeb, R. T. (1999). Multipotentiality, giftedness, and career choice: A review. *Journal of Counseling & Development, 77*, 423–430. doi:10.1002/j.1556-6676.1999.tb02469.x

Salchegger, S. (2016). Selective school systems and academic self-concept: How explicit and implicit school-level tracking relate to the big-fish–little-pond effect across cultures. *Journal of Educational Psychology, 108*(3), 405–423. doi:10.1037/edu0000063

Sampson, J. P., & Chason, A. K. (2008). Helping gifted and talented adolescents and young adults make informed and careful career choices. In. S. I. Pfeiffer (Ed.), *Handbook of giftedness in children: Psychoeducational theory, research, and best practices* (pp. 327–346), New York, NY: Springer-Verlag.

Southern, W. T., & Jones, E. D. (2015). Types of acceleration: Dimensions and issues. In S. G. Assouline, N. Colangelo, J. VanTassel-Baska, & A. Lupowski-Shoplik (Eds.), *A nation empowered: Evidence trumps the excuses holding back America's brightest students* (pp. 9–18). Iowa City, IA: Connie Belin & Jacqueline N. Blank International Center for Gifted Education and Talent Development.

Stambaugh, T., & Ford, D. Y. (2015). Microaggressions, multiculturalism, and gifted individuals who are Black, Hispanic, or low income. *Journal of Counseling & Development, 93*(2), 192–201. doi:10.1002/j.1556-6676.2015.00195.x

Subotnik, R. F., Olszewski-Kubilius, P., & Worrell, F. C. (2011). Rethinking giftedness and gifted education: A proposed direction forward based on psychological science. *Psychological Science in the Public Interest, 12*(1), 3–54. doi:10.1177/1529100611418056

Watters, J. J. (2010). Career decision making among gifted students: The mediation of teachers. *Gifted Child Quarterly, 54,* 222–238. doi:10.1177/0016986210369255

Wood, S., Portman, T. A. A., Cigrand, D., & Colangelo, N. (2010). School counselors' perceptions and experience with acceleration as a program option for gifted and talented students. *Gifted Child Quarterly, 54*(3) 168–178. doi:10.1177/0016986210367940

Yoo, J. E., & Moon, S. M. (2006). Counseling needs of gifted students: An analysis of intake forms at a university-based counseling center. *Gifted Child Quarterly, 50,* 52–61.

9

Personal/Social Counseling and Mental Health Concerns

JEAN SUNDE PETERSON

A speech/theater teacher at a large urban high school refers Andrew (pseudonym for a composite profile), 16, to the school counselor because "he's out of control and living dangerously." The counselor, who routinely examines the student's school file before such a meeting, finds standardized test percentiles in the high 90s, a good attendance record, and regular participation in the arts, but also a high incidence of lateness to class and an academic record that has deteriorated in high school. Family information shows an older brother attending a distant university, parental divorce when Andrew was 5, and, at age 12, Andrew relocating with his brother and mother when she remarried.

Andrew presents as personable, verbal, socially smooth—and somewhat arrogant. He claims he can raise his current low grades before the semester ends. Missed assignments are the key. He says he adds provocative comments to class discussion, and teachers like him.

His best friend lives 2000 miles away, where Andrew lived prior to his move at age 12. Andrew has gravitated toward dramatic females locally, and his current girlfriend is in high conflict at home. His grades deteriorated after becoming involved with her. He has run away several times and now has thoughts of running away with her. He mentions a special relationship with a male friend. When he drinks, he drinks too much, and his friends worry about him.

Andrew believes the psychologists he saw in the past did not understand him. He was diagnosed with attention deficit hyperactivity disorder (ADHD) and depression, but was noncompliant with medication. He recognizes that he makes poor choices. He claims not to be suicidal currently, but has been in the past. He has self-harmed. He says his father has almost no contact with him, but his father does have a close relationship with his brother. Andrew says his own problems resemble his highly intelligent father's. Andrew has been exploring anarchic and white supremacist groups online.

The counselor plans to meet with him in a week, but will informally check on him daily and then meet with him and his mother together, a meeting Andrew quickly agrees to. Regardless of whether a referral will be made eventually, the counselor hopes to build a therapeutic relationship with Andrew to be able to provide ongoing support at school as needed.

A few days after the school counselor's meeting with Andrew, his mother contacts the counselor because of the girlfriend. She says Andrew struggles with impulse control, is easily distracted and affected emotionally, has difficulty managing emotions, and escalates conflict quickly when sad or angry. He resists authority at home, and his arguments with her leave her worn out and sad. She says her husband, Andrew's stepfather, ignores Andrew and does not understand giftedness.

● ● ●

PERTINENT RESEARCH AND CLINICAL LITERATURE

Circumstances and Needs

This chapter is a discussion of the construct of giftedness as it intersects with the practice of counseling. The vignette may seem extreme, but the circumstances (e.g., divorce, remarriage, relocation), behaviors (e.g., academic underachievement, poor relationship skills, running away, substance use), and emotions (e.g., depression, anxiety, fear of abandonment, loneliness, agitation) are not uncommon, as any school counselor who works with adolescents knows. Though researchers have typically not compared gifted and general-population youth on most of these concerns, clinicians focused on gifted youth are familiar with stories like Andrew's—probably not with a similar full array of concerns, but at least with some or many of them. Like any adolescents, gifted teens are growing up, navigating complex peer and family relationships, and feeling frantic at times. Unfortunately, over many decades, the gifted-education field has paid relatively little attention to social and emotional development, compared with attention to academic curriculum and performance. "Needs" are often discussed, but usually only in connection with appropriate rigor in academic curriculum. Research attention to actual counseling approaches in the field (e.g., Hébert, 2000; Jen, 2015; Kerr & Kurpius, 2004; Mofield & Chakraborti-Ghosh, 2010; Peterson, 2013; Peterson & Lorimer, 2011, 2012; Pfeiffer, 2013a; Wood, 2010) and book chapters about counseling approaches for gifted students (e.g., Peterson, 2012a; Pfeiffer, 2013b) are both rare. Both school and community counselors can benefit from such guidance, especially when working with complex situations like Andrew's, but in more limited circumstances.

Though long discussed in gifted-education literature by stalwart advocates (e.g., Betts & Kercher, 1999; Gowan, 1972; Hollingworth, 1926; Whitmore, 1980), only in recent decades has social, emotional, and career development had a consistent, significant presence in the field, with many well-attended program sessions at gifted-education conferences. In counselor education, unfortunately, individuals with exceptional ability are typically not viewed as a special population that warrants differentiated counseling approaches, unlike persons with physical, intellectual, or emotional disability. *Giftedness* and *high ability* are not included among demographic variables in the current Council of Accreditation of Counseling and Related Educational Programs standards (CACREP, 2016), and giftedness continues to have little or no presence in school counselor preparatory curriculum (Peterson & Wachter, 2010).

Serious Concerns

Areas such as disordered eating, self-injury, sexual abuse, parent–child conflict, arrested development, and asynchronous development have generally not been studied, per se, related to giftedness. However, S. M. Wood and Craigen (2011) thoroughly examined research related to self-injury and included speculation about factors contributing to gifted persons' susceptibility to it: lack of expressive language (Levenkron, 1998), not feeling connected to the body (Favazza & Conterio, 1988), high sensitivity to emotions and sensory stimuli (Conterio, Lader, & Bloom, 1998), maladaptive perfectionism (Dixon, Lapsley, & Hanchon, 2004), and negative reactions to perceived failure (Roberts & Lovett, 1994). Krafchek (2017), in a recent qualitative dissertation, found that the role of academic achievement changed and self-worth contingencies shifted prior to disordered eating in high-achieving and gifted females. A school counselor might see anxiety (Gaesser, 2014), depression (Jackson & Peterson, 2003), stress and disruptive behavior (Peterson, Duncan, & Canady, 2009), bullying and thoughts of violence (Peterson & Ray, 2006a, 2006b), and fears related to sexual orientation (Peterson & Rischar, 2000) in gifted students. School counselors should keep in mind the characteristics of giftedness discussed in Chapter 3 of this book, as they may intensify factors contributing to any of these challenges as well as how they are experienced by gifted students. As with any other population, when social and emotional concerns interfere with schoolwork, relationships, or well-being, they warrant the attention of helping professionals.

KEY CONCEPT

Beware of Assumptions About Achievement

Stereotypes of both gifted high achievers and gifted low achievers abound. The default profile of the former is a conscientious, culturally advantaged, eager, compliant, respectful, positive "good kid" who does not struggle academically. For their peers and the adults around them, high achievers may epitomize "giftedness." The profile of the latter, especially during adolescence, is someone resistant to authority and external expectations, lazy, uninterested in learning, and cynical about school—that is, someone who *won't* perform.

These stereotypes are unfair and potentially dangerous—for gifted students in both broad categories. When there is no room in peers' and invested adults' assumptions about high achievers for self-doubt, sense of vulnerability, stress from their own and others' expectations, and painful and unsettling experiences, then negative outcomes, when they occur, are a surprise. High achievers who struggle socially and emotionally during the school years may be struggling with depression and even silently flirting with suicide. Most will likely survive "growing up," but the school years might be lonely and frightening—even for those who are well liked, even popular, and excel in activities and academics. Because of their good record, school counselors might not think to ask open-ended questions about worries or stress during a perfunctory meeting about a class schedule, a letter of recommendation, or college plans. Later, agency counselors and psychologists may see such individuals more than school counselors did, when the image of success during the school years has become less important and maturity has allowed them to seek support. Some are sad and adrift in college, after leaving a strong, positive identity behind.

High achievers may become underachievers in late elementary or middle school (Peterson, 2002; Peterson & Colangelo, 1996), and teachers and counselors at the next school level may not be aware of their level of intelligence, now overshadowed by negative behavior or listlessness. A multitude of factors can contribute to underachievement, of course—peer and family relationships, horrendous life experiences, learning preferences, even cultural values that celebrate humility—

(continued)

KEY CONCEPT *(continued)*

not "showing what you know" (Peterson, 1999). Unfortunately, low-achieving gifted children and teens may not be on the gifted-education radar (e.g., entered the district after the identification year; teachers, unaware of student history, not examining low performance with giftedness in mind; each year, a different teacher; multiple teachers during middle and high school; learning disabilities becoming newly and increasingly problematic; no parent or guardian advocacy; lack of consistent family leadership; difficult family economic circumstances). They may then miss opportunities to interact with intellectual peers and to feel validated for their intellectual strengths, creative talent, outside-of-the-box thinking, insights about people and historical contexts—and resilience. School counselors may forget to ask about change and loss: "What's different this year, compared to last year?" "I'm wondering if something has been left behind." "What has changed in your life?"

When educators get to know high and low performers beyond the stereotypes, they discover that these students, regardless of their place on a broad continuum of motivation to achieve, are much more complex than is usually evident at a superficial (and possibly judgmental) level. High achievers probably welcome a school counselor's *not* being in awe of their performance, instead being genuinely interested in their well-being, holistically. Underachievers are likely to welcome respectful counselor curiosity about how they are experiencing school, developmental challenges, life transitions, and current contexts. Interest in how both achievers and underachievers experience the asset–burden paradox of giftedness is likely to open the gate to meaningful conversation that helps them feel that they "matter" in school—beyond what they do or do not do. School counselors can have great impact on the current and future life of these students. Important to remember is that both high and low achievers during the school years may be surprisingly different in college (Peterson, 2000, 2002) and as adults (Peterson, 2001b). It is easy to forget that reality in the present moment.

Underachievement

For mental health concerns, school counselors are likely to see more gifted underachievers than high achievers. High achievers' concerns may be masked by stellar academic or talent performance. Especially pertinent to Andrew's challenges are findings in Peterson's (e.g., 2000, 2001b, 2002; Peterson & Colangelo, 1996) several studies of underachievers, which offer hope that adolescents who feel developmentally stuck regarding identity, direction, relationships, autonomy, or conflict at home during high school can change.

School-File Patterns

In a study of patterns in the school files of 153 gifted achievers and underachievers (Peterson & Colangelo, 1996), 20% of students still classified as underachievers had raised their academic performance by a full grade point by graduation. Findings warn against making assumptions about learning based on academic performance: 20 of the 49 underachievers had ACT scores at or above the 90th percentile. School counselors can consider that extremely able children and teens might be missed during identification for special programs, given that episodic underachievement, in response to life events, for example, might affect their classroom grades and scores on standardized assessments for a few years. If they are not able to be involved in some form of differentiated programming, they cannot benefit from interaction with intellectual peers during a difficult developmental period.

Four Years Later

A 4-year follow-up study (Peterson, 2000) of 73% of the original sample in the study mentioned earlier found that 87% of underachievers (versus 100% of achievers) went to college, 52% of all underachievers had 4 years of college (compared with 83% of achievers), 56% of extreme underachievers had 4 years of college, and 41% of all underachievers performed better academically in college than in high school. Those percentages can be viewed positively, since parents, teachers, administrators, gifted-education personnel, and school counselors probably did not expect such postsecondary results, especially from the extreme underachievers. Episodic (versus chronic) underachievement in high school and improvement before graduation were associated with improvement during college. Financial and other nonacademic factors may have impact on whether college attendance is sustained steadily.

The main challenges of all 97 participants, according to responses to an open-ended question on the survey, were related to developmental tasks: autonomy (for 61%), a significant relationship (24%), identity (21%), and career direction (19%). Other concerns were related to academics (51%), social concerns (27%), a new environment (24%), a critical life event (21%), and finances (18%). These narrative responses argue that nonacademic challenges warrant attention before and during gifted students' college years.

At-Risk Gifted Adolescents

Peterson (2002) also followed 14 of the original participants qualitatively (inviting a letter every 6 months) and quantitatively (initial assessments of perceptions of family cohesion, communication, stress, and satisfaction, and a recurring brief survey asking for scaled responses about direction, maturity of relationships, autonomy, and conflict with parents). This mixed group of gifted high (one) and moderate (one) achievers and moderate (four) and extreme (eight) underachievers were all considered at risk for poor outcomes because of depression, severe family conflict, family situation, or underachievement and might be typical of gifted students who are referred to the school counselor. Some resembled Andrew.

After 4 years, three were college graduates, five others had at least 3 years of college, seven had made notable progress in at least three areas of development, and two extreme underachievers had had 4 years of college. For half, conflict with family had provoked the most writing and was still salient. One high achiever and one moderate underachiever, both National Merit Scholars, had dropped out of college after 2 years, had returned to college by the end of the study, but reported no progress in three areas of development. Initial level of family cohesion seemed to be related to outcomes.

Though some of the study participants did not move out of stuckness, others had had unusual experiences in an environmental program, a Semester at Sea, or international hitchhiking funded by periodic work in Alaska fisheries, for example, with developmental progress in identity, direction, relationships, autonomy, and resolution of conflict with family. Findings suggested that convergence of developmental task accomplishments is related to ability to focus on school, and silent distress is associated with stress-related disorders, including misuse of substances and depression.

Successful Former Underachievers

In a retrospective study of 30 successful adults who once were adolescent underachievers (Peterson, 2001b), with the emphasis on school and family, a general profile emerged: difficult to raise; family and/or school factors associated with decline; one uninvolved parent; friends and siblings who achieved; one parent a nonacademic achiever; "no fuss" about achievement; unpredictable teacher feedback; conflict with same-gender parent; an achieving adult model elsewhere; and a positive developmental event associated with change in achievement late in college. Leaving home appeared to be associated with change, differentiation from parents occurred in the late 20s, and career direction then emerged. Interactive systemic factors seemed to be associated with underachievement.

As with the other Peterson studies of underachievement, developmental stuckness and task accomplishment were associated with negative and positive changes, respectively, in motivation to achieve.

Important for school counselors to keep in mind is that change is possible. Predictions about future outcomes should not be based on behaviors and academic performance during one stage of development or one school level. These studies underscore that systemic factors may affect motivation or ability to achieve. Circumstances can change, life transitions can be traversed successfully, and even one developmental task accomplishment (e.g., finding direction, experiencing a mature relationship) may lead to others—and to better results academically. Assumptions about gifted students like Andrew, whose life circumstances have changed, whose history is not known by educators, and whose cocky protective cover belies insecurity, self-doubt, fears, toxic relationships, and misuse of substances, may not only be inaccurate, but also prevent them from getting much needed help as they run off the rails. Their high intelligence is both asset and burden (Peterson, 2012), and the burdens may not be obvious.

High Achievement

Assumptions that high achievers have few or no mental health concerns are potentially dangerous. Several studies have found that these individuals tend to hide their distress for fear of the toxic effect on others of their telling (e.g., Jackson & Peterson, 2003, Peterson, 2002), to protect a positive social image (Peterson & Rischar, 2000), or to honor a belief that they should resolve their problems themselves (Peterson & Ray, 2006a, 2006b). Andrew is currently not a high achiever, but if he had engaged with a school counselor during earlier school years, some of the information and discussion here might have been helpful.

In the Peterson (2000) follow-up study mentioned earlier, 9% of former high achievers and 41% of former moderate achievers became underachievers in college. Those findings again suggest that preparing gifted students for "launching" (Peterson, 2002) by attending to current and anticipated social and emotional concerns systematically during secondary-level education is important. Pertinent to identity development and representative of the former underachievers in the follow-up study, one female student with an exceptionally high IQ reported that her dramatic rebellion was done by the time she graduated from high school, and she achieved well in college.

Developmental impasse is not unique to underachievers. Some high achievers may feel stuck in a narrow performance-oriented identity, feeling no permission to explore areas of interest beyond those in which they are confident of success, or to consider a career path not supported by their parents. They may also not feel encouraged to balance academics with recreation and social relationships, or to address debilitating perfectionism. Some may never have expressed strong feelings, fears, and doubts, or a need for guidance.

Peterson, Duncan, and Canady (2009) found that stress levels increased steadily throughout the school years, and overcommitment was a major theme in that regard. Peterson's (2013) study of school counselors working with young gifted children during a summer program found that the counselors had not expected the great differences between the gifted children and those in the general population with whom they worked during the school year. They saw anxiety and high stress when the former compared themselves with others in the summer program and acknowledged a knowledge gap. Some perceived each activity as a "test," and they were anxious when not bringing prior knowledge into a new curriculum component. Keeping these findings about high achievers in mind might help school counselors at all school levels to feel compassion and to be able to build therapeutic relationships with them.

Andrew's Mental Health

Positive Disintegration

Andrew's responses to his environment and to intense, uncomfortable feelings reflect developmental potential, according to Polish psychiatrist, psychologist, and theorist Dabrowski (1967). Dabrowski noticed the intensity, sensitivity, and emotional extremes of intellectually and artistically gifted youth, in addition to their urge toward internal development (Daniels & Piechowski, 2009). Dabrowski's (1967; see also Mendaglio, 2008) theory of positive disintegration offers a framework for understanding the extreme distress Andrew is feeling during early and middle adolescence. Intense upheaval, doubt, and internal and external conflict push him toward support, but only after considerable and extended emotional pain. The components of his developmental potential are high general intelligence, overexcitabilities, and the capacity for self-directed emotional growth and self-determination (Daniels & Piechowski, 2009). Perhaps Andrew cannot believe that he has potential for growth during his darkest times, but it may be propelling him forward. Chapter 5 offers additional information about this theory.

Overexcitabilities

Cognitive sensitivity (Mendaglio, 2007), connected with overexcitabilities (OEs) and discussed briefly in Chapter 3 (see also Piechowski, 1999; Tieso, 2007), also seems to apply to Andrew. Daniels and Piechowski's (2009) attention to OEs in their book on intensity prompts speculation about Andrew's sensitivity to change—even as related to medications. How he experienced the developmental transitions related to parental divorce and remarriage, his loss of friends and a familiar context through relocation, and changes he observed in his three family contexts likely reflects characteristics associated with giftedness.

All five areas of OE are of interest here. Andrew's active, physical restlessness suggest psychomotor OE. His sensory OE is manifested in emotional extremes, in reactivity demanding action, and perhaps in being drawn to alcohol-induced and other altered states. Intellectual OE is manifested in being eager to learn, loving ideas, and wanting to make sense of himself, his brother, and his three parents. Imaginational OE is probably most apparent in his fantasies about the future when in intense, conflict-ridden relationships. Emotional OE is reflected in intense mood swings, provoking his family at home, and complexly loving his friends. It would be easy to miss Andrew's concern for others, including his current and former girlfriends, given his often scattered self-examination and sense of urgency to calm himself through action—running away and cutting. Insights and creative impulses, if kept internal, may contribute to distress, according to Daniels and Piechowski (2009). Applying that perspective here, Andrew might be viewed as desperately trying to maintain stability.

In a longitudinal study of a gifted survivor of multiple trauma (Peterson, 2012, 2014), one theme was that out-of-control feelings generated a sense of urgency to gain control, which in turn led to making impulsive, dramatic decisions, cutting, bingeing and purging, defending or advocating for other victims, and dropping out of school. Andrew does not have disordered eating, but has run away, cut, made impulsive decisions, and rescued troubled girlfriends. Though he may not have experienced the abuse the traumatized research subject experienced, his feeling abandoned by his father, ignored by his stepfather, and bereft of a familiar context during a vulnerable developmental period suggests posttraumatic stress. His behaviors and emotional reactions may be frantic responses to his complex world, recursively made more volatile by his choices and behaviors. He wants intimacy—close friendship with one or two peers, not huge groups of acquaintances (see Gross, 2004). Characteristics associated with giftedness are an overlay.

Underachievement

Gifted males and females who underachieve in middle school may have achieved well during elementary school (Peterson, 1997, 1998, 2001a), but life events, circumstances, and confusing emotions and thoughts during puberty may affect motivation to achieve and ability to focus (Peterson, 2002). Underachievers may test the limits of others' acceptance and tolerance, as Andrew apparently does, but adults should not assume that underachievers have low self-esteem regarding ability (McCoach & Siegle, 2003). Andrew talks confidently about his intelligence, but also offers that he might not be investing because he may not be able to deliver. "Smart" is the component of his identity he has felt best about.

Tardiness

Regarding his tardiness, underachievers in Peterson and Colangelo's (1996) study were late much more than high achievers were. The researchers speculated that lateness might reflect passive aggression—more socially acceptable than blatant hostility. Females were late more often than males were, perhaps because they did not have other outlets for anger.

Substances

Substance use has had little research attention in the gifted-education field, but three studies are pertinent. High intelligence at age 10 correlated positively with alcohol use at age 30 in the United Kingdom (Batty et al., 2008), and Wilmoth (2012) found a positive correlation between intelligence and past recreational drug use in the United States. The latter researcher speculated that substance use might reflect valuing novelty and being unconcerned about addiction because of confidence in self-control (Schmeichel, Vohs, & Baumeister, 2003). At the highest intelligence levels, Winner's (2000) correlations were less positive, perhaps because of less social connection at those levels.

Not Feeling Understood

Andrew's feeling that psychologists and psychiatrists did not understand him reflects findings in Yermish's (2010) dissertation study of 30 highly gifted individuals who had experienced therapy. Therapeutic rupture (Safran, Muran, & Shaker, 2014) occurred when the helping professionals seemed to lack understanding of giftedness, including that it affects all of life, and showed no curiosity about how giftedness was experienced. When rupture occurred, it seemed impossible to recover the therapeutic relationship, yet compliant young clients continued to attend sessions their parents had arranged.

● ● ●

COUNSELOR POSTURE

Conceptualization

During the second meeting with the school counselor, Andrew attributes his poor grades to peer and family stressors and his own internal conflict. He describes himself as full of shame and regret and intensely influenced by mood and contexts. He says he thinks too much and is always restless. When he considers developmental tasks, he says he feels "stuck" not only in identity, but also with relationships, including with his family. He wants proof of caring from people he cares about, and he fears being left behind. He lacks confidence about decision making and relies on peers to make decisions for him. He seems to have a dependent attachment to his current girlfriend. He wants teachers to like him, but his respect for them is conditional. He can talk comfortably with one of them. He cares about learning, and he likes the art and order of technology. He says he wants to feel better, control impulses better, make better decisions, and be able to quiet himself. Strategies he has tried, including meditation, have not worked. He worries that he is a "bad person"—bisexual, without direction, and immoral.

The school counselor conceptualizes Andrew's behavioral difficulties as extreme risk-taking and difficulty concentrating on homework outside of class. Emotionally, the counselor identifies anger and anxiety connected to perceived threats of abandonment, and ongoing adjustment issues related to family relocation and altered family constellation. These concerns affect academic motivation and performance.

Entering Andrew's World With Nonjudgment, Compassion, Curiosity, and Respect

Andrew's initial self-presentation may affect the counseling relationship negatively. A counselor's poise, warmth, confidence, and unconditional respect can quietly assure him that neither awe nor negative judgment will characterize their interaction. He will be alert to signs that the counselor is genuinely and nonvoyeuristically curious about his life as a gifted person.

He may particularly watch the counselor's reaction to details about substance use, running away, sexual activity, and flirting with dangerous online groups. His interest in those groups may reflect what Deikman (1994) discussed in connection with vulnerability to cults, occurring commonly in response to yearnings for meaning and purpose, for service, to be taken care of, to be accepted, and to have a strong leader or organization to depend on. Andrew's concern about sexual orientation may add an extra layer to his fear of abandonment by friends and family, according to Peterson and Rischar's (2000) retrospective study of school experiences of 18 gifted gay, lesbian, bisexual, and transgender (GLBT)-gifted young adults. Some underachieving adolescents like Andrew may reject guidance by adults at a time when it is crucial for their development, distancing themselves from parents, being sexually active young, and claiming maturity, but actually being in toxic, nonegalitarian romantic relationships (Bourque, 2006). Fortunately, Andrew feels some closeness to a teacher.

If Andrew is to invest in counseling at school or in the community, a trusting and sustained therapeutic relationship is essential. The school counselor may feel tested and challenged, but embracing Andrew's complexity and relying on solid counseling skills and ethical behavior can support work with Andrew as much as with any other gifted child or adolescent. Even young gifted children are likely to engage easily when a counselor approaches them with respectful interest, avoids "talking down" to them, and appeals to cognitive strengths while still focusing on emotional health and development. Chapter 7 includes additional information about counseling approaches, particularly in the form of classroom guidance and small-group discussion.

Self-Monitoring for Bias

Wise and aware school counselors, like any other adults who work with gifted students in schools, know the importance of self-monitoring regarding pertinent positive or negative biases (Peterson, 2011). How do they feel and what do they believe about high achievers? About gifted underachievers? About the parents of each? What are their impulses when interacting with high-ability children and teens? Do they feel competitive—with humor or with knowledge? Do they need to show gifted students how intelligent they themselves are? Do they feel an urge to "knock them down a notch"? How comfortable and secure do they feel when interacting with gifted kids? Positive bias may be in the form of "being in awe of" impressive talents and intellectual strengths. Unfortunately, when a gifted student senses awe, a therapeutic relationship may be difficult to establish, since the student may hesitate to be genuine and vulnerable, protecting the positive public image.

• • •

CONCLUDING THOUGHTS AND RECOMMENDATIONS

Boredom Versus Engagement

Noteworthy is that neither Andrew nor his mother refers to boredom—a common default complaint with implied criticism of teachers when gifted children and teens are having problems at school. Andrew likes to be in class and generally feels comfortable with his teachers. He is taking challenging classes, meeting affinity needs related to incorporating giftedness into his identity (Mahoney, Martin, & Martin, 2007). Hyperactivity affects him negatively mostly outside of class—when he feels anxious, lonely, awkward, untrusting, and adrift. Andrew may not be typical in his good fortune of having classes that engage him. However, it is important that educators and counselors resist blaming teachers for gifted students' concerns in schools and instead consider problems complexly, perhaps with the help of a school psychologist, who can assess for disability or need for intensive, longer-term mental health support outside of school.

If a gifted student mentions being bored, school counselors and teachers can probe for further information: "Tell me about *bored*. Help me understand what that word means for you." "What does it feel like? When do you feel it most?" Boredom may, of course, be a very real problem when curriculum and teaching approaches are not differentiated, and when teachers simply assign even more redundant assignments. A school counselor might then, perhaps through role-playing, help a bored child self-advocate for an appropriately differentiated curriculum in a particular class. Advocating inappropriately by pushing a teacher into a defensive posture with the word *bored*, and not considering the importance of a collaborative posture and a focus on needs, wastes an opportunity to rectify a problematic situation.

However, first it is helpful to ascertain whether having multiple teachers in middle school instead of one main teacher, or having smaller print in larger textbooks with fewer illustrations or pictures, or not being with friends in some classes is playing a role. Common stereotypes notwithstanding, all gifted children and teens are not avid and able readers, and reading longer assignments at each new grade level might in fact be overwhelming for a gifted student with even a mild reading disability. Being tested on facts from long readings, instead of broad themes, might contribute to anxiety, translated as boredom. Regardless, discussing boredom with a child or teen can help the student develop expressive language about concerns.

Referral

In situations involving students in complicated situations and with high-risk behavior, like Andrew's, a referral to a mental health provider in the community should be considered seriously. Concerns about equity of access and time limitations, due to school counselors' heavy student loads, argue against long-term, regular sessions in school.

When a student in crisis appears to need to step away from the present context to focus on urgent issues, one option, if affordable, and regardless of whether it would be involuntary, is a private residential facility for troubled youth, with programming geared toward well-being, not punishment. Andrew might benefit from the individual mentoring, careful monitoring of medication, and frequent therapy at such places. Improved relationship skills, self-awareness, self-management, and self-confidence, as well as a better verbal "filter," more appropriate openness, the ability to discern and respond to caring, less dramatic and more nurturing friendships, better fitness and health, and a vision of the future might result. Subsequently, online classes to finish high school and explore interest areas could also help Andrew move out of stuckness and toward a positive future.

• • •

REFERENCES

Batty, G. D., Deary, I. J., Schoon, I., Emslie, C., Hunt, K., & Gale, C. R. (2008). Childhood mental ability and adult alcohol intake and alcohol problems: The 1970 British cohort study. *American Journal of Public Health, 98,* 2237–2243.

Betts, G. T., & Kercher, J. K. (1999). *Autonomous Learner Model: Optimizing ability.* Greeley, CO: ALPS.

Bourque, J. V. (2006). *Academically underachieving and achieving adolescent girls: Quantitative and qualitative differences in self-efficacy, planning, and developmental asynchrony* Unpublished dissertation, York University, Toronto, ON, Canada.

Conterio, K., Lader, W., & Bloom, J. (1998). *Bodily harm: The breakthrough healing program for self-injurers.* New York, NY: Hyperion.

Council for Accreditation of Counseling and Related Educational Programs. (2016). 2016 CACREP standards. Retrieved from http://www.cacrep.org/wp-content/uploads/2016/06/2016-Standards-with-Glossary-rev-2.2016.pdf

Dabrowski, K. (1967). *Personality-shaping through positive disintegration.* Boston, MA: Little, Brown.

Daniels, S., & Piechowski, M. M. (2009). *Living with intensity: Understanding the sensitivity, excitability and emotional development of gifted children, adolescents and adults.* Scottsdale, AZ: Great Potential Press.

Deikman, A. (1994). *The wrong way home: Uncovering the patterns of cult behavior in American society.* Boston, MA: Beacon Press.

Dixon, F. A., Lapsley, D. K., & Hanchon, T. A. (2004). An empirical typology of perfectionism in gifted adolescents. *Gifted Child Quarterly, 48,* 95–106.

Favazza, A. R., & Conterio, K. (1988). The plight of chronic self-mutilators. *Journal of Community Mental Health, 24,* 22–30.

Gaesser, A. H. (2014). *Interventions to reduce anxiety for gifted children and adolescents.* Unpublished doctoral dissertation, University of Connecticut, Storrs, CT. Retrieved from http://digitalcommons.uconnedu/dissertations/377

Gowan, J. C. (1972). Issues on the guidance of gifted and creative children. In J. C. Gowan, G. D. Demos, & C. J. Kokaska (Eds.), *The guidance of exceptional children* (2nd ed., pp. 3–9). New York, NY: David McKay.

Gross, M. U. M. (2004). *Exceptionally gifted children* (2nd ed.). London, UK: Routledge Falmer.

Hébert, T. P. (2000). Helping high ability students overcome math anxiety through bibliotherapy. *Journal of Secondary Gifted Education, 8,* 164–178.

Hollingworth, L. S. (1926). *Gifted children: Their nature and nurture.* New York, NY: Macmillan.

Jackson, P. S., & Peterson, J. S. (2003). Depressive disorder in highly gifted adolescents. *Journal for Secondary Gifted Education, 14*(3), 175–186.

Jen, E. (2015). *Incorporating a small-group affective curriculum model into a diverse university-based summer residential enrichment program for gifted, creative, and talented youth.* Unpublished doctoral dissertation, Purdue University, West Lafayette, IN.

Kerr, B., & Kurpius, S. E. (2004). Encouraging talented girls in math and science: Effects of a guidance intervention. *High Ability Studies, 15*, 85–102. doi:10.10 80/1359813042000225357

Krafchek, J. (2017). *Stress and coping in academically high-achieving females before the onset of disordered eating: The role of academic achievement.* Unpublished doctoral dissertation, Monash University, Melbourne, Australia.

Levenkron, S. (1998). *Understanding and overcoming self-mutilation.* New York, NY: W. W. Norton.

Mahoney, A. S., Martin, D., & Martin, M. (2007). Gifted identity formation: A therapeutic model for counseling gifted children and adolescents. In S. Mendaglio & J. S. Peterson (Eds.), *Models of counseling gifted children, adolescents, and young adults* (pp. 199–230). Austin, TX: Prufrock Press.

McCoach, D. B., & Siegle, D. (2003). Factors that differentiate underachieving gifted students from high-achieving gifted students. *Gifted Child Quarterly, 47*, 144–154.

Mendaglio, S. (2007). Affective-cognitive therapy for counseling gifted individuals. In S. Mendaglio & J. S. Peterson (Eds.), *Models of counseling gifted children, adolescents, and young adults* (pp. 35–68). Waco, TX: Prufrock Press.

Mendaglio, S. (Ed.). (2008). *Dabrowski's theory of positive disintegration* (pp. 13–40). Scottsdale, AZ: Great Potential Press.

Mofield, E. L., & Chakraborti-Ghosh, S. (2010). Addressing multidimensional perfectionism in gifted adolescents with affective curriculum. *Journal for the Education of the Gifted, 33*, 479–513.

Peterson, J. S. (1997). Bright, troubled, and resilient, and not in a gifted program. *Journal of Secondary Gifted Education, 8*, 121–136.

Peterson, J. S. (1998). Six exceptional young women at risk. *Reclaiming Children and Youth, 6*, 233–238.

Peterson, J. S. (1999). Gifted—through whose cultural lens? An application of the postpositivistic mode of inquiry. *Journal for the Education of the Gifted, 22*, 354–383.

Peterson, J. S. (2000). A follow-up study of one group of achievers and underachievers four years after high school graduation. *Roeper Review, 22*, 217–224.

Peterson, J. S. (2001a). Gifted and at risk: Four longitudinal case studies. *Roeper Review, 24*, 31–39.

Peterson, J. S. (2001b). Successful adults who were once adolescent underachievers. *Gifted Child Quarterly, 45*, 236–249. doi:10.1177/001698620104500402

Peterson, J. S. (2002). A longitudinal study of post-high-school development in gifted individuals at risk for poor educational outcomes. *Journal for Secondary Gifted Education, 14*, 6–18.

Peterson, J. S. (2011). The counseling relationship. In T. R. Cross & J. R. Cross (Eds.), *Handbook for counselors serving students with gifts and talents: Development, relationships, school issues, and counseling needs/interventions* (pp. 443–459). Waco, TX: Prufrock Press.

Peterson, J. S. (2012a). Differentiating counseling approaches for gifted children and teens: Needs and strategies. In T. R. Cross & J. R. Cross (Eds.), *Handbook for counselors serving students with gifts and talents: Development, relationships, school issues, and counseling needs/interventions* (pp. 681–698). Waco, TX: Prufrock Press.

Peterson, J. S. (2012b). The asset–burden paradox of giftedness: A 15-year phenomenological, longitudinal case study. *Roeper Review, 34,* 1–17. doi:10.1080/02783193.2-12.715336

Peterson, J. S. (2013). School counselors' experiences with children from low-income families and other gifted children in a summer program. *Professional School Counseling, 16,* 194–204. doi:10.5330/PSC.n.2013-16.194

Peterson, J. S. (2014). Giftedness, trauma, and development: A longitudinal case study. *Journal for the Education of the Gifted, 37,* 295–318.

Peterson, J. S. (2017). Counseling gifted children and teens. In S. Pfeiffer, M. Nicpon Foley, & E. Shaunessy-Dedrick (Eds.), *APA handbook of giftedness and talent* (pp. 511–527). Alexandria, VA: American Psychological Association.

Peterson, J. S., & Colangelo, N. (1996). Gifted achievers and underachievers: A comparison of patterns found in school files. *Journal of Counseling & Development, 74,* 399–407. doi:10.1002/j.1556-6676.1996.tb01886.x

Peterson, J. S., Duncan, N., & Canady, K. (2009). A longitudinal study of negative life events, stress, and school experiences of gifted youth. *Gifted Child Quarterly, 53,* 34–49. doi:10.1002/j.1556-6676.1996.tb01886.x

Peterson, J. S., & Lorimer, M. R. (2011). Student response to a small-group affective curriculum in a school for gifted children. *Gifted Child Quarterly, 55,* 167–180. doi:10.1177/0016986211412770

Peterson, J. S., & Lorimer, M. R. (2012). Small-group affective curriculum for gifted students: A longitudinal study of teacher-facilitators. *Roeper Review, 34,* 158–169. doi:10.1080/02783193.2012.686423

Peterson, J. S., & Ray, K. E. (2006a). Bullying among the gifted: The subjective experience. *Gifted Child Quarterly, 50,* 252–269.

Peterson, J. S., & Ray, K. E. (2006b). Bullying and the gifted: Victims, perpetrators, prevalence, and effects. *Gifted Child Quarterly, 50,* 148–168.

Peterson, J. S., & Rischar, H. (2000). Gifted and gay: A study of the adolescent experience. *Gifted Child Quarterly, 44,* 149–164.

Peterson, J. S., & Wachter, C. A. (2010). Understanding and responding to concerns related to giftedness: A study of CACREP-accredited programs. *Journal for Education of the Gifted, 33,* 311–336.

Pfeiffer, S. I. (2013a). *Serving the gifted: Evidence-based clinical and psychoeducational practice.* New York, NY: Routledge.

Pfeiffer, S. I. (2013b). Treating the clinical problems of gifted children. In L. Grossman & S. Walfish (Eds.), *Translating research into practice: A desk reference for practicing mental health professionals* (pp. 57–63). New York, NY: Springer Publishing.

Piechowski, M. M. (1999). Overexcitabilities. In M. A. Runco & S. R. Pritzker (Eds.), *Encyclopedia of creativity* (Vol. 2, pp. 325–334). San Diego, CA: Academic Press.

Roberts, S. M., & Lovett, S. B. (1994). Examining the "F" in gifted: Academically gifted adolescents' psychological and affective responses to scholastic failure. *Journal for the Education of the Gifted, 17,* 241–259.

Safran, J. D., Muran, J. C., & Shaker, A. (2014). Research on therapeutic impasses and ruptures in the therapeutic alliance. *Contemporary Psychoanalysis, 50,* 211–232.

Schmeichel, J., Vohs, K. D., & Baumeister, R. F. (2003). Intellectual performance and ego depletion: Role of the self in logical reasoning and other information processing. *Journal of Personality and Social Psychology, 85*, 33–46.

Tieso, C. L. (2007). Patterns of overexcitabilities in identified gifted students and their parents: A hierarchical model. *Gifted Child Quarterly, 51*, 11–22.

Whitmore, J. R. (1980). *Giftedness, conflict, and underachievement.* Boston, MA: Allyn & Bacon.

Wilmoth, D. R. (2012). Intelligence and past use of recreational drugs. *Intelligence, 40*, 15–22.

Winner, E. (2000). The origins and ends of giftedness. *American Psychologist, 55*, 159–169.

Wood, S. M. (2010). Best practices in counseling the gifted in schools: What's really happening? *Gifted Child Quarterly, 54*, 42–58. doi:10.1177/0016986209352681

Wood, S. M., & Craigen, L. M. (2011). Self-injurious behavior in gifted and talented youth: What every educator should know. *Journal for the Education of the Gifted, 34*, 839–859.

Yermish, A. (2010). *Cheetahs on the couch: Issues affecting the therapeutic working alliance with clients who are cognitively gifted* [Doctoral dissertation]. Available from ProQuest Dissertations and Theses Database. (UMI No. 3415722).

Collaboration, Consultation, and Systemic Change: Creating a Supportive School Climate for Gifted Students

SUSANNAH M. WOOD

Stewart and Tray are the seventh- and eighth-grade school counselors in a new middle school in a large urban district with a diverse student population. Wintercrest Middle School has been a magnet school for science, technology, engineering, and mathematics (STEM) for only 3 years. Currently students can take Algebra I, Geometry, Honors Biology, and semester classes in Advanced Computing, Introduction to Physics, Robotics, and Trigonometry. Logistically, the magnet school functions as a school within a school, with students attending classes in one wing of the school building. Teachers and students who are not involved in the magnet school are located in two other wings on the opposite side of the school. During the past school year, Tray and Stewart have sensed tensions in the school in various relationships, including within, between, and among teams of teachers, between parents and teachers, among students, and between administrators and teachers. Mr. Wallace, their building principal, has seen the explosive outcomes of some of these tensions and has encouraged the counselors to investigate the current school climate.

Stewart and Tray have several challenges ahead of them in their quest to ameliorate the tensions and improve the climate of their school. The concept of school climate is complex, with scholars often referring to the "personality" (Reinke & Herman, 2002) of the unique "system" of school members and interactions (American School Counselor Association [ASCA], 2012). Hernandez and Seem (2004, p. 256) defined *school climate* as the "related factors of attitude, feeling, and behavior of individuals within the school system."

School climate, school culture, and *school community* are terms that are frequently used interchangeably. However, although the concepts are similar, they are not the same. The concept of school culture is more anthropological, encompassing the group's norms, beliefs, and values, which are difficult to measure (MacNeil, Prater, & Busch, 2009). School climate, in contrast, refers to the attitudes and behavior of the individuals who create the group and the overall quality of the school's environment, which is easier to assess (MacNeil et al., 2009). As Gruenert (2008) noted, "If culture is the personality of the organization, then climate represents that organization's attitude. It is much easier to change an organization's attitude (climate) than it is to change its personality (culture)" (p. 58). Addressing school climate has traditionally been the purview of the lead administrators in a school building, but responding to diverse needs of K–12 personnel is a shared responsibility among *all educators*, including school counselors.

Literature in the school counseling field has suggested that because of their training in group dynamics, individual counseling, utilization of data, consultation, and advocacy, school counselors can and should be leaders in creating systems change to promote safe school climates and students' academic success (ASCA, 2012; Hernandez & Seem, 2004; Lindwall & Coleman, 2008). ASCA, along with other national organizations such as the National Association of School Psychologists and the National Association of Secondary Principals, created a *Framework for Safe and Successful Schools*. According to the authors of the framework, "school counselors work to promote safe learning environments for all members of the school community and regularly monitor and respond to behavior issues that impact school climate, such as bullying, student interpersonal struggles, and student–teacher conflicts" (Cowan, Vailancourt, Rossen, & Politt, 2013, p. 11).

Gifted students are among the "all members" who deserve a safe and effective learning environment. Stewart and Tray must identify and investigate assumptions that affect attitudes and behaviors of members of the school community, implicit and explicit norms and policies that drive decision making, and expectations and beliefs about control, academic expectations, and the degree to which members feel connected and bonded with the school (Hernandez & Seem, 2004; Reinke & Herman, 2002). However, these school counselors must accomplish this with an eye toward how the magnet school-within-a-school is affecting the overall school climate and the needs of the gifted and talented students. There are both advantages and disadvantages to the school-within-a-school framework (Matthews & Kitchen, 2007). This chapter describes Stewart and Tray's journey of addressing issues related to school climate, and identifying concerns specific to gifted students, while working within their roles as counselors, collaborators, and consultants.

● ● ●

SCHOOL CLIMATE AND GIFTED STUDENTS

School climate (i.e., its attitude) is generated by complex social relationships and interactions. School climate is also rooted in the assumptions of the students, educators, parents, and community members interacting in a building (Hernandez & Seem, 2004). Assumptions drive how school community members treat one another, which rules are acceptable, which behaviors are not acceptable, how expectations are established, and of whom expectations exist. Attitudes, relationships, assumptions, and expectations all play a role in the school climate at Wintercrest. Tray and Stewart will explore the numerous relationships within the school building and determine the degree to which those relationships contribute to a sense of connection and a positive learning environment.

Connection With Teachers

Croft (2003) asserted that gifted students "appear to be [more] profoundly impacted by their teachers' attitudes and actions than are other students" (p. 558). The connection that begins as a clash between gifted student and teacher, but develops into a deeper, more positive, longer-lasting relationship "is crucial" and "makes all the difference" to the gifted student (Robinson & Bryant, 2012, p. 427). Lee (2016) stated that, in fact, "teachers' influences on talent development are the most significant and observable results documented in recent literature" (p. 194). The Teacher Knowledge and Skills Standards authored by National Association for Gifted Children (NAGC) and the Council for Exceptional Children (2013, Standard 2) underscore the importance of gifted-education professionals who create "safe, inclusive and culturally responsible learning environments so that individuals with gifts and talent become effective learners and develop social and emotional well-being" (p. 2). According to Robinson and Bryant (2012), these standards acknowledge that a responsive learning environment that provides opportunity for intellectual stimulation and authentic learning is vital to the relationship between gifted student and teacher. The standards also acknowledge that not all gifted students are well behaved, conforming, and easily likable; they may need support in negotiating an educational system that is not always empathetic about their learning needs (Robinson & Bryant, 2012).

Many studies have examined the relationship between gifted students and their teachers as well as teachers' perceptions and attitudes toward gifted students and gifted students' expectations of their teachers. According to findings in these studies, effective teachers of gifted students (a) personalize/individualize students' education (Siegle, Rubenstien, & Mitchell, 2014); (b) demonstrate competence, high quality, and efficiency in a variety of instructional methods, including differentiation (Siegle et al., 2014), and have strong subject matter expertise (Milgram, 1979); (c) listen, are available outside of class hours, and take constructive feedback (Buser, Stuck, & Casey, 1974); (d) provide informal mentoring and opportunities to explore for possible college and/or career paths (Watters, 2010); (e) demonstrate a positive attitude toward the subject matter (Choi & Choi, 2012); (f) demonstrate certain personal characteristics that students respond well to and have personal characteristics that are preferred over their intellectual characteristics (Vialle & Tischler, 2005); (g) help students master content, encourage academic confidence, praise students for positive attitudes, and support students' growth toward the next level of comprehension and/or accomplishment (Choe, Choi, Kim, Yoon, & Kwon, 2012); (h) connect academic learning to real-life issues and concerns and increase meaning and relevance of learning (Coxbill, Chamberlin, & Weatherford, 2013); (i) provide flexible/permissive and stimulating learning environments, including self-directed learning (Chang, 2013); and (j) demonstrate acceptance of students' gifts and facilitate a sense of belonging (Garces-Bascal, Cohen, & Tan, 2011). In essence, "all of these results bolster the view that highly competent teachers are knowledgeable about content and also efficient in adapting instruction to the diverse needs of students" (Lee, 2016, p. 195).

Educator Perceptions of Gifted Students

Studies pertaining to teachers' (both preservice and current-service teachers) perceptions and attitudes toward gifted students have provided a mixed and clouded picture (Robinson & Bryant, 2012). Some research findings have led to the conclusion that, after teachers have training and professional development, their attitudes are more positive toward gifted students (Megay-Nespoli, 2001).

In 2008, Geake and Gross surveyed 377 teachers from Scotland, England, and Australia and found that teachers may be suspicious of gifted students' intellectual precocity and, therefore, have negative feelings toward the students themselves. Suspicions appeared to be rooted in gifted students' nonconforming behaviors (e.g., insensitivity toward others, social isolation, or disrespect for authority) as well as their ability to be highly articulate. These researchers also found that professional development pertinent to giftedness had a positive impact on teachers' attitudes toward gifted children. However, McCoach and Siegle (2007) did not find this effect. They found that, in general, teachers were supportive of gifted education but had ambivalent opinions about acceleration. Training was found to be positively related to teachers' perception of themselves as gifted, but not to their attitudes toward gifted students.

Unfortunately, classroom teachers without training in gifted education have more challenges when identifying gifted students than those who do have such training (Croft, 2003). Educators without pertinent knowledge or formal training may fall prey to the numerous myths and stereotypical thinking about giftedness or assume it is equated with well-behaved, high-achieving students who do not question authority. Assumptions affect how counselors work with gifted students, contribute to the overall school climate, and develop "attitudes" about these students and services focused on their needs. Addressing assumptions and beliefs requires self-reflection.

Stewart and Tray might begin their investigation of the school climate by conducting group interviews with students enrolled, and not enrolled, in the STEM magnet school. Open-ended questions might focus on how much these students feel connected to their magnet teachers and to teachers in nonmagnet classes. Tray and Stewart might inquire about the degree of academic challenge in the advanced coursework as well as students' stress level. Individual and group meetings with Wintercrest teachers may help these counselors determine how gifted students are perceived and to what extent the teachers see compliance and uniformity of behavior as a requirement for participation in gifted-education programming. Teachers who have worked with gifted students might have valuable insights about how to work effectively with behaviors and characteristics that affect classroom dynamics, such as questioning authority, adult-like humor, and heightened sensitivity. Further conversations might explore teachers' need and desire for professional development and teacher comfort level with curriculum differentiation. Tray and Stewart may also want to collect some quantitative data on their school's climate, using instruments available online without cost, focused on determining needs of schools. In addition, Tray and Stewart could collect data on teachers' perceptions of gifted students. Their findings might illuminate how these perceptions are affecting the magnet wing and the school in general.

● ● ●
_____

GIFTED STUDENTS' NEED FOR A SAFE ENVIRONMENT

Tray wonders if the students in the honors courses in the STEM magnet are being targeted for bullying by their nonmagnet peers, and vice versa. Stewart is worried that there are instances of bullying they, as school counselors, are not aware of in those classes and in the magnet wing as a whole. He and Tray also are concerned about how students are reacting to some teachers' negative attitudes about them and the STEM magnet program. Studies in the gifted and talented field pertaining to school climate are rare. However, several researchers have explored how gifted and talented students navigate their social worlds, as related to peer culture, social coping, academic self-concept, and stigma.

Peer perception and acceptance become increasingly important as students move into adolescence and early adulthood and have implications for academic and social success. Coleman (1985, 2012) introduced the stigma of giftedness paradigm (SGP), which had, as one of its primary tenets, the idea that gifted students, like all students, want normal interactions with their peers. However, the research literature suggests that these interactions are challenging and complex. Some studies suggest that gifted students in elementary school are accepted by peers, but this acceptance changes during adolescence (Rimm, 2002). At that point, a gifted identity is considered positive when it pertains to academic benefits, but negative in terms of peer relationships (Kerr, Colangelo, and Gaeth, 1988). Manaster, Chan, Watt, and Wiehe (1994) found that although they viewed themselves mostly positively, gifted students also perceived that they were treated differently by their classmates. Peer attitudes and behaviors changed in degree from mostly positive in those who knew the gifted students, to increasingly negative as familiarity with the student decreased (Manaster et al., 1994). Some gifted students accept being known as studious or academically inclined, but not to the extent that these activities ostracize them from their peers or create a negative peer perception of them (Brown & Sternberg, 1990; Cross, Coleman, & Terhaar-Yonkers, 1991).

The SGP's second tenet suggests that gifted students become aware that they are being perceived and treated differently by their peers when their gift or talent is known (Coleman, 2012). A study of students in honors programs and in accelerated courses (Bishop et al., 2004) found that harassment by peers was greater for students who perceived that there was an anti-intellectual or anti-learning peer crowd with social dominance in the school. Participants in the study were viewed by their nonhonors program peers as not socializing much, having "geeky interests," dressing unfashionably, lacking in self-confidence, saying "stupid things," and competing for grades (Bishop et al., 2004, p. 249). According to the SGP (Coleman, 2012), to cope with possible harassment and bullying, gifted students may choose to manage information about themselves and their gifts, talents, and/or academic achievement, including playing down or denying being identified as gifted, hiding their gifts, deflecting attention from themselves, and using humor (Cross et al., 1991; Swiatek, 2012). However, Lee, Olszewski-Kubilius, and Thomson (2012), in their study of 1526 gifted students who had participated in talent-development programming, found that these students did not believe their giftedness led to negative peer pressure. In fact, these students reported (a) being content with the number of relationships they had, (b) having positive perceptions of their relationships, and (c) feeling comfortable/competent in social interactions.

Given school counselors' mandate to address bullying concerns in their building, Tray and Stewart must investigate and intervene. First, they can consult district policies on bullying and cyberbullying. Second, they can examine office referrals for behavior related to bullying and then disaggregate these data based on grade level and/or school teams. The data may reveal that the magnet school has an inordinate amount of bullying. Third, Tray and Stewart might

Bullying and the Gifted Student

Jean Sunde Peterson

Scholars focused on bullying are no longer merely measuring prevalence and correlates. Recent studies have not only used more precise definitions and gone beyond vague time spans, but also explored psychological contributors, teacher–student relationships, social networks, school climate and school culture, and impact on mental health, for example. They are studying cyberbullying, which may be used to target gifted youth, but also may be a readily available, anonymous venue for payback. Bullying words do not go away; going home does not leave cyberbullying behind; and any bullying might be relentless.

In the early 2000s, U.S. researchers began to catch up with the well-established international attention to bullying. Related to giftedness, Peterson and Ray's seminal quantitative (2006b) and qualitative (2006a) retrospective studies of bullying of and by gifted eighth-graders raised awareness of the phenomenon with this population, and four comparative studies have since appeared. Findings have not shown more or less prevalence among gifted youth, but that in itself argues against assuming less vulnerability.

School counselors know that bullying often happens under the radar—in restrooms, lunchrooms, bus lines, locker rooms, buses, and classrooms. They may see gifted victims referred for flat affect, absenteeism, or fighting—just like any other student. However, because of positive biases, teachers may not consider that gifted children are being targeted and are perpetrating bullying (Estell et al., 2009). Counselors can encourage parents to inquire about bullying with open-ended questions (e.g., "I'm curious. What would I see if I stood in the bus line or ate at your table or rode your bus?"). Media accounts have illuminated that the loneliness of differentness and the tendency not to ask for help put gifted children and teens at risk for self-harm, violent thoughts (Peterson & Ray, 2006b), and violent actions (cf. Delisle, 2014).

(continued)

KEY CONCEPT *(continued)*

Characteristics associated with giftedness may exacerbate the impact of bullying. Even a single incident may have long-term effect (Peterson & Ray, 2006a), challenging definitions that make repetition of deliberately hostile behaviors, with a power imbalance, a key ingredient.

Researchers have concluded that effects on bystanders may be worse for some children than being a victim, perhaps especially for intense gifted children with heightened sensitivity to injustice, emotional intensity, psychic overexcitabilities, and existential depression (see Chapter 3). Educators and counselors should also be concerned about the mental health of bullies, because they may carry bullying behaviors into future employment, parenting, and partnerships. In adulthood, bullying behaviors may qualify as assault, battery, libel, or slander. Bully victims (i.e., being both) and bullies are at risk for poor mental health.

convene teams of teachers and groups of parents to discuss their perceptions of, and experiences with, various types of bullying in the school. Subjective data from these discussions might be quite helpful. Tray and Stewart might also create and deploy a student survey of pertinent perceptions and experiences. Some school districts have mandated bullying curricula to be utilized by school counselors; often these curricula that come with assessment measures.

• • •

FACILITATING CONNECTIONS: COLLABORATION AND CONSULTATION

According to ASCA (2012), to facilitate community and a common goal of "equity, access, and academic success for every student" (p. 6), the school counselor should act as a collaborator. This role involves understanding how all stakeholders contribute to the success of every student and encouraging collaboration between educators and students. Effective collaborative relationships have open communication, a shared vision, opportunities to contribute ideas, and shared decision-making.

School counselors also have a consultant role. Consultation generally refers to school counselors working with another professional, the consultee (e.g., teacher or administrator), to develop knowledge and skills to use on behalf of a student (Perera-Diltz, Moe, & Mason, 2011; Peterson, 2007). According to ASCA (2012), this role is indirect—advocating for a student, receiving information about student needs, and offering teachers ideas to improve student achievement.

Stewart and Tray are already experienced in consultation and collaboration. However, they know they need to expand the number of their allies to address the current climate issues. When supporting gifted students, school counselors may collaborate and consult with teachers, gifted-education coordinators, and school psychologists in, or connected with, the school. To be effective, they need additional knowledge about the education of gifted children and teens. The next section describes how school counselors can prepare to collaborate and consult with a variety of stakeholders to address academic, career, and personal/social needs of high-ability students.

Collaborating and Consulting With Classroom Teachers

According to Ray et al. (2007), school counselors can enhance school climate through positively collaborating with classroom teachers. Through invited observation and follow-up discussion, for example, school counselors can raise teachers' awareness about how a classroom functions and gather student input on its climate. In addition, school counselors can work in partnership with teachers to facilitate character education programs, host classroom meetings, work with small groups, and codevelop lesson plans (Peterson, 2007; Ray et al., 2007). School counselors can consult with general-education and gifted-education teachers about integrating social and emotional development into the current classroom curriculum in a way that promotes students' self-reflection (Peterson, 2007; see Chapter 7 for more information). The following additional areas are discussed in detail in other chapters of this book: (a) responding to underachievement (Chapter 9); (b) assisting with college and career decisions (Chapter 8); (c) preparing and supporting teachers who facilitate group discussions (Chapter 7); (d) helping with identification and assessment (Chapter 6); (f) guiding parental advocacy (Chapter 11); and (g) providing referrals to community agencies.

Teachers may also seek assistance when they need to respond to parent concerns and questions. Both teachers and school counselors are points of contact when a parent has questions about identification, programming, acceleration, or other services for a gifted student (Chandler, 2012). Questions may arise over identification or how students are being taught (or being challenged academically), especially when the school has no formal program. When a program does exist, parents may feel disconnected from it or confused about its requirements. Already stressed general-education teachers may be overwhelmed by the number of academic accommodations they are responsible for, and they may not have had any training in curriculum differentiation for gifted students (Peterson, 2007).

In these situations, tensions and flaring tempers may reflect worry, fear, confusion, frustration, and perceptions of disrespect—or simply poor communication. School counselors can be mediators in meetings that become tense. Meetings with parents and/or teachers are prime opportunities for school counselors to use not just their problem-solving skills, but their active-listening and individual and group counseling skills as well. Parents may feel reassured when a school counselor volunteers to observe classrooms and work with teachers to address academic and social concerns. School counselors may realize that needed supports go beyond what the school can provide and so make referrals to community resources for counseling and treatment, for example (Peterson, 2007). Chapter 11 has additional information on how school counselors can help support families of gifted students by collaborating with their teachers.

Just as teacher–student relationships are crucial to a healthy school culture, so are teacher–school counselor relationships. Wood's (2012) qualitative study investigated gifted-education teachers' experiences and working relationships with school counselors. Both parties were similar in feeling alone, devalued by colleagues, and isolated by the nature of their roles and functions. Both experienced a lack of resources, ineffective communication, and difficult professional schedules, all of which contributed to a lack of trust and respect from fellow educators and poor communication and sharing of information. Some of these teachers felt that their counseling colleagues did not understand the teachers' roles, responsibilities, and general job description. Others noted that the overall school culture and the stance of school administrators toward gifted students and gifted-education programming detracted from the teachers' ability to collaborate with counselors and other educators as needed. Gifted-education teachers did not feel support for collaboration. Matthews, Foster, Gladstone, Schieck, and Meiners (2007, p. 334) argued that "administrative support is essential to teachers' effective participation in ongoing collaborative relationships" in gifted education. Lack of support is frequently a symptom of an unhealthy school climate (Bemak, 2000).

However, gifted-education teachers in the Matthews et al. (2007) study described a great need and desire to work with school counselors. To promote this collaboration, Wood (2012) suggested that both parties trade and discuss their job descriptions, identifying areas in which their expertise complements or overlaps (e.g., working together to resolve a complex scheduling concern for a student). School counselors might take a "one-down" position and abdicate their power while building these relationships, with the understanding, for example, that the gifted-education teacher is the expert in educating gifted students (Wood, 2012). Respecting the expertise of the counselor, the teacher might also assume a one-down posture regarding social, emotional, and career development. A healthy, productive, mutually beneficial relationship between counselor and gifted-education teacher can provide the school with a model of effective collaboration.

Collaborating With Building Administrators

Strong, positive leadership can mean the difference between toxic and healthy school climates for all students, including gifted students. According to Wood and Peterson (2014), "Principals who agree with and are invested in the district definition of giftedness and general program philosophy can offer crucial support for students and programs" (p. 633). As a leader in the building, the administrator must be able to assume several roles (Chandler, 2012; Speirs Neumeister & Burney, 2011; Wood & Peterson, 2014): (a) acting as a liaison between the central office and the school building with special attention to programming; (b) being fluent in local and state policies and plans; (c) supporting differentiated learning and monitoring teacher effectiveness in delivering it; (d) providing resources for students, parents, and teachers; and (e) working with parents of high-ability learners.

Principals are in a vital position to advocate for gifted-education programs and hire knowledgeable and competent teachers. However, administrators may face challenges when attempting to secure enough staff and physical resources to manage the logistical challenges inherent in these programs. Regardless, they can support and encourage not only collaboration but also professional development for educators serving gifted students (Wood & Peterson, 2014). Finally, building leaders can make sure that any written plan (e.g., professional development, school improvement, and strategic planning) includes gifted education so that it "will become an integral part of the school program, as opposed to an add-on that is easy to ignore" (Chandler, 2012, p. 563). A healthy gifted-education program, "directed with energy, especially those with some components open to the entire student body, can help to create a school culture characterized by learning, challenge, and respect for intellect" (Wood & Peterson, 2014, p. 636).

• • •

CONCLUDING THOUGHTS AND RECOMMENDAITONS

Tray and Stewart realize that relationships are at the heart of the Wintercrest climate. Relationships between and among teachers, students, administration, and parents all hold Wintercrest together, but are also susceptible to tensions. As Tray and Stewart investigate, they may find that implicit biases and myths about gifted students and gifted-education programs are creating tensions felt within the magnet school. Students in the magnet wing could be perceiving a lack of teacher interest and support or a more overtly hostile climate punctuated by bullying. Depending on their perceptions of acceptance by peers, gifted students may opt to hide or deny their gifts or, in contrast, invest intensely in coursework and extracurricular activities. However, Tray and Stewart should carefully consider that magnet students might also be contributing to tension with arrogant behavior and bullying (see Peterson & Ray, 2006a). To create positive change at Wintercrest, the building principal can provide the gifted-education teacher with the time and support needed to collaborate and have access to more professional development. As Tray and Stewart open-mindedly examine the current school climate and, if warranted, work toward changing it, they will likely strengthen their relationships with teachers, school psychologists, and administrators.

By nature of their position in the school, school counselors are in a prime position to be the "pulse-checkers" of their school climates. School climate is based on both perception and relationship. School counselors can use this chapter to guide their examination of their own school climates, including staff perceptions and beliefs about giftedness and/or how bullying is currently having an impact on school climate. Counselors working in magnet or school-within-a-school settings may already be noticing differences in the educational experience of their students and staff in those environments. School counselors are relationship brokers and relationship builders. They understand the necessity of consistently building and strengthening the relationships they need to be effective counselors and collaborators. This chapter provides some suggestions for revisting relationships and for establishing entirely new relationships in the interest of fostering a positive educational environment for gifted students.

● ● ●

REFERENCES

American School Counselor Association. (2012). *ASCA National Model: A framework for school counseling programs* (3rd ed.). Alexandria, VA: Author.

Bemak, F. (2000). Transforming the role of the counselor to provide leadership in educational reform through collaboration. *Professional School Counseling, 3,* 323–332.

Bishop, J. H., Bishop, M., Bishop, M., Gelbwasser, S. G., Peteron, E., Rubinsztaj, A., & Zuckerman, A. (2004). Why we harass nerds and freaks: A formal theory of student culture and norms. *Journal of School Health, 74*(7), 235–251.

Brown, B. B., & Steinberg, L. (1990). Skirting the "brain-nerd" connection: Academic achievement and social acceptance. *Education Digest, 55,* 57–60.

Buser, R. A., Stuck, D. L., & Casey, J. P. (1974). Teacher characteristics and behaviors preferred by high school students. *Peabody Journal of Education, 51,* 119–123.

Chandler, K. (2012). The role of central office and building administration in serving gifted students. In T. L. Cross & J. R. Cross (Eds.), *Handbook for counselors serving students with gifts and talents: Development, relationships, school issues, and counseling needs/interventions* (pp. 555–567). Waco, TX: Prufrock Press.

Chang, I. (2013). The role of teacher as "learning-mate" in gifted education using technology. *Journal of the Korean Society for Gifted and Talented, 12,* 117–134.

Choe, S., Choi, H., Kim, H, Yoon, H., & Kwon, K. (2012). Factors influenced Korean gifted girls and boys to become International Math and Science Olympians. *Journal of Gifted/Talented Education, 12,* 31–60.

Choi, Y., & Choi, K. (2012). Science experience's type and meaning of Korean middle school science gifted students in parent, school, out-of-school institution. *Journal of Korean Association for Science Education, 32,* 1580–1598.

Coleman, L. J. (1985). *Schooling the gifted.* Menlo Park, CA: Addison-Wesley.

Coleman, L. J. (2012). Lived experience, mixed messages, and stigma. In T. L. Cross & J. R. Cross (Eds.), *Handbook for counselors serving students with gifts and talents: Development, relationships, school issues, and counseling needs/interventions* (pp. 371–392). Waco, TX: Prufrock Press.

Cowan, K. C., Vailancourt, K., Rossen, E., & Politt, K. (2013). *A framework for safe and successful schools* [Brief]. Bethesda, MD: National Association of School Psychologists.

Coxbill, E., Chamberlin, S. A., & Weatherford, J. (2013). Using model-eliciting activities as a tool to identify and develop mathematically creative students. *Journal for the Education of the Gifted, 36,* 176–197.

Croft, L. J. (2003). Teachers of the gifted: Gifted teachers. In N. Colangelo & G. A. Davis (Eds.), *Handbook of gifted education* (3rd ed., pp. 558–571). Needham Heights, MA: Allyn & Bacon.

Cross, T. L., Coleman, L. J., & Terhaar-Yonkers, M. (1991). The social cognition of gifted adolescents in schools: Managing the stigma of giftedness. *Journal for the Education of the Gifted, 15,* 44–55.

Delisle, J. (2014, November). *Shock and awe: Mass murderers among gifted youth.* Baltimore, MD: National Association for Gifted Children.

Estell, D. B., Farmer, T. W., Irvin, M. J., Crowther, A., Akos, P., & Boudah, D. J. (2009). Students with exceptionalities and the peer group content of bullying and victimization in late elementary school. *Journal of Child and Family Studies, 18,* 136–150.

Garces-Bascal, R. M., Cohen, L., & Tan, L. S. (2011). Soul behind the skill, heart behind the technique: Experiences of flow among artistically talented students in Singapore. *Gifted Child Quarterly, 55,* 194–207.

Geake, J. G., & Gross, M. U. M. (2008). Teacher's negative affect toward academically gifted students: An evolutionary psychological study. *Gifted Child Quarterly, 52*(3), 217–231. doi:10.1177/0016986208319704

Gruenert, S. (2008, March/April). School culture, school climate: They are not the same thing. *Principal, 87*(4), 56–59.

Hernandez, T. J., & Seem, S. R. (2004). A safe school climate: A systemic approach and the school counselor. *Professional School Counseling, 7*(4), 256–262.

Kerr, B., Colangelo, N., & Gaeth, J. (1988). Gifted adolescents' attitudes toward their giftedness. *Gifted Child Quarterly, 32,* 245–247.

Lee, S.-Y. (2016). Supportive environments for developing talent. In M. Neihart, S. I. Pfeiffer, & T. L. Cross (Eds.), *The social and emotional development and gifted children: What do we know?* (2nd ed., pp. 191–204). Waco, TX: Prufrock Press.

Lee, S.-Y., Olszewski-Kubilius, P., & Thomson, D. T. (2012). Academically gifted students' perceived interpersonal competence and peer relationship. *Gifted Child Quarterly, 56*(2), 90–104. doi:10.1177/0016986212442568

Lindwall, J. L., & Coleman, H. L. K. (2008). The elementary school counselor's role in fostering caring school communities. *Professional School Counseling, 12*(2), 144–148.

MacNeil, A. J., Prater, D. L., & Busch, S. Angus J. (2009) The effects of school culture and climate on student achievement. *International Journal of Leadership in Education, 12*(1), 73–84. doi:10.1080/13603120701576241

Manaster, G. J., Chan, J. C, Watt, C., & Wiehe, J. (1994). Gifted adolescents' attitudes toward their giftedness: A partial replication. *Gifted Child Quarterly, 38*, 176–178.

Matthews, D., Foster, J., Gladstone, D., Schieck, J., & Meiners, J. (2007). Supporting professionalism, diversity, and context within a collaborative approach to gifted education. *Journal of Educational and Psychological Consultation, 17*(4), 315–345. doi:10.1080/10474410701634161

Matthews, D., & Kitchen, J. (2007). School-within-a-school gifted programs: Perceptions of students and teachers in public secondary schools. *Gifted Child Quarterly, 51*(3), 256–271.

McCoach, B. D., & Siegle, D. (2007). What predicts teachers' attitudes towards the gifted? *Gifted Child Quarterly, 51*(3), 246–255. doi:10.1177/0016986207302719

Megay-Nespoli, K. (2001). Beliefs and attitudes of novice teachers regarding instruction of academically talented learners. *Roeper Review, 23*, 178–182.

Milgram, R. M. (1979). Perception of teacher behavior in gifted and non-gifted children. *Journal of Educational Psychology, 71*, 125–128.

National Association for Gifted Children & Council for Exceptional Children. (2013). NAGC–CEC teacher preparation standards in gifted and talented education. Retrieved from http://www.nagc.org/sites/default/files/standards/NAGC-%20 CEC%20CAEP%20standards%20%282013%20final%29.pdf

Perera-Diltz, D. M., Moe, J. L., & Mason, K. L. (2011). An exploratory study in school counselor consultation engagement. *Journal of School Counseling, 9*(13). Retrieved from http://www.jsc.montana.edu/articles/v9n13.pdf

Peterson, J. S. (2007). Consultation related to giftedness: A school counseling perspective, *Journal of Educational and Psychological Consultation, 17*(4), 273–296. doi:10.1080/10474410701634096

Peterson, J. S., & Ray, K. E. (2006a). Bullying among the gifted: The subjective experience. *Gifted Child Quarterly, 50*, 252–269.

Peterson, J. S., & Ray, K. E. (2006b). Bullying and the gifted: Victims, perpetrators, prevalence a, and effects. *Gifted Child Quarterly, 50*, 148–168.

Ray, S. L., Lambie, G., & Curry, J. (2007). Building caring schools: Implications for professional school counselors. *Journal of School Counseling, 5*(14). Retrieved from http://jsc.montana.edu/articles/v5n14.pdf

Reinke, W. M., & Herman, K. C. (2002). Creating school environments that deter antisocial behaviors in youth. *Psychology in the Schools, 39*(5), 549–559. doi:10.1002/pits.10048

Rimm, S. (2002). Peer pressures and social acceptance of gifted students. In M. Neihart, S. M. Reis, N. M. Robinson, & S. M. Moon (Eds.), *The social and emotional development of gifted children: What do we know?* (pp. 13–18). Waco, TX: Prufrock Press.

Robinson, A., & Bryant, L. (2012). Gifted students and their teachers: Relationships that foster talent development. In T. L. Cross & J. R. Cross (Eds.), *Handbook for counselors serving students with gifts and talents: Development, relationships, school issues, and counseling needs/interventions* (pp. 427–442). Waco, TX: Prufrock Press.

Siegle, D., Rubenstein, L. D., & Mitchell, M. S. (2014). Honors students' perceptions of their high school experiences: The influence of teachers on student motivation. *Gifted Child Quarterly, 58,* 35–50.

Speirs Neumeister, K. L., & Burney, V. H. (2011). *An introduction to gifted education: Quick start guide.* Waco, TX: Prufrock Press.

Swiatek, M. A. (2012). Social coping. In T. L. Cross & J. R. Cross (Eds.), *Handbook for counselors serving students with gifts and talents: Development, relationships, school issues, and counseling needs/interventions* (pp. 665–680). Waco, TX: Prufrock Press.

Vialle, W., & Tischler, K. (2005). Teachers of the gifted: A comparison of students' perspectives in Australia, Austria and the United States. *Gifted Education International, 19,* 173–181.

Watters, J. J. (2010). Career decision making among gifted students: The mediation of teachers. *Gifted Child Quarterly, 54,* 222–238. doi:10.1177/0016986210369255

Wood, S. M. (2012). Rivers' confluence: A qualitative investigation into gifted educators' experiences with collaboration with school counselors. *Roeper Review, 34*(4), 261–227.

Wood, S. M., & Peterson, J. S. (2014). Superintendents, principals, and counselors: Facilitating secondary gifted education. In S. Moon & F. A. Dixon (Eds.), *The handbook of secondary gifted education* (pp. 627–649). Waco, TX: Prufrock Press.

11

Empowering Parents of Gifted Students

SUSANNAH M. WOOD AND CARRIE LYNN BAILEY

Angela was extremely excited to begin school as a kindergarten student and was matched with a supportive teacher for her first year in the rural community in which her family lived. She was lively and talkative around adults, and her parents worked hard to find opportunities for Angela to connect with kids her own age. However, in their small community there were limited possibilities for connection, and Angela often retreated physically behind her parents in public.

During the first parent–teacher conference for Angela, her parents were surprised at the teacher's observations that Angela was reading well beyond the level of her peers. Not knowing many other children with whom to compare Angela's abilities, they had assumed she was on par with most other kids her age. While there were no services available in their school system until the third grade, the kindergarten teacher remarked that the Lees might want to look into additional enrichment opportunities for Angela elsewhere. However, the teacher was eager to provide additional reading opportunities. Because reading was one of Angela's favorite activities, this arrangement seemed to be a good fit.

It was during Angela's third-grade year that challenges began for her at school. She often came home upset that she was reprimanded at school, and she rarely talked about positive interactions with her peers. She shared with her parents that she did not have much in common with many of the girls in her class, and that they often teased her about her friendship with a boy in the class they all thought was "weird." This social tension was exacerbated when she was reprimanded for not showing her work in math class. She expressed her frustration with "Why do I need to write out all the steps for something when I just know the answer!" A friend of Angela's parents worked in the school Angela attended and shared with them that contacting the school counselor might be the best next step.

School counselors are aware of a wide array of possible presenting issues and needs in families—especially in the children from those families. In comprehensive school counseling programs and in school systems in general (American School Counselor Association [ASCA], 2016), counselors are charged with the often challenging task of promoting, facilitating, and advocating for collaboration with families. Gifted students can benefit from such partnerships as they navigate an educational terrain their parents may not understand, and, as indicated in previous chapters, parents can also benefit when they learn more about the unique educational, social, and emotional characteristics of their gifted students.

To personalize this collaborative process, this chapter follows the Lee family, presenting a sampling of challenges and issues that they encounter, individually and together, during the educational journey of their daughter Angela and their son Joe, with the main focus on Angela. The Lee family's story is based upon a compilation of families with whom Carrie Lynn has worked in various settings over many years and highlights some of the challenges school counselors face when working with families of gifted students. While theirs is but one story, it illuminates a number of opportunities counselors usually have to connect with families and empower them to advocate for their students. Angela and Joe are the children of a middle-class, two-parent family; both parents have postsecondary educations. While they may not be typical of families and concerns across school settings, the Lees' situation reflects some common challenges that gifted students and their families face. Some significant and problematic intersections of giftedness and education are explored at the close of the chapter.

• • •

WHAT DO SCHOOL COUNSELORS NEED TO KNOW?

Unique Characteristics and Needs of Families of Gifted Students

While a research and clinical foundation for understanding the unique needs and characteristics of gifted students has been interspersed throughout this text, there is much less research and clinical literature that specifically explores the unique needs and characteristics of gifted families, particularly those representing cultural or other diversity. Yet school counselors may be one of the first educators whom parents approach for support and guidance regarding their gifted student. School counselors should expect that parents may need information, resources, and support around the following concerns (Colangelo, 2003; Hermann & Lawrence, 2012; Schader, 2008; Silverman & Golon, 2008): (a) parenting strategies and parenting efficacy; (b) understanding family dynamics after the label *gifted* is introduced; (c) locating resources and opportunities for intellectual challenge and stimulation; (d) helping their gifted children and teens develop social skills and strategies; (e) advocating for services while maintaining a positive relationship with the school; and (f) finding parents of other gifted students.

Talent "Spotting"

Several studies have underscored that parents can identify precocity in their children, especially when advanced reasoning or reading ability sets them apart from other children of the same age (Robinson, Shore, & Enerson, 2007; Silverman & Golon, 2008). Robinson et al. (2007) wrote that "parents of gifted children are notoriously accurate in identifying their child's abilities" (p. 7). They suggested that talent identification is usually the first area of interaction between parents and schools (Robinson et al., 2007). When Garn, Matthews, and Jolly (2010) interviewed mothers of gifted students, a parents-as-experts theme emerged in the language of the majority. Because these mothers had daily interaction with their gifted children, and thus a deeper understanding of their children's unique strengths, the mothers believed they were experts on their children's motivation, even if they were frustrated in trying to develop it.

To foster positive school interactions and increase the likelihood of future positive support for gifted students, school counselors should embrace parents as allies and welcome their information and insight about their children's abilities (Robinson et al., 2007). These precocious behaviors (see Chapter 3) are likely evident even before preschool; however, formal identification of gifted students (Chapter 6) may not occur until grade 3, depending on district policies and practices. Parents may therefore wonder if their child is gifted, but "unfortunately by the time parents seek counseling to answer this question, they have often become frustrated. They want a simple answer and the answer is never simple" (Hertzog, 2012, p. 196). And, as was the case for the Lee family, parents may have concerns about their gifted children even before they are identified for services.

Characteristics Associated With Giftedness at Home

Because Angela's experiences fit with characteristics commonly associated with giftedness, an appropriate starting point is helping parents better understand those characteristics, especially when they seem to affect others in the home. The most common traits and behaviors of gifted students, as identified by scholars and clinical professionals, are presented in Chapter 3. Each of these has ramifications for parenting and family functioning.

For example, parents may feel frustrated and exhausted over trying to provide novel experiences for mental stimulation (Keirouz, 1990; Lovecky, 1992; Silverman & Golon, 2008). Their bright, energetic children may need less sleep and more time to think and "play" with ideas and creative outlets. In addition, gifted children who display intensity and divergent thinking often ask questions, including about the reasons for rules and boundaries (Lovecky, 1992; Probst & Piechowski, 2012; Silverman & Golon, 2008). Parents' confidence as parents may be shaken when their gifted children question authority or are argumentative or defiant (Morawska & Sanders, 2008). Parents may find themselves frustrated with highly intense and sensitive children whose unique traits do not allow them to "get over it." Gifted children inclined toward introversion need relatively more solo and quiet time than their age-peers do, but their parents may worry about that withdrawal from social interaction.

Perceptive gifted adolescents may be familiar with negative family dynamics, but not have the language to describe how enmeshment or triangulation feels. Parents may be confused and frustrated when asynchronous development (see Chapter 3) is manifested in paradoxical behaviors (Colangelo, 2003; Silverman, 2012). For example, Silverman and Golon (2008) wrote that "the same child who can communicate his love of dolphins by reciting the Latin names of virtually every species can be found moments later arguing over toys" (p. 205). In addition, as has been highlighted elsewhere in this text, gifted students are challenged with developmental tasks such as establishing autonomy and independence from their parents, a process their nongifted peers also experience. Finally, research suggests that the families of gifted students often include other gifted individuals with the characteristics associated with giftedness seen in both parent and child (Fornia & Frame, 2001). These families have challenges that other families also experience, but often with added intensity and sensitivities. The challenge is even more significant if the student has extreme abilities or is considered highly gifted.

The Gifted Label

Post (2013) wrote, "Your child is gifted. Those words validate, inform, confirm, enlighten, challenge, frighten, and confuse. They engender pride, excitement, relief, fear, and guilt" (p. 1). Literature in both gifted education

Extreme Ability

Jean Sunde Peterson

The IQ range of approximately 95% of students in the general population is approximately 60 points, depending on the instrument used, from two standard deviations above the mean to two standard deviations below it. In the extremes of ability found in the "ends" of a bell curve of intellectual ability to learn are individuals who differ greatly from the "middle" two-thirds, if a full range of ability exists in a classroom. At the "top" end are children and teens who may have the *gifted* label. Because of co-occurring learning disabilities, adverse life circumstances, or social or emotional factors, some individuals with such high levels of ability might not have the label if high classroom performance is required. Important to consider here is that the range beyond two standard deviations at the upper end—that is, the potentially "gifted" range—can be as broad as the entire range in a general-education classroom (i.e., 130–190 and even beyond).

It is important for educators and counselors to keep that range in mind. "Gifted kids" are highly idiosyncratic, and therefore statements beginning with "gifted kids are . . ." (including in this book), though efficient and pragmatic, are inappropriate generalizations. In addition, adult school personnel should consider that those persons in the "exceptionally gifted" range (1:10,000, at or above 155) or "extremely gifted" range (1:100,000, at or above 165; Gagné, 2007) likely have no or only rare readily available mind-mates and perhaps no one who shares their intense interests. Even basic conversational skills may be lacking. Extreme loneliness, frustration, anger, discouragement, and sadness may be their daily companions. It is not helpful to tell children at this level that they are "the same" as anyone else. Yes, they do share some important aspects with their age-peers, such as physical and emotional development. That reality is important for them to keep in mind for the sake of empathy and ethical behavior. But they are indeed different in most other aspects—even from most others with the *gifted* label, and they probably feel that difference intensely.

(continued)

KEY CONCEPT *(continued)*

Their parents and siblings may or not be similarly endowed. If either parent is, or if both have extreme ability, school counselors may find that such extreme ability, with concomitant levels of intensity and sensitivity affecting perspectives and behavior, may make conversations about advocacy, student behavior, and needs stressful. Keeping the information in mind may be helpful when talking with parents of an extremely gifted child, including simply noting, on a bell curve, that social challenges and intensities make sense at that level. Validation of the complexity of parenting an extremely able child may be rare for them. The concept of disenfranchised grief (Thornton & Zanich, 2002), referring to grief that is unrecognized or unsanctioned, may apply here if acquaintances cannot relate to their "loss" of anticipated positive aspects of raising a gifted child. The presence of the child with the most extreme ability, especially if that child is an outlier in the family, likely also affects the family system—communication, family leadership, child and parent roles, and the parents' relationship (cf. Breunlin, Schwartz, & Mac Kune-Karrer, 1992).

Mental health issues should not be assumed with this extreme population, although some feelings or behaviors might indeed reflect a disorder. Important to consider is the possibility of a misdiagnosis of extreme levels of characteristics of giftedness (e.g., intensity, sensitivities) as pathology or *a missed diagnosis* because behaviors in children and teens with extreme ability are dismissed as simply "odd." Homogeneously grouped gifted students in small-group discussion, with periodic brief social-skills training, interspersed noncompetitive activities requiring conversation (e.g., writing and sharing small poems in response to prompts; giving and receiving compliments), and psychoeducational information, can help extremely gifted students feel understood, connected to peers, and "not crazy" at a crucial time in their development.

and counseling suggests that, for better or for worse, once a child is identified and labeled as "gifted," the label creates a unique experience for parents and families (Cornell, 1983; Fornia & Frame, 2001; Hermann & Lawrence, 2012; Jenkins-Friedman, 1992; McMann & Oliver, 1988). Because each family is unique, their experiences are as well. However, school counselors may wish to consider the following points when collaborating with parents subsequent to the identification process.

Jenkins-Friedman (1992) wrote that the gift and the gifted child can become the family "re-organizer," with families renegotiating how time, resources, or attention to the gift are provided. This reorganization may mean that decisions must be made about whether the family can afford private lessons or summer enrichment opportunities. Families must determine whether there is time for libraries, museums, lessons, and other experiences to nurture talent, and how those decisions will affect siblings, especially if siblings are not also identified as gifted (McMann & Oliver, 1988). Siblings who have not been identified may question their role and value in the family system. Confusion can be compounded if a nongifted sibling was not identified because of a difference of only one or two points on a test used by the district during assessment for eligibility (Jenkins-Friedman, 1992; Moon & Hall, 1998). On the one hand, family support is vital to talent development; on the other hand, reorganizing family life around the gifted child can unbalance the family system with varying results (Colangelo, 2003).

The label *gifted* may also lead to assumptions about the child. When gifted students, due to asynchronous development and an advanced vocabulary, seem older than they are and communicate with parents as if they themselves were adults, the result may be confusion in boundaries between them and family members (Keirouz, 1990; Moon & Thomas, 2003). If a family does reorganize itself around the gift, the child may then have undue "power" in the home, with parents deferring to the child inappropriately. Having a gifted child may mean to some parents that these children should have more responsibilities at home or behave in a more adult way. Colangelo (2003, p. 380) explained that a behavior may be tolerated in one family because the parents perceive that "this is how it is with a gifted child," while in others the same behavior is not tolerated because "such behavior should not come from a gifted child" (p. 380).

The "Otherness" of Parenting Gifted Children

The school counselor first meets with Angela's teachers to hear their concerns. She listens empathically to what is worrisome to them and seeks to learn more about Angela from their perspective. Then she meets with Angela's parents. While listening to Angela's parents, the school counselor begins to sense other family challenges. They moved to this state for employment reasons, knowing that the community was small and rural. When Angela begins to struggle in third grade, they find they have few people in their new community to talk with about their concerns. They left good friends and family members in their previous state. Phone calls "home" seem to create more frustration as their friends describe their children as thriving and happy in their schools. Angela's mother is inundated with conflicting advice from her family and her friends. She confides to the school counselor that she and her husband typically feel more confused, misunderstood, and isolated after conversations with old friends and family members than before they picked up the phone. Angela's mother says, "Everyone tells us they envy us for having it so easy parenting a child like Angela, but they're not listening. It's not easy. It's scary and overwhelming, and most of the time I feel like I'm pretty much alone in figuring all of this out."

Feldman and Piirto (2002) wrote, "Although few would sympathize with parents who find themselves trying to raise a child with exceptional intellectual talent, it is in fact one of the most daunting and often discouraging challenges that family life has to offer" (p. 195). Fornia and Frame (2001) suggested that parents of gifted students view this circumstance as being both a blessing and a curse. Messages such as the ones Angela's parents are hearing about their "luck" in having a gifted child or her ability to "figure" her way out of her current struggles can leave parents feeling frustrated, confused, misunderstood, and isolated. While friends and family may be eager to give advice, they are not really hearing—or empathizing—with what Angela's mother is trying to communicate. This lack of felt support may be due to the many myths and stereotypes that surround the concept of giftedness. According to Alsop (1997), parents of gifted children encounter the "stigma" attached to giftedness even before their child enrolls in school: "Well intentioned friends and relatives offer advice meant to minimize differences which parents, especially mothers, observe in daily interactions between their child[ren] and those of those neighborhood" (Alsop, 1997, p. 28). Parents in Alsop's study expected that they would be able to discuss issues tied to their children's giftedness with family and friends. But parents also reported not being able to obtain practical advice from family and friends.

Depending on context, families of gifted students may not be able to find or connect with other families who also have gifted students in their communities. Fornia and Frame (2001) noted that parents wonder how other members of their neighborhood or community will treat their gifted child after it is known that the child has that label. Parents of gifted students may tread cautiously when entrusting friends, neighbors, and even family with information about and access to their gifted child. This caution can, in turn, reinforce the parents' experience of feeling misunderstood and isolated even in their own neighborhood. However, with the expansion of the Internet, and the availability of devices like digital phones and tablets or "apps," families now have a range of communication systems that can put them in contact with parents of other gifted students.

The Internet does provide a virtual "meeting place" for parents of gifted students. Online blogs (the resource section in the back of this text lists several) can provide an empathic sounding board on which parents can read the thoughts of other parents who are struggling with challenges unique to this population. Post (2013), in her blog, discussed the "guilty thoughts" of parents of gifted students. Not all are brimming with joy or pride. In fact, parents can wish their child were "normal" or able to "fit in." Other parents struggle with lukewarm or even antagonistic relationships with their local schools.

Sarah Robbins, author of *Everything Parent's Guide to Raising a Gifted Child*, has her own blog with topics ranging from obedience to acceleration to responding to boredom in the home. Regardless of meeting place—the Internet, at school, a parent advocacy group—parents of gifted students who find other parents to talk with experience a sense of relief in knowing that they are not alone (DeVries, 2011). Helping parents to connect with each other may be one of the most important services a school counselor can provide to parents of a gifted student. Another is smoothing pathways to other educators so that family interaction with the school is not fraught with antagonism or, worse, apathy.

Interactions With Schools

In Angela's case, her parents are disappointed to learn that although students were identified in third grade, few additional supports were available until middle school. However, the school counselor provides information about summer enrichment programs and assures them that Angela will take part in the process of assessment for eligibility for gifted-education programming, with testing administered to all students at that school during the third-grade year. Angela is soon identified and is then moved to an Advanced Reading class.

At the beginning of Angela's fourth-grade year, a new principal implements a different class assignment policy in which the highest-achieving students are grouped with the lowest-achieving students in an effort to bolster the school's achievement scores. High-achieving students are paired with low-performing students to assist them with their work. While this arrangement is challenging for Angela, she at times enjoys being able to help others. However, it is difficult for her to explain concepts and processes to her low-performing age-peers. She therefore feels further isolated and misunderstood by her classmates. Angela's mother contacts the teacher to set up a meeting, but becomes frustrated and distraught when the teacher is dismissive of her concerns.

Because values are often transferred from one generation to the next, how gifted students feel about school and what they believe about education are informed by their parents' or guardians' experiences, beliefs, and values (Hermann & Lawrence, 2012). If the parents of a gifted student are gifted themselves, their experiences, particularly as related to giftedness and education, may have left emotional residue (Henshon, 2012). The school counselor can act not only as an advocate for gifted students and their parents, but also as a collaborator and a presence that can ameliorate tensions between family and school.

Tensions can arise from a lack of communication, trust, or relationship-building between families and schools. On the one hand, parents of gifted students can find themselves questioning whether they should trust the school about accuracy of assessment during identification and about provision of adequate services (e.g., Do we trust educators to assess our child's abilities fairly and accurately? Do we trust the school to provide what is best for our child? Fornia & Frame, 2001). While mistrust may be rooted in parents' past experiences or in fear and worry about their student's well-being, teachers and educators are probably alert to parental suspicion. Teachers, in turn, may feel threatened or devalued when well-intentioned, well-informed parents question their abilities, expertise, and training (Schader, 2008). Both parties can lack confidence in each other's ability to identify talent and provide adequate enrichment to nurture that talent at home or at school (Hodge & Kemp, 2006). On the other hand, parents who do not have social capital to help them navigate complex relationships with school personnel may not know which questions to ask, and of whom, leaving the onus of communication on the school (Schader, 2008). Lack of trust and lack of communication can lead to an "us-versus-them" stance when parents meet with school personnel to discuss the needs of their student (Reinisch & Reinisch, 1997, p. 248).

Parents face additional difficulties in decision-making related to identification and service if they hear conflicting messages. Parents want their gifted students to be both challenged in academics and safe and supported in school. However, making decisions about which types of programming are appropriate can be difficult when parents are confronted with mixed messages from school personnel, friends, community members, research in books and magazines, and the general media (Schader, 2008). This quandary can lead to parents "making decisions based on unfounded information, misinformation or even disinformation" without clear guidance from educators who understand both research and policy (Schader, 2008, p. 479). Schools that do not communicate with parents about policy and procedures related to identification and academic programming leave families floundering or force parents to assume responsibility for advocacy even if they have incomplete information.

Educators in a "passive" school, which does not regularly communicate with parents, may be operating under the assumption that the typical school curriculum suffices and a student's talent will develop without assistance. This type of interaction describes *Natural Development*, which is one of four interactions schools have with gifted students as suggested by Colangelo and Dettman (1983). School counselors employed in a school that takes this stance need to harness multiple stakeholder groups and work toward providing appropriate gifted-education programming in their schools (see Chapter 12 in this volume).

A Type III interaction, *Interference*, is typified by schools that wish to provide services to gifted students, but parents who may not want to take advantage of the services. In this interaction, parents are concerned about the impact of the *gifted* label on their students' social relationships but some fear students may be set apart in a negative way if they participate in gifted-education programming (Colangelo & Dettman, 1983). To alleviate their fears, school counselors can talk with parents about the latter's beliefs about gifted education. Counselors can also acquaint them with research on the effect of gifted programming, including acceleration, on their students' social development (see Key Concept: Acceleration, in Chapter 8).

Unfortunately, many parents experience what Colangelo and Dettman call a Type II interaction, a type of relationship with their student's school reflected in the name of the interaction: *Conflict*. Here, parents advocate for appropriate gifted programming, but educators in the school believe that special programming is a priority only for students with special needs (i.e., disabilities). The stance of the school is that the regular curriculum is adequate for gifted students. Parents blame the school for not providing adequate services and feel they must be aggressive to get what their students need. School personnel, in response, dig in their heels regarding existing policies. If parents believe the school will never provide gifted programming, they may allow their students to undermine teachers and tacitly condone negative attitudes toward school work and education. Some parents withdraw their students from the school altogether if they have the financial means to enroll them in a private school, for example. School counselors may find themselves in the crossfire in situations like this; however, they can also exert leadership toward changing school climate, advocating for resources, and altering policies.

For family–school interaction, "the most workable and successful plans are those that center on building communication skills, sharing information about the nature and needs of gifted children, and experiencing the viewpoints of others" (Robinson et al., 2007, p. 10). This description would fit the Type I, or *Cooperation*, interaction between families and schools. Such an interaction is characterized by operation and trust. Both family and school share information and operate from the belief that both parties are active participants in a gifted student's talent development. The school takes responsibility for providing appropriate educational challenge through specific gifted-education programming. Parents are advocates for keeping that programming in place.

Angela's parents are in regular contact with the school counselor, who provides them with an opportunity to voice their concerns about the school policies and helps coordinate meetings with various professionals as needed. The counselor works with other allies within the system to try to foster a more positive climate for both gifted students and their families, as many of the parents of gifted students have expressed the perception that they have felt pushed away by the current administration. The parents of the small group of identified gifted students at the elementary school begin to form an informal support network, with whom the school counselor and the gifted-education coordinator meet regularly, and for whom they provide information about giftedness, about pertinent resources in the larger community, and about how to best advocate for their children within the school system.

Collaborating with the school counselor, Angela's parents meet with the principal, the gifted-education coordinator, and Angela's teachers to develop a Differentiated Learning Plan (similar to an Individualized Education Plan) in response to the parents' assertion that the school is not adequately meeting Angela's learning needs. The parents found this language in the resources provided by the school counselor about the legal rights of parents of gifted children. That language helps them convey their concerns more effectively.

The school counselor studies the results from the achievement and aptitude testing that has been done and reviews and interprets the results with Angela's parents. They learn that she is performing well above her age-peers and her grade level and outlines the limited options available: grade acceleration, continued differentiation in the classroom, or alternative schooling options such as a private school. The school counselor provided additional information about each of those options for the parents to review and schedules a follow-up meeting to discuss the benefits and challenges of each.

● ● ●

RECOMMENDATIONS FOR PRACTICE

School counselors have a critical role in the lives of gifted students and their families. They act as empathic listeners, counselors, advocates, and coordinators of resources. In this chapter's vignette, Angela's school counselor is effective in all four areas. The following are recommendations for school counselors who wish to empower parents and create alliances between them and school personnel so that their gifted students thrive. School counselors should do the following:

1. **Have a thorough understanding of traits, development, and academic needs of gifted students.** Both authors were practicing school counselors. One of their primary challenges in that role was that many school-system professionals simply did not have a clear understanding of the unique characteristics, needs, and concerns of gifted students. To connect with and empower families of gifted students, school counselors need to build their own pertinent knowledge base so that they can educate their colleagues. Being able to understand the concerns parents bring to their attention enables school counselors to demonstrate empathy and concern, effectively advocate for those families, and help them advocate for their children themselves.

2. **Provide parents and families with research-based information and resources.** Research-based books and articles can help parents to better understand their gifted students. With resources and information, parents may have less anxiety about whether professionals and websites are credible and more confidence about making informed choices about services. School counselors should be able to direct parents to talent searches and weekend/summer enrichment options at local universities, policy and practice regarding acceleration, information about achievement and career planning, and resources for supporting social and emotional well-being. As they would for any other student population, school counselors should be ready with a list of external supports such as community-based counselors and family therapists. However, they also need to be familiar with service providers who can work effectively with gifted youth and to help parents prepare questions to ask counselors or therapists before deciding to send their children to them. School counselors can utilize the list of resources in the back of this book to begin or expand their role as a resource coordinator.

3. **Take time to listen to the fears and worries of parents of gifted children.** School counselors can put their active listening and reflecting skills to work here. Parents of gifted students often have characteristics associated with giftedness themselves and may mask deep, intense emotions by focusing on cognitive concerns. Being alert to underlying emotions and reflecting them enables school counselors to hear concerns and convey understanding, so that they are better able to address the issues for which the parent is seeking support. To build a greater network of support, the professional school counselor can provide parents with connections to resources, organizations that support gifted children, and even families of other gifted students (Reinisch & Reinisch, 1997; Stephens, 1999).

4. **Involve parents in the identification process and honor their perspectives.** As Griffin and Wood (2015) observed, "Parent involvement is not a novel idea, as it has long been a strategy for increasing academic achievement of all students. Indeed, researchers, federal policymakers, and school stakeholders assert that there is a direct link between parents' participation and students' academic achievement, making parental involvement and its relationship to academic achievement a central focus in educational research" (p. 297). Schools and districts may sometimes give lip service to parent involvement but not actually promote and practice it. School counselors can meet with both parents and students to share the district rationale and process for nominating or not nominating students for participation in programming. While educators should

be trained so that they can discuss the unique traits, characteristics, and development of gifted students knowledgeably, parents should also be accorded respect and space to talk about what they observe in their child at home, as gifted attributes may be demonstrated differently depending on the context (Griffin & Wood, 2015). In addition, elementary school counselors who educate parents about the language of the school system and the legal rights and limitations of the identification process can prepare parents for possible future challenges related to placement during middle and high school.

5. **Consistently work on building relationships.** School counselors understand the need to communicate regularly with parents to build trust and credibility. Mutual respect and understanding are the hallmarks of collaborative relationships with parents. School counselors who focus on relationship-building move the focus of discussions "above and beyond academics and toward family support and developing parental efficacy, which is the parents' sense of ability to positively affect their children's achievement" (Griffin & Wood, 2015, p. 307). Relationship-building, trust, and communication are particularly vital for parents of culturally and economically diverse gifted children. Griffin and Steen (2010) suggested that facilitating a deeper relationship with parents increases mutual understanding between home and school and allows educators and school counselors to better understand the strengths and needs of parents.

6. **Strive for cultural competence in all areas of parent collaboration.** School counselors need to consider which areas of outreach to parents might benefit from more cultural competence in those attempting to engage them. Dissemination of information regarding identification and service to culturally diverse groups should be done in small groups. In that format, parents of gifted students from diverse backgrounds can hear questions other parents may ask, leading to increased connection and normalization of parenting experiences (Griffin & Wood, 2015). Outreach can strategically target groups that have not had a history of access to education. Families from high-poverty backgrounds, especially generational poverty, may be unaware of educational opportunities such as identification during elementary school of gifted students for special programs. Lack of information and access can have an impact on student placement and identification of giftedness at later stages (Griffin & Wood, 2015). Stronger alliances with parents can decrease educator bias and reduce educators' deficit assumptions about gifted students of color (Bower & Griffin, 2011; Griffin & Steen, 2010).

7. Model and practice appropriate advocacy. Parents of gifted students benefit from school counselors who actively advocate for resources that support gifted students' learning (Silverman & Golon, 2008). School counselors can act as both sounding board and strategist as they help families respond to potential pushback from the school system as they advocate for students. Some gifted students have additional differences that can compound their need for support in learning, such as minority status, socioeconomic status, twice-exceptionality, sexual orientation, gender identity, physical disability, or mental health concerns, to name but a few. These students may require advocacy on multiple fronts. Chapter 4 describes options for school counselor advocacy for an African American twice-exceptional student. Chapter 12 provides suggestions for school counselor advocacy.

8. Utilize family resources to empower them. School counselors can connect with professional organizations (the American School Counselor Association, the American Counseling Association, and the National Association for Gifted Children) for continuing education, professional development opportunities, networking, and support. Keeping abreast of current research, policy, and practice can help school counselors address the needs of their students and maintain their own sense of professional identity. School counselors should not be afraid to reach out to others to bolster their own resources and efficacy. In the process, they can build a network of resources to pass along to the families of gifted students, including local agencies, colleges, counselors, libraries, and arts centers.

● ● ●

CONCLUDING THOUGHTS AND RECOMMENDATIONS

Angela and her parents provided an opportunity to explore a number of issues that families of gifted children may face in the course of their children's education. Within the Lee family's story are embedded a number of critical skills and attitudes that school counselors can integrate into their work with parents of gifted students, such as being an informed advocate, a skilled and empathic listener, and a competent collaborator. One gift school counselors can give these families is themselves as knowledgeable professionals who have a thorough understanding of gifted students' unique characteristics and their district's and school's policies and procedures for identification and programming. Knowledgeable school counselors can help parents navigate the complexities of school systems and to secure needed services for their gifted children. An informed advocate can help to change the minds of school personnel who are reluctant to support programming for gifted children and teens. A competent collaborator can work with parents to identify their family's and their student's unique needs and concerns and create a plan to utilize local, state, and national resources to address them. However, the counselor as empathic listener is crucial for understanding and validating what parents and guardians of gifted students face as they attempt to support talented children at home and secure appropriate services at school. A professional school counselor empowers families by acting in each of these roles and creating powerful alliances with them.

• • •

REFERENCES

Alsop, G. (1997). Coping or counseling: Families of intellectually gifted students. *Roeper Review, 20*(1), 28–35.

American School Counselor Association. (2016). The school counselor and school–family–community partnerships. Retrieved from https://www.schoolcounselor .org/asca/media/asca/PositionStatements/PS_Partnerships.pdf

Bower, H. A., & Griffin, D. (2011). Can the Epstein model of parental involvement work in a high minority, high poverty elementary school? A case study. *Professional School Counseling, 15,* 77–87.

Breunlin, D. C., Schwartz, R. C., & Mac Kune-Karrer, B. (1992). *Metaframeworks: Transcending the models of family therapy.* San Francisco, CA: Jossey-Bass.

Colangelo, N. (2003). Counseling gifted students. In N. Colangelo & G. A. Davis (Eds.), *Handbook of gifted education* (3rd ed., pp. 373–387). Needham Heights, MA: Allyn & Bacon.

Colangelo, N., & Dettman, D. F. (1983). A conceptual model of four types of parent–school interactions. *Journal for the Education of the Gifted, 5,* 120–126.

Cornell, D. G. (1983). Gifted children: The impact of positive labeling on the family system. *American Orthopsychiatric Association, 53*(2), 322–335.

DeVries, A. (2011). What I've learned from parents of gifted children. Retrieved from http://sengifted.org/what-ive-learned-from-parents-of-gifted-children

Feldman, D., & Piirto, J. (2002). Parenting talented children. In M. Bornstein (Ed.), *Handbook of parenting: Practical issues in parenting* (Vol. 5, pp. 195–219). Mahwah, NJ: Lawrence Erlbaum.

Fornia, G. L., & Frame, M. W. (2001). The social and emotional needs of gifted children Implications for family counseling. *Family Journal: Counseling and Therapy for Couples and Families, 9*(4), 384–390.

Gagné, F. (2007). Ten commandments for academic talent development. *Gifted Child Quarterly, 51,* 93–118. doi:10.1177/0016986206296660

Garn, A. C., Matthews, M. S., & Jolly, J. L. (2010). Parental influences on the academic motivation of gifted students: A self-determination theory perspective. *Gifted Child Quarterly, 54*, 263–272.

Griffin, D., & Steen, S. (2010). School–family–community partnerships: Applying Epstein's theory of the six types of involvement to school counselor practice. *Professional School Counseling, 13*, 218–226.

Griffin, D., & Wood, S. (2015). "Mommy, I'm bored": A dialectical exploration of school–family–community approaches to working with gifted, Black males in rural school environments. In T. Stambaugh & S. Wood (Eds.), *Serving gifted students in rural settings* (pp. 87–98). Waco, TX: Prufrock Press.

Henshon, S. E. (2012). Wise, holistic thinking: An interview with Jean Sunde Peterson. *Roeper Review, 34*, 139–144.

Hermann, K. M., & Lawrence, C. (2012). Family relationships. In T. L. Cross & J. Cross (Eds.), *Handbook for counselors serving students with gifts and talents: Development, relationships, school issues, and counseling needs/interventions* (pp. 393–408). Waco, TX: Prufrock Press.

Hertzog, N. B. (2012). Counseling for young gifted children. In T. L. Cross & J. R. Cross (Eds.), *Handbook for counselors serving students with gifts and talents: Development, relationships, school issues, and counseling needs/interventions* (pp. 195–208). Waco, TX: Prufrock Press.

Hodge, K. A., & Kemp, C. R. (2006). Recognition of giftedness in the early years of school: Perspectives of teachers, parents, and children. *Journal for the Education of the Gifted, 30*(2), 164–204.

Jenkins-Friedman, R. (1992). Families of gifted children and youth. In M. J. Fine & C. Carlson (Eds.), *Handbook of family school interventions: A systems perspective* (pp. 175–187). Boston, MA: Allyn & Bacon.

Keirouz, K. S. (1990). Concerns of parents of gifted children: A research review. *Gifted Child Quarterly, 34*(2), 56–63.

Lovecky, D. V. (1992). Exploring social and emotional aspects of giftedness in children. *Roeper Review, 15*(6), 18–25.

McMann, N., & Oliver, R. (1988). Problems in families with gifted children: Implications for counselors. *Journal of Counseling & Development, 66*, 275–278.

Moon, S., & Hall, A. S. (1998). Family therapy with intellectually and creatively gifted children. *Journal of Marital and Family Therapy, 24*(1), 59–80.

Moon, S., & Thomas, V. (2003). Family therapy with gifted and talented adolescents. *Journal of Secondary Gifted Education, 14*(2), 107–113.

Morawska, A., & Sanders, M. R. (2008). Parenting gifted and talented children: What are the key child behaviour and parenting issues? *Australian and New Zealand Journal of Psychiatry*, 819–827.

Post, G. (2013). Guilty thoughts: What parents of gifted children really think. Retrieved from http://giftedchallenges.blogspot.com/2015/01/guilty-thoughts-what-parents-of-gifted.html

Probst, B., & Piechowski, M. (2012). Overexcitabilities and temperament. In T. L. Cross & J. R. Cross (Eds.), *Handbook for counselors serving students with gifts and talents: Development, relationships, school issues, and counseling needs/interventions* (pp. 53–74). Waco, TX: Prufrock Press.

Reinisch, S. A., & Reinisch, L. (1997). One year at a time: Parents' perspectives on gifted education. *Peabody Journal of Education, 72*(3/4), 237–252.

Robinson, A., Shore, B., & Enerson, D. (2007). Parent involvement. In A. Robinson, B. Shore, & D. Enerson (Eds.), *Best practices in gifted education: An evidence-based guide* (pp. 7–14). Waco, TX: Prufrock Press.

Schader, R. M. (2008). Parenting. In J. A. Plucker & C. M. Callahan (Eds.), *Critical issues and practice in gifted education* (pp. 479–492). Waco, TX: Prufrock Press.

Silverman, L. K. (2012). Asynchronous development: A key to counseling the gifted. In T. L. Cross & J. R. Cross (Eds.), *Handbook for counselors serving students with gifts and talents: Development, relationships, school issues, and counseling needs/interventions* (pp. 261–280). Waco, TX: Prufrock Press.

Silverman, L. K., & Golon, A. S. (2008). Clinical practice with gifted families. In S. Pfeiffer (Ed.), *Handbook of giftedness in children: Psychoeducational theory, research, and best practices* (pp. 223–246). New York, NY: Springer-Verlag.

Stephens, K. R. (1999). Parents of the gifted and talented: The forgotten partners. *Gifted Child Today, 22*(5), 38–43.

Thornton, G., & Zanich, M. L. (2002). Empirical assessment of disenfranchised grief: 1989–2000. In K. J. Doka (Ed.), *Disenfranchised grief: New directions, challenges, and strategies for practice*. Champaign, IL: Research Press.

12

School Counselors as Leaders and Advocates for Gifted Students

SUSANNAH M. WOOD, ERIN M. D. LANE, AND MATTHEW J. BECK

Samantha has been the middle school counselor in a small rural district in the Midwest for the past 3 years. She has spent most of her time in program development and building relationships with students, parents, staff, and community partners. Currently, she is working with community and district administrators to increase access to Internet and other technology in her building for more program options; unfortunately, the district's increasingly tight budget precludes upgrades to current systems. As the academic year comes to a close, she talks with Rachel, a veteran teacher with considerable experience in differentiation. Rachel is concerned about some of her math students. By year's end, due to her differentiated curriculum, at least seven will have completed Algebra 1, the most advanced math class at the school. Rachel wonders what can be planned for them for next year. A few parents have expressed concerns about future classes as these students progress. She asks to meet with Samantha about this situation.

Samantha is in a position to be an advocate for her students and a leader in her building and district. The American School Counselor Association (ASCA) National Model identifies leadership, advocacy, collaboration, and acting as a systemic change agent as major skill sets all school counselors should develop (ASCA, 2012). School counselors who take on these roles "promote student achievement and systemic change that ensure equity and access to rigorous education for every student and lead to closing achievement opportunity and attainment gaps" (ASCA, 2012, p. 1). According to the ASCA Ethical Standards for School Counselors (2016, p. 9), an advocate is "a person who speaks, writes or acts to promote the well-being of students, parents/guardians and the school counseling profession." *Advocacy* and *leadership* are terms often used interchangeably. While there are similarities in the characteristics, roles, and responsibilities of advocates and leaders, there are also differences. This chapter describes the concepts of leadership and advocacy, explores traits and characteristics of leaders and advocates, suggests ideas for leadership and advocacy pertaining to gifted and talented students, and provides possible responses to difficult questions school counselors may be asked when engaged in leadership and advocacy for this population.

• • •

LEADERSHIP AND ADVOCACY: DEFINITIONS AND CONCEPTS

Mason and McMahon (2009) suggested that leadership is a complex concept that is difficult to define but could be seen as the foundation for other skill sets such as advocacy and collaboration. Several types of leadership models have been proposed in the school counseling literature. ASCA (2012) recommended that school counselors utilize four contexts of leadership (structural, human resource, political, and symbolic) as developed by Bolman and Deal (2008), and the organization provided leadership activities and connections between these activities and the National Model. Findings from recent studies investigating the nature of school counseling leadership have suggested that *school counselor leadership should include advocacy in some way* (Young & Bryan, 2015; Young, Dollarhide, & Baughman, 2015).

The concept of advocacy has evolved from disciplines such as sociology, feminism, psychology, political science, religion, and social work. Within the counseling literature, advocacy is tied to social justice. Counselors practice advocacy in counseling by "helping clients challenge institutional and social barriers that impede academic, career, or personal–social development" (Lee, 1998, pp. 8–9). Specific to school counselors, advocacy is linked with systemic change in a way that counselors to "right injustices, increase access, and improve educational outcomes for all students" (Ratts, DeKruyf, & Chen-Hayes, 2007, p. 90). ASCA (2012) provided a helpful conceptual framework for how school counselors can practice systems change and social justice advocacy counseling at the micro (student) and macro (school, community, and state) levels by merging principles from the ASCA National Model with the American Counseling Association (ACA) Advocacy Competencies (Lewis, Arnold, House, & Toporek, 2002).

In the case of Samantha, several avenues for advocacy and opportunities for leadership are available. However, advocating for and on behalf of high-ability students is not always an easy process, given the nature of the specific situations and considering the emotionally charged constructs and labels of *gifted*, *talented*, and *high ability*.

● ● ●

CHARACTERISTICS OF LEADERS AND ADVOCATES

Several researchers in the counseling and school counseling fields have explored qualities and characteristics of leaders and advocates (Kiselica & Robinson, 2001; Ratts et al., 2007; Shillingford & Lambie, 2010; Young et al., 2015). For some researchers characteristics merge into practices; in other words, leaders and advocates *are what they do*. For school counselors to be able to lead and advocate, they must nurture specific dispositions, understand the cultural norms of their schools, and develop strategic relationships.

Nurturing Dispositions

Because gifted and talented students are a unique population, school counselors' development of personal advocacy and leadership dispositions can be a crucial to their being able to meet these students' unique academic, personal–social, and career counseling needs. School counselor advocates and leaders model compassion, empowerment, inspiration, insightfulness, and empathy (Dahir & Stone, 2012). Characteristics such as proactivity, tenacity, and challenge-seeking are important skills school counselors can infuse into their work as advocates (McMahan, Singh, Urbano, & Haston, 2010). Dispositions include being aware of self (McMahan et al., 2010), assessing strengths and limitations (Ratts et al., 2007), and reflecting upon worldviews, values, and beliefs (Byrd & Hays, 2012). McMahan et al. (2010) found that school counselors often reflect, identify, and incorporate their personalities in their advocacy work. School counselors who reflect on and acknowledge both key strengths and areas for personal growth likely find themselves well prepared when confronted by barriers and resistance in the form of "we've tried that before" and "your ideas won't work" (Dahir & Stone, 2012, p. 129). Self-reflection can also help to address internalized biases and dispel myths pertaining to high-ability or twice-exceptional students.

Understanding School Culture

Leadership and advocacy skills for school counselors can also be specific to school culture and climate (Trusty & Brown, 2005). Navigating politics within the school system requires school counselors to model the skills of communication, collaboration, and intentionality (McMahan et al., 2010). Due to the nature of schools as systems and subsystems (e.g., teachers, students), school counselors should recognize that some schools welcome change for the sake of students, whereas others "maintain a culture of conformity" (Trusty & Brown, 2005, p. 261). Nonetheless, school counselors need knowledge related to the worldviews, policies, and cultural norms of their stakeholders (i.e., board members, administrators, parents, community members, and elected officials) as well as the relationships and dynamics between and among these stakeholders at each institutional level. Their problem-assessment and conflict-resolution skills can be matched to the specific situation and culture in which the school counselor is engaged in advocacy (Trusty & Brown, 2005). Knowledge of the organizational dynamics and policies in the school building and district can strengthen the ability of school counselors to be politically savvy when speaking up for high-ability students (Trusty & Brown, 2005).

Developing Strategic Relationships

Purposeful collaboration and communication with all members of the school community have been identified as important skills for school counselor advocates and leaders (Singh, Urbano, Haston, & McMahan, 2010). However, it is important to note that developing relationships in schools takes time, and school counselors should be aware that school professionals (i.e., teachers, principals, and board members) might not always understand the role and function of counselors as advocates. Therefore, perspective-taking skills may help school counselors to view concerns and events through an alternate lens. Specifically, school counselors should anticipate, and practice with colleagues, how administrators or other professionals may respond to their advocacy. As a result, school counselors might develop mind-sets similar to those of their colleagues and school community members, and thus be in a better position to advocate on behalf of gifted students.

* * *

LEADERSHIP AND ADVOCACY FOR GIFTED STUDENTS IN ACTION

ASCA (2012) suggest leadership and advocacy competencies for school counselors which complement the major areas found within the ACA Competencies (Toporek, Lewis, & Crethar, 2009). School counselors act with students (empowerment), and on behalf of them through providing individual student assistance, promoting school–community collaboration, identifying systemic barriers, working with the community, and involving themselves in social and political advocacy (ASCA, 2012). When discussing how counselors can advocate on behalf of their students and clients (micro level), Ratts and Hutchins (2009) suggested 13 strategies, which can be condensed to three major themes: identification, planning, and assistance. These three themes also roughly correspond to the phrases suggested by Grantham, Frasier, Roberts, and Bridges (2005) suggested phases: needs assessment, development of advocacy plans, implementation, and evaluation/follow-up. In the following paragraphs, we describe how Samantha and Rachel can apply the three themes to social justice advocacy for their students (Ratts & Hutchins, 2009) and add the final step of evaluation and follow-up.

Identification of Allies, Resources, and Potential Barriers

Samantha and Rachel begin by identifying resources, barriers, and potential allies (Ratts & Hutchins, 2009). Investigating stakeholders' experiences and thoughts about this situation also enables the duo to determine who has a stake in it and some possible effects of resolution. Some stakeholders might be uncomfortable with Rachel and Samantha's questions; however, taking risks and questioning current practices and processes is an effective leadership practice (Kouzes & Posner, 2003). Table 12.1 illustrates the questions and topics Rachel and Samantha use to better understand the issues from each stakeholder's perspective. School counselors interested in advocating for gifted students may wish to use the questions to explore current policy and practice. School counselors should also expect to be asked questions pertaining to student needs, the building as a resource, and possible outcomes to various situations. These questions are also listed in Table 12.1. The last section of this chapter offers questions and answers that can help school counselors prepare for future conversations.

Samantha also needs to talk with her high school counterparts, potential allies in her quest to make academic challenge possible for this group of students. Those counselors can identify potential obstacles and barriers from their perspective. Having middle school students in a high school math class will add logistical burdens. While administrators will contend with issues like classroom space, qualified teachers, buses, budget, and technology, high school counselors will have to address concerns pertaining to credit hours, dual enrollment, and scheduling. In addition, the counselors may wonder if the current situation will be a long-term problem requiring planning for the future. Undoubtedly there have been and will continue to be middle school students ready for advanced coursework in math and in other areas. High school counselors and administrators at both levels may be concerned about limitations on what they can provide in services and logistics.

Fortunately for Samantha and Rachel, the high school counselors engaged in community asset mapping last year. The high school counselors offer their findings related to resources in the immediate community, and at the state level.

TABLE 12.1

SAMPLE QUESTIONS AND CONVERSATION TOPICS WITH VARIOUS STAKEHOLDER GROUPS

	Students	Teachers	Parents/Guardians	Administrators
Questions to stakeholders	• What has been your experience with your math classes thus far? • How would you describe your feelings toward your math classes? • If you could choose the focus of your next math class, would you want a more advanced course with new information like geometry, or a class that had more complex information about algebra? • Would you want another math course at all if you had your choice?	• What do you believe all students need to know about math? • To what extent do you believe the current math class structure meets the needs of college-bound students? • What specifically does this group of students need, considering they have already mastered the last math class in the sequence here? • What has been done in similar situations in the past? What worked? What didn't? • Which options do you believe are open to you and to these students (e.g., taking class at a high school and online learning)? Can we brainstorm ideas you would be willing to try?	• What do you want for your children? • How is success discussed/defined in your home? How is happiness discussed/defined? • What are your thoughts about college and career paths for your child? • If college is the advanced path you would like for your student, what do you think your student will need to know when they get there? What knowledge and skills will be needed to be prepared? What will you need help understanding?	• What do you want for our students? • What do you believe our school does well to meet the academic needs of students? • To what extent do you believe the current math class structure meets the needs of college-bound or high-ability students? • What specifically does this group of students need, considering they have already mastered the last math class in the sequence that this building has? • What has been done in similar situations in the past? What worked? What didn't?

TABLE 12.1 (continues)

SAMPLE QUESTIONS AND CONVERSATION TOPICS WITH VARIOUS STAKEHOLDER GROUPS

Students	Teachers	Parents/Guardians	Administrators
• What do you think you will need to have learned math if you are planning on going to college after high school? Or a job? • How would you feel if you were to be placed in a more advanced or complex course? • How motivated would you be if you were in more advanced math course? • What would you be willing to do to explain to the principal or school board that this is a class you need (e.g., emails or letters)?	• What are your worries or concerns about the various options we've discussed? • If another advanced math class is to be offered here, to what extent do you believe you are prepared to teach it? What would a teacher in charge of that kind of class need to know? • If another or different class is not an option, to what extent do you believe you are willing and/or able to go "deeper" with the content with these students? Or to differentiate the content for these students?	• What do you believe about kids having advanced classes during middle school? • If an advanced math course were to be offered, what would be your concerns about your student participating in that class? • If this is something you would want for your student, what is your level of willingness to write to or speak to the school board to discuss the need for this class?	• Which options do you believe are open to you and to these students (e.g., taking class at a high school and online learning)? • What are your worries or concerns about the various options? • What resources do we need to consider for these options (e.g., time, human resources, finances, logistics, and technology)?

(continued)

TABLE 12.1 *(continues)*

SAMPLE QUESTIONS AND CONVERSATION TOPICS WITH VARIOUS STAKEHOLDER GROUPS

	Students	Teachers	Parents/Guardians	Administrators
Possible questions/ comments from stakeholders	• Would I still get to be with my friends if I took this class? • Would I have to go to the high school to take the class? • Do I need this class for college? • How much will it cost? • Would I have to give up a class? • What if my friends think this is a dumb idea? • What if my parents don't want me to do this? • Will there be a lot of homework?	• If I agree to teach an advanced class, will I be asked to do this every year? • Is it fair to the other students to offer a different class at this level? Shouldn't it be open to everyone? • Will I have support from the parents/guardians when I ask the students to take on more challenging work? • Is there a specific curriculum I should use or do I use the high school curriculum? • How will this affect the student's future math curriculum in high school? • Can we consult the high school math teacher before making any decision?	• What if my student doesn't want to take another math class in middle school? How does this affect his or her path to college, if at all? • I don't want my kids putting on airs. They know their place in the community. • My student wants another math class, but if it means more homework, that could be a problem. We work, and he or she takes care of his/ her brothers and sisters and the house/property.	• Who would coordinate logistics required for a new class? • Which community resources do we have to make this work? • How do you see this new class working? • If we do this for this one group of students, what happens to the next group who wants accommodations? • Who will pay for this? • What new technology is required? • What does the high school have to say about this? The com- munity college? • What will the students' transcripts look like?

(continued)

TABLE 12.1 *(continues)*

SAMPLE QUESTIONS AND CONVERSATION TOPICS WITH VARIOUS STAKEHOLDER GROUPS

Students	Teachers	Parents/Guardians	Administrators
• I want to write an email/letter. What do I say? How do I say it? Who can help me? Should someone proofread it?		• How many girls would be in this class? Would my child be the only one? • Wouldn't my teen be better off spending time working, babysitting, or taking an elective class? • What would taking another math class at a high school mean for my teen's friendships? Will these students be hanging out with older kids? Won't that be a bad influence? How will they fit in? • What happens if they run out of math classes at the high school level?	• Will students get high school credit for this advanced class that they take in middle school? If they do get high school credit, will it count for the total number they need for graduation?

Griffin and Farris (2010, p. 249) defined community asset mapping as "drawing of a map" that has, as a primary component, a list of resources that have been identified and compiled by multiple stakeholders. For school counselors, community asset mapping has traditionally meant identifying agencies and referral resources for families and students struggling with a various issues, including mental health concerns, special needs, and homelessness. However, community asset mapping can lead to identifying resources to support schools, students, and families in multiple areas, including the academic needs of gifted students. Griffin and Farris (2010) suggested that three levels of assets be considered: (a) abilities, gifts, and skills of individuals residing in the community; (b) local community associations facilitating collaboration between agencies and individuals toward common goals; and (c) local businesses and government facilities such as hospitals, human services agencies, colleges, and universities (Griffin & Farris, 2010). Mapping requires that members of the school and community come together to talk, work, and identify the resources they are aware of.

Creating a Plan

Rachel and Samantha will likely have to create a plan to resolve the situation, provide options for solutions, and present the plan to administrators and school board members. In addition, Rachel and Samantha should be prepared to address concerns and answer questions. Perhaps most important, they need to communicate a common or shared vision of what is needed in a way that can inspire and enable these stakeholders to become active collaborators in the plan. First, Rachel and Samantha need to identify the number of students the issue currently affects as well as present comparisons of the aggregated standardized test results of the group of advanced students with the aggregated standardized test results of the rest of their graduating class. Rachel should also present the completed curriculum and assessment results for the group of gifted students. Additionally, they should be able to describe similar situations from the past, if any, and explain how they were resolved. These two professionals might also argue for the likelihood of the situation happening again, whether with the math sequence or in other core subjects.

Just as important, Rachel and Samantha should come to the meeting with the stories and experiences of their stakeholders. In our experience, numbers *and* the voices of students and parents can deepen administrators' and school board officials' understanding of the current situation. Rachel's students might self-advocate by writing letters and emails to the middle school and high school principals and school board members. This exercise would be an opportunity for Rachel and Samantha to work with the students on appropriate voice and tone of professional letters and to model language and tone for the students through role-playing meetings with educators. In doing so, Samantha might discover that some of the students have been angry about feeling bored in other classes, being with peers who do not value education or who misbehave in class, and being ridiculed by teachers for asking questions. She can arrange individual counseling sessions with them if needed.

Perhaps the most difficult part of the process is *presenting both the vision and the plan* to address the needs of these students. Samantha and Rachel, with the support of their building principal, can present their ideas to the school board. In doing so, the two educators are engaging in political leadership (Bolman & Deal, 2008), utilizing their interpersonal influence (Young & Bryan, 2015) and challenging current barriers to students' academic success (Shillingford & Lambie, 2010). As they address the school board, Samantha and Rachel must demonstrate leadership attributes such as confidence and innovation, relationship attributes such as being open and approachable, and communication and collaboration skills such as listening and building rapport (Young et al., 2015).

While this may be a new experience for counselor and teacher, between the two of them they have the skills essential for effective advocacy. Rachel can describe her experiences and interactions with students, parents, and fellow educators. Samantha can use words such as *we*, and acknowledge concerns and possible areas of resistance in the room. Because they have planned ahead, both educators will be prepared to answer difficult questions and provide additional information about changes that school board members seem reluctant to embrace. As a school counselor, Samantha complements Rachel's knowledge with her skills in group facilitation and processing of emotions. Some of the most basic counseling skills, such as reflection, linking, and immediacy, can be powerful in these kinds of situations. Kiselica and Robinson (2001, p. 394) suggested that effective advocates demonstrate the following skills: (a) flexibility and willingness to compromise; (b) awareness of the effect of their personality on others; (c) warmth, openness, and empathy toward others; (d) openness to understanding how systems work; and (d) setting realistic goals. Samantha and Rachel will need a positive collaborative alliance with the school board. To gain this they will have to be open to considering what the school board believes and values, their collective ability to make change, and their limitations. Counselor and teacher must both be flexible, open, and warm in their approach if they are to "avoid the pitfalls of overzealousness and blind idealism" that they could inadvertently create by attacking the school board or district administrators or disparaging current practices or professionals in the district (Kiselica & Robinson, 2001, p. 394).

Risk-taking and Counselors' Self-efficacy

After talking with the school board, Samantha and Rachel will probably have differing perspectives about that experience. They both will have taken risks in advocating for a group of students whose needs may not be well understood. Rachel may be more confident in this type of advocacy as she has done it many times for students. However, she has not engaged much in political leadership. In contrast, Samantha is in only her third year as a school counselor, and advocacy may be an uncomfortable experience for her. If any stakeholder in this scenario is significantly and negatively resistant, Samantha may experience a dip in her sense of self-efficacy and an increase in self-doubt. She may believe she should have been more effective or more competent (Mason & McMahon, 2009)—a common experience with school counselors with only a few years of experience. However, this may be both a developmental issue (Mason & McMahon, 2009) and a learning opportunity for her. In addition, Samantha may benefit from considering where resistance occurred in this situation, and the extent to which she may be personalizing the problem (Dollarhide, Gibson, & Saginak, 2008). Regardless, learning to lead means taking advantage of opportunities to lead and advocate. Shillingford and Lambie (2010) recommended that school counselors engage in "challenging the process" successively over time. Doing so allows them to be "more self-enhanced in making their presence felt" (p. 214).

Both Rachel and Samantha may also consider that even a small step toward their goal of securing needed academic services is a significant step (e.g., provision for this class of students, but no plans for future accommodations). Small, focused, and attainable goals are an important part of leadership (Dollarhide et al., 2008). Regardless of how well the teacher and counselor plan and how collaboratively the school board works with them to resolve the current issue, there will likely be both anticipated and unanticipated outcomes. Both Rachel and Samantha should prepare themselves, the students, and the parents for next steps.

Assistance

Ideally, Rachel and Samantha's collaborative relationship will not end when they leave the school board meeting. As the plan unfolds, they can maintain responsibility for serving these students, the parents, and students who may be in a similar situation in the future. Leaders identified as successful in Dollarhide et al.'s (2008) study "took responsibility and empowered themselves to bring out change, even in the face of resistance, doubt and lack of initial support. This would suggest that willingness to bring about change must be coupled with determination and resolve" (p. 267). To prepare them for advanced classes, Samantha can make plans to work with the students individually and in small or classroom-size groups, proactively, in the areas of time management, working with more challenging content, concerns about failure, and organizational skills. Together she and Rachel can help the students identify possible mentors in the community as well as high school mentors in advanced math classes. Samantha can also continue to work with the high school counselors, hoping that eventually they can establish a stable plan for students in similar situations—not only in math, but also in other core areas even earlier than eighth grade. Rachel can continue to build relationships with school board members, high school teachers, and community college faculty and to provide them with updates on how the plan is evolving. She can also work with Samantha to generate more social and emotional supports for parents and teachers.

Follow-Up and Evaluation

For school counselors engaging in advocacy and leadership, implementation of a plan is not the end of the process. Samantha and Rachel need to continue to check in with the students and parents to address any concerns with the plan, work with school counselor and teacher colleagues in the district to handle similar and future concerns, and be willing to present their advocacy and leadership experiences to others in the field. Samantha and Rachel should assess their plan so they can identify any unforeseen consequences as it unfolds and evaluate the overall degree of success once the plan has been completed. Evaluation of an advocacy plan can include follow-up conversations with the key stakeholders to adjust the plan during the school year as well as at the end of year, after determining strengths and weaknesses. In addition, Samantha can monitor the students' progress in accelerated math class by obtaining data about homework completion, test scores, and end-of-period grades so that interventions can address concerns.

In addition, Samantha and Rachel may wish to extend their leadership and advocacy to larger arenas, including state and national leadership. After a year they may wish to consider presenting their experiences at the state school counseling and state talented and gifted conferences. These presentations may lead to projects involving both ASCA and the National Association for Gifted Children (NAGC). School counselors and gifted-education teachers might benefit from learning how Samantha and Rachel collaborated as advocates, specially how they fielded questions from stakeholders and school board members. Effective advocates are prepared to address questions and navigate areas of resistance or systemic barriers.

KEY CONCEPT

Preparing for Leadership and Advocacy on Behalf of Gifted Students

When school counselors engage in advocacy and leadership related to gifted and high-ability students, they typically encounter questions, concerns, doubts, and myths about exceptional ability. This section addresses common stakeholder questions and concerns and expands on responses provided by NAGC (n.d.) to common misperceptions about gifted-education programming and academic provisions for gifted students.

Do gifted students really need a differentiated curriculum? As was noted in Chapter 1, many educators have doubtful reactions when approached about accommodating academically gifted students. Teachers may believe that accelerating a student or creating faster-paced courses places gifted students unfairly at the "top" of a hierarchy. In this mind-set, the concept of equality means sameness (e.g., all students), with equity or the provision of educational interventions such as acceleration in proportion with the student need. Those who do acknowledge giftedness may claim that acceleration is unnecessary, because teachers can create sufficient accommodations.

Recently, this issue has been evident in the continued expansion of the "excellence gap," a growing discrepancy between gifted students' abilities and their achievement scores. Although the current educational focus is on ensuring that every student meets a minimum academic standard, recent data suggest that this goal may be detrimental to students at higher ability levels, particularly in certain subgroups (Plucker, Burroughs, & Song, 2010). A lack of academic challenge results in a general trend toward mediocre achievement, even by those who are capable of producing at high levels. If confronted with this type of response, school counselors can produce research findings that explain why gifted students need alternative acceleration options (see Assouline, Colangelo, & VanTassel-Baska, 2015).

School counselors can also make comparisons with a population that is more familiar to educators who resist services for academically gifted students: athletes. Consider this example: A coach sees a ninth-grade basketball player who shows superior skills and abilities on the court

(continued)

when compared to her peers. The player has the ability to play at the varsity level immediately. The coach decides the player should be advanced to the varsity team even though she is in ninth grade and should be on the ninth grade or junior varsity team. This type of acceleration is not uncommon in our schools. Why is acceleration of a gifted athlete acceptable and academic acceleration for students with exceptional intellectual abilities discouraged or not allowed? Such a scenario allows people to see that educators do already treat some giftedness in a different way; even so, academic accommodations are often met with resistance. This comparison may start a conversation about why an educator, administrator, or school system is resisting these accommodations.

Why should we reward students with additional activities if they are not finishing homework or getting high grades and are behaving poorly in class? This question assumes that gifted-education programming is a reward for achievement and good behavior, not an educational intervention to address academic needs. It also assumes that a "gifted student" looks and acts according to common stereotypes. Best practice in the identification of gifted students is that school districts have multiple measures for decision-making, including standardized test scores, portfolios, teacher and parent checklists, and peer and self-nominations (see Chapter 6). When districts begin the identification process with a referral from teachers or parents, those nominations tend to "favor high-achieving, compliant students" who fit the mold of the ideal student (Robinson, Shore, & Enersen, 2007, p. 238). For this reason universal screening of students using multiple measures is preferred instead of, or in addition to, the nomination process (see Chapter 6). In addition, providing professional development to educators regarding the varied characteristics and traits associated with giftedness across all backgrounds has resulted in increased referrals for nonconforming gifted students (Robinson et al., 2007).

There may be times when educators or administrators are resistant to identifying or offering gifted programming to students who are lax with homework or whose behavior challenges teachers in the classroom. These educators may have equated "gifted" with

(continued)

"perfect," or they may believe that gifted students should not be "rewarded" with special programming if they fail to meet certain expectations. School counselors' advocacy and collaboration efforts are extremely important in addressing this resistance, as they will need to raise teachers' and administrators' awareness about expectations and assumptions about giftedness. According to ASCA (2013), school counselors should consider it their responsibility to advocate for equitable identification procedures and gifted-education programming. The Every Student Succeeds Act (ESSA) includes provisions that Title I funding can be used for identification and programming for gifted students. Additionally, any Title II Professional Development funds can be used to train teachers in identification or programming of gifted students (NAGC, 2015). Therefore, school counselors should look into leadership or advocacy opportunities provided by this legislation and take advantage of them.

Why should I work this hard for the gifted kids when I have so many other kids in crisis? Aren't they smart enough to just figure it out on their own? This question assumes that students' giftedness acts as a buffer or even a bulletproof vest to protect them from, or help them during, problems and crises. While a gifted student may appear to have success and good mental health, gifted students tend not to seek help even if they are in crisis or have serious academic or personal concerns. Their reluctance may be due to a societal perception that they should be able to handle their issues on their own (Peterson, 2015). However, due to characteristics associated with giftedness, these students may actually experience academic, personal, and social concerns with unusual intensity. Peterson, in Chapter 3, discusses several pertinent concerns such as existential depression, anxiety, perfectionism, and underachievement. Many gifted students encounter bullying at some point during the school years and often lack supportive environments in which they can display their gifts safely. The climate of a school may send an implicit message: "Excel, but don't set yourself apart too much." That message reflects the tug-of-war between equity and excellence that schools and educators often experience.

● ● ●

CONCLUDING THOUGHTS AND RECOMMENDATIONS

This chapter followed Samantha and Rachel as they investigated the needs of gifted students in their school and created an advocacy plan to address those needs. At each step the counselor and the gifted-education teacher practiced, refined, or even developed new leadership dispositions such as risk-taking and self-reflection. Together they examined the school climate and the cultural norms and beliefs around gifted education, and then identified and collaborated with potential allies to enact their plan. Last, Rachel and Samantha laid the groundwork for future advocacy efforts by evaluating the degree of the plan's success and suggesting recommendations for future collaborative efforts.

School counselors may see their own leadership and advocacy strengths reflected in Samantha or Rachel. Part of the school counselor's role is raising uncomfortable questions as part of an effort to acknowledge, explore, and redress barriers to students' educational progress. Advocacy for and leadership around educational access for gifted students is similar in nature, although the barriers may be different depending on the school and the counselor. This chapter provided suggestions for effective strategies for leadership and advocacy, and it closed with a series of questions and responses to help school counselors prepare to address stakeholders' questions when enacting advocacy plans.

● ● ●

REFERENCES

American School Counseling Association. (2012). *The ASCA National Model: A framework for school counseling program* (3rd ed.). Alexandria, VA: Author.

American School Counselor Association. (2013). *The school counselor and gifted and talented programs*. Alexandria, VA: Author.

American School Counselor Association. (2016). *Ethical standards for school counselors*. Alexandria, VA: Author.

Assouline, S. G., Colangelo, N., & VanTassel-Baska, J. (2015). *A nation empowered: Evidence trumps the excuses holding back America's brightest students* (Vol. 1). Iowa City, IA: Belin-Blank Center.

Bolman, L. G., & Deal, T. E. (2008). *Reframing organizations: Artistry, choice, and leadership* (4th ed.). San Francisco, CA: Jossey-Bass.

Byrd, R., & Hays, D. G. (2012). School counselor competency and lesbian, gay, bisexual, transgender, and questioning (LGBTQ) youth. *Journal of School Counseling, 10*(3). Retrieved from http://jsc.montana.edu/articles/v10n3.pdf

Dahir, C. A., & Stone, C. B. (2012). School counselors as advocates. In C. A. Dahir & C. B. Stone (Eds.), *The transformed school counselor* (pp. 123–146). Belmont, CA: Brooks/Cole.

Dollarhide, C., Gibson, D., & Saginak, K. (2008). New counselors' leadership efforts in school counseling: Themes from a year-long qualitative study. *Professional School Counseling, 11*(4), 262–271. doi:10.5330/PSC.n.2010-11.262

Grantham, T. C., Frasier, M. M., Roberts, A. C., & Bridges, E. M. (2005). Parent advocacy for culturally diverse gifted students. *Theory Into Practice, 44*(2), 138–147. doi:10.1207/s15430421tip4402_8

Griffin, D., & Farris, A. (2010). School counselors and collaboration: Finding resources through community asset mapping. *Professional School Counseling, 13*(5), 248–256.

Kiselica, M. S., & Robinson, M. (2001). Bringing advocacy counseling to life: The history, issues, and human dramas of social justice work in counseling. *Journal of Counseling and Development, 79*(4), 387–397. doi:10.1002/j.1556-6676.2001.tb01985.x

Kouzes, J., & Posner, B. (2003). *Credibility: How leaders gain and lose it, why people demand it.* San Francisco, CA: Jossey-Bass.

Lee, C. C. (1998). Counselors as agents of social change. In C. C. Lee & G. R. Walz (Eds.), *Social action: A mandate for counselors* (pp. 3–14). Alexandria, VA: American Counseling Association & Educational Resources Information Center Counseling and Student Services Clearinghouse.

Lewis, J. A., Arnold, M. S., House, R., & Toporek, R. L. (2002). ACA advocacy competencies. Retrieved from https://www.counseling.org/Resources/Competencies/Advocacy_Competencies.pdf

Mason, E. C., & McMahon, H. G. (2009). Leadership practices of school counselors. *Professional School Counseling, 13*, 107–115. doi:10.5330/PSC.n.2010-13.107

McMahan, E. H., Singh, A. A., Urbano, A., & Haston, M. (2010). The personal is political: School counselors' use of self in social justice advocacy work. *Journal of School Counseling, 8*(18), 1–29. Retrieved from http://jsc.montana.edu/articles/v8n18.pdf

National Association of Gifted Children. (n.d.). Myths about gifted children. Retrieved from http://www.nagc.org/resources-publications/resources/myths-about-gifted-students

National Association of Gifted Children. (2015). Questions and answers about the Every Student Succeeds Act. Retrieved from http://www.nagc.org/sites/default/files/Advocacy/ESSA%20Q%20%2B%20A.pdf

Peterson, J. S. (2015). School counselors and gifted kids: Respecting both cognitive and affective. *Journal of Counseling & Development, 93*, 153–162. doi:10.1002/j.1556-6676.2015.00191.x

Plucker, J. A., Burroughs, N., & Song, R. (2010). *Mind the (other) gap!: The growing excellence gap in K–12 education.* Bloomington, IN: Center for Evaluation and Education Policy.

Ratts, M. J., DeKruyf, L., & Chen-Hayes, S. F. (2007). The ACA advocacy competencies: A social justice advocacy framework for school counselors. *Professional School Counseling, 11*(2), 90–97. doi:10.5330/PSC.n.2010-11.90

Ratts, M. J., & Hutchins, A. M. (2009). ACA advocacy competencies: Social justice advocacy at the client/student level. *Journal of Counseling & Development, 87*(3), 269–275. doi:10.1002/j.1556-6678.2009.tb00106.x

Robinson, A., Shore, B. M., & Enersen, D. L. (2007). *Best practices in gifted education: An evidence-based guide.* Waco, TX: Prufrock Press.

Shillingford, M., & Lambie, G. (2010). Contribution of professional school counselors' values and leadership practices to their programmatic service delivery. *Professional School Counseling, 13*(4), 208–217. doi:10.5330/PSC.n.2010-13.208

Singh, A. A., Urbano, A., Haston, M., & McMahan, E. (2010). School counselors' strategies for social justice change: A grounded theory of what works in the real world. *Professional School Counseling, 13*(3), 135–145. doi:10.5330/PSC.n.2010-13.135

Toporek, R. L., Lewis, J. A., & Crethar, H. C. (2009). Promoting systemic change through the ACA advocacy competencies. *Journal of Counseling & Development, 87*(3), 260–268. doi:10.1002/j.1556-6678.2009.tb00105.x

Trusty, J., & Brown, D. (2005). Advocacy competencies for school counselors. *Professional School Counseling, 8*(3), 59–265. doi:10.5330/PSC.n.2010-11.90

Young, A., & Bryan, J. (2015). The school counselor leadership survey: Instrument development and exploratory factor analysis. *Professional School Counseling, 19*(1), 1–15. doi:10.5330/1096-2409-19.1.1

Young, A., Dollarhide, C. T., & Baughman, A. (2015). The voices of school counselors: Essential characteristics of school counselor leaders. *Professional School Counseling, 19*(1), 36–45. doi:10.5330/1096-2409-19.1.36

13

Concluding Thoughts

JEAN SUNDE PETERSON

Giftedness is both asset and burden, both protection and vulnerability. It affects all areas of life, not just academic and talent performance. Giftedness makes a difference—and differentness. School counselors respond every day to students who feel different, perhaps painfully different, from those around them—at home, at school, or in the community. Those counselors are distinguished in the school context by rare skills and perspectives that can be used to help gifted students make sense of themselves, value their differentness, and embrace their complex feelings and sometimes perplexing behaviors. School counselors, affirming gifted students as among the *all* students in their care, can help them navigate their complex internal and external worlds in the present. By responding to them with respect, nonjudgment, and genuine interest in the overlay of giftedness on who they are and on all they do, they can help these students prepare for future relationships, development, and experiences and find satisfaction and well-being. By being alert, in routine interactions, to high ability that is hidden, not validated, or viewed by gatekeepers as "not deserving," school counselors can advocate for opportunities for "missed" gifted students to interact with intellectual and talent peers in stimulating program options.

The chapters in this volume have covered a wide range of theories, concerns, and perspectives. Chapter content has implications for policy and practice. School professionals can incorporate the information and recommendations in them into their current services to ensure that gifted students receive needed support. Brief summaries of the chapters follow here.

- In **Chapter 1**, "Counseling Gifted and Talented Students," gifted students are described as a diverse group, misunderstood or ignored because of pervasive myths about giftedness. Characteristics, differing in degree from those of nongifted age-peers, set them apart. However, regardless of their impressive strengths, these students need support and can benefit from differentiated approaches to academic, career/college, and personal–social counseling. School counselors are ethically mandated to serve all students, and gifted students are among those, of course.
- **Chapter 2**, "Aligning Service to Gifted Students With the ASCA National Model," highlights an American School Counselor Association (ASCA) position statement that offers guidance for interacting with gifted-education programs and gifted students. Using the statement in tandem with the ASCA National Model, school counselors can address unique academic, career, and personal–social needs. They can reconceptualize their work in each of the model's quadrants (Foundation, Accountability, Delivery, and Management) and determine how they can be leaders, advocates, and change agents for this population.
- **Chapter 3**, "Characteristics and Concerns of Gifted Students," offers some detail about various phenomena and concerns related to giftedness in the literature: heightened sensitivity, intensity, asynchronous development, anxiety, perfectionism, introversion, existential depression, denied emotions, academic underachievement, career indecision, a desire to learn, the asset–burden paradox of giftedness, multipotentiality, a strong sense of justice and fairness, and the potential for misdiagnosis. Any of these aspects might be components of presenting issues in counseling.
- In **Chapter 4**, "Diverse Gifted Students: Intersectionality of Cultures," the emphasis is on gifted students as a diverse population. By recognizing that each component of identity contributes uniquely, school counselors can better understand the intersectionality of affiliations (e.g., twice-exceptional, African American, rural). In their multiple roles, they can facilitate services, locate resources, support parents, and help students make meaning of their multiple identities. Through partnerships and supported by professional development focused on embracing cultural diversity, school counselors can advocate for gifted students from marginalized populations.

- **Chapter 5**, "Theories That Support Programs and Services in Schools," attends to both achievement-based theories (i.e., with performance and progress measured) and development-oriented theories (i.e., focused on social and emotional growth). Theories developed by Gagne, Renzulli, and Moon represent the former, and theories developed by Dabrowski, Silverman, Colangelo, and Betts the latter. Unrecognized and unacknowledged cultural values can influence identification of gifted students. Knowledgeable school counselors can advocate on behalf of underachievers and other often-missed students.
- **Chapter 6**, "Identifying Gifted and Talented Learners in Schools: Common Practices and Best Practices," argues that school counselors have advantages as talent scouts. When working with students, they can be alert to abilities, interests, and dual exceptionality. But they may not be aware of best practices related to equitable talent identification. Thus, school counselors need to stay current on assessments and strategies. As they routinely monitor school climate, they can identify mismatches among students' gifts, gifted-education programming, and cultural values. As collaborators and resource coordinators, they can advocate for appropriate programming.
- **Chapter 7**, "Working With Classrooms and Small Groups," offers detailed guidance about how teachers and school counselors can collaborate to create classroom affective curriculum. Examples of components in core academic areas are provided, as well as suggestions for helping teachers develop listening skills and an ethical sense about privacy. A discussion of logistics, rationale, and topics for nonacademic, noncompetitive small-group discussions for gifted students follows. Facilitating groups can help school counselors learn about needs and concerns in this population.
- **Chapter 8**, "Academic Advising and Career Planning for Gifted and Talented Students," presents a theory-informed framework for optimizing learning, experience, insight, and investment related to gifted students' career development. Barriers such as stereotype threat, life events, unique concerns, mismatched personal strengths and programming, and limited resources can affect self-confidence and opportunities. Suggested interventions are aligned with developmental processes here. Too often and inappropriately, gifted youth are expected to find direction intuitively.

- In **Chapter 9**, "Personal/Social Counseling and Mental Health Concerns," a composite profile of a gifted adolescent with concerns reflecting change, loss, and characteristics associated with giftedness draws attention to serious concerns that do not fit common positive stereotypes of gifted students. Discussed are common mistaken assumptions about high and low academic achievers and positive and negative biases about gifted students that can affect the counseling relationship. Concluding the chapter are reminders about the importance of respectful interest in how giftedness is experienced.

- In **Chapter 10**, "Collaboration, Consultation, and Systemic Change: Creating a Supportive School Climate for Gifted Students," the emphasis is on relationships, which, with norms, beliefs, and visions, are aspects of school culture. As collaborators, consultants, and change agents, school counselors can identify school-climate concerns, such as bullying, that negatively affect the career development and academic, personal, and social functioning of gifted students. School counselors can help teachers and administrators understand, appreciate, and support gifted students.

- **Chapter 11**, "Empowering Parents of Gifted Students," acknowledges that parenting a gifted child can be challenging. Parents must deal with the often confusing identification process and programming options, possibly unreceptive school personnel, the weight of the *gifted* label, and their own complex emotions. School counselors can support parents in interactions with the school, provide information, facilitate connections with other parents of gifted students, and collaborate with resources. Most important, school counselors can listen. Parents often need a safe space to talk about their concerns.

- In **Chapter 12**, "School Counselors as Leaders and Advocates for Gifted Students," leadership and advocacy are described as having overlapping and complementary skill sets. Gifted students may not typically be viewed as warranting advocacy, but they are a population that can benefit from school counselor leadership and advocacy. School counselors understand school culture and should be able to identify potential allies, foster relationships, and create action plans. They need to act with compassion, empathy, and tenacity; be aware of potential barriers; and be able to explain the need for specialized services.

Broad themes emerged in the chapters, collectively. Foremost is that school counselors can attend to concerns of gifted youth as part of their conscientious support of *all* students in their care. They are also in an advantageous position to help teachers understand gifted students, behave ethically, and gain listening and group discussion skills.

Second is the importance of knowledge and awareness of this special population, including understanding that characteristics associated with giftedness may intensify responses to life events and circumstances and exacerbate difficulties related to developmental transitions. Also important are knowledge and awareness of potential barriers to well-being, the effect of stereotypes on whether needs are recognized and acknowledged, the need for an appropriate match between a student's strengths and available programming, and challenges related to parenting gifted children. In addition, self-awareness about potential biases related to giftedness may help to nurture and avoid rupturing the therapeutic relationship.

Third is that school counselors can offer gifted children and teens compassion, nonjudgment, and respectful curiosity about how giftedness is experienced. A one-down, nonexpert posture is especially important for inviting these students to teach counselors about their internal world, which may hide doubt, deep distress, and even violent thoughts.

Fourth is the importance of psychoeducational information in helping gifted youth make sense of feelings and behaviors. Important information about development, stress, mental health concerns, substance use and abuse, and even giftedness, for example, usually appeals to the cognitive strengths of gifted individuals and groups and can help them make sense of themselves and others.

Last is the empirically supported assertion that predicting the future lives of gifted high achievers and underachievers based on one stage of life is unwise. Change can happen in either direction because of life events or circumstances. Moving beyond impasse and accomplishing developmental tasks can contribute to increased motivation for underachievers, for example. School counselors who meet gifted students where they are stay open to possibilities.

Appendix

RESOURCES BY TOPIC AND TYPE

CHAPTER 1 COUNSELING GIFTED AND TALENTED STUDENTS

Articles

Levy, J. L., & Plucker, J. A. (2008). A multicultural competence model for counseling gifted and talented children. *Journal of School Counseling, 6*(4). Retrieved from http://jsc.montana.edu/articles/v6n4.pdf

Moon, S. M. (2009). Myth 15: High-ability students don't face problems and challenges. *Gifted Child Quarterly, 53,* 274–276. doi:10.1177/0016986209346943

Olszewski-Kubilius, P., Subotnik, R. F., & Worrell, F. C. (2015). Conceptualizations of giftedness and the development of talent: Implications for counselors. *Journal of Counseling & Development, 93,* 143–152.

Peterson, J. S. (2009). Myth 17: Gifted and talented individuals do not have unique social and emotional needs. *Gifted Child Quarterly, 53,* 280–282. doi:10.1177/0016986209346946

Peterson, J. S. (2015). School counselors and gifted kids: Respecting both cognitive and affective. *Journal of Counseling & Development, 93,* 153–162. doi:10.1002/j.1556-6676.2015.00191.x

Peterson, J. S., & Wachter Morris, C. (2010). Preparing school counselors to address concerns related to giftedness: A study of accredited counselor preparation programs. *Journal for the Education of the Gifted, 33,* 311–366.

Books

Cross, T. L., & Cross, J. R. (2012). *Handbook for counselors serving students with gifts and talents: Development, relationships, school issues, and counseling needs/interventions.* Waco, TX: Prufrock Press.

Mendaglio, S., & Peterson, J. S. (Eds.). (2007). *Models of counseling: Gifted children, adolescents, and young adults* (pp. 1–6). Waco, TX: Prufrock Press.

Neihart, M., Pfieffer, S., & Cross, T. L. (Eds.). (2016). *The social and emotional development of gifted children: What do we know?* (2nd ed.) Waco, TX: Prufrock Press.

Websites

American School Counselor Association. (2013). The school counselor and gifted and talented programs. Retrieved from https://www.schoolcounselor.org/asca/media/asca/PositionStatements/PS_Gifted.pdf

National Association for Gifted Children. (n.d.). Myths about gifted students. Retrieved from http://www.nagc.org/myths-about-gifted-students

National Association for Gifted Children. (n.d.). Social and emotional issues. Retrieved from   https://www.nagc.org/resources-publications/resources-parents/social-emotional-issues

National Association for Gifted Children. (2009). Position paper: Nurturing social and emotional development of gifted children. Retrieved from https://www.nagc.org/sites/default/files/Position%20Statement/Affective%20Needs%20Position%20Statement.pdf

National Association for Gifted Children. (2014). Position paper: Collaboration among all educators to meet the needs of gifted learners. Retrieved from https://www.nagc.org/sites/default/files/Position%20Statement/Collaboration%20Among%20Educators.pdf

Supporting Emotional Needs of Gifted. Mental health professionals. Retrieved from http://sengifted.org/resources/recognized-professionals

Thomas B. Fordham Institute. (2008). Executive summary. Retrieved from http://www.nagc.org/sites/default/files/key%20reports/High_Achieving_Students_in_the_Era_of_NCLB_Fordham.pdf

Thompson, M. C. (1998, April). All children are gifted. Keynote speech presented at the annual conference of the Indiana Association for the Gifted, Indianapolis, IN. Retrieved from http://giftedkids.about.com/od/gifted101/a/gifted_response.htm

• • •

CHAPTER 2 ALIGNING SERVICE TO GIFTED STUDENTS WITH THE ASCA NATIONAL MODEL

Articles

Peterson, J. S. (2003). An argument for proactive attention to affective concerns of gifted adolescents. *Journal of Secondary Gifted Education*, *14*(2), 62–70.

Peterson, J. S., & Wachter Morris, C. (2010). Preparing school counselors to address concerns related to giftedness: A study of accredited counselor preparation programs. *Journal for the Education of the Gifted*, *33*, 311–366.

Wood, S. (2009). Counseling concerns of gifted and talented adolescents: Implications for school counselors. *Journal of School Counseling*, *7*(1). Retrieved from http://www.nagc.org/myths-about-gifted-students

Wood, S. (2010). Best practices in counseling the gifted in schools: What's really happening? *Gifted Child Quarterly*, *54*, 42–58.

Wood, S. M. (2010). Nurturing a garden: A qualitative investigation into school counselors' experiences with gifted students. *Journal for the Education of the Gifted, 34*(2), 261–302.

Wood, S. M. (2012). Rivers' confluence: A qualitative investigation into gifted educators' experiences with collaboration with school counselors. *Roeper Review, 34*(4), 261–274.

Books

Cross, T. L., & Cross, J. R. (2012). *Handbook for counselors serving students with gifts and talents: Development, relationships, school issues, and counseling needs/interventions.* Waco, TX: Prufrock Press.

Neihart, M., Pfieffer, S., & Cross, T. L. (Eds.). (2016). *The social and emotional development of gifted children: What do we know?* (2nd ed.). Waco, TX: Prufrock Press.

Silverman, L. K. (Eds.) (1993). *Counseling the gifted and talented.* Denver, CO: Love.

VanTassel-Baska, J., Cross, T. L., & Olenchak, R. (Eds.). (2009). *Social–emotional curriculum with gifted and talented students.* Waco, TX: Prufrock Press.

Websites

American School Counselor Association. (n.d.). Executive summary. Retrieved from https://www.schoolcounselor.org/asca/media/asca/ASCA%20National%20Model%20Templates/ANMExecSumm.pdf

American School Counselor Association. (2013). The school counselor and gifted and talented programs. Retrieved from https://www.schoolcounselor.org/asca/media/asca/PositionStatements/PS_Gifted.pdf

National Association for Gifted Children. (2009). Position paper: Nurturing social and emotional development of gifted children. Retrieved from https://www.nagc.org/sites/default/files/Position%20Statement/Affective%20Needs%20Position%20Statement.pdf

• • •

CHAPTER 3 CHARACTERISTICS AND CONCERNS OF GIFTED STUDENTS

Articles

Greenspon, T. S. (2000). "Healthy perfectionism" is an oxymoron! Reflections on the psychology of perfectionism and the sociology of science. *Journal of Secondary Gifted Education, 11*, 197–208.

Jackson, P. S., & Peterson, J. S. (2003). Depressive disorder in highly gifted adolescents. *Journal for Secondary Gifted Education, 14*(3), 175–186.

Mendaglio, S. (2003). Heightened multifaceted sensitivity of gifted students: Implications for counseling. *Journal of Secondary Gifted Education, 14*(2), 72–82.

Neville, C. S., Piechowski, M. M., & Tolan, S. S. (2014). *Off the charts: Asynchrony and the gifted child.* Unionville, NY: Royal Fireworks Press.

Peterson, J. S. (2012). The asset–burden paradox of giftedness: A 15-year phenomenological, longitudinal case study. *Roeper Review, 34,* 1–17. doi:10.1080/02783193. 2-12.715336.

Peterson, J. S., & Colangelo, N. (1996). Gifted achievers and underachievers: A comparison of patterns found in school files. *Journal of Counseling & Development, 74,* 399–407. doi:10.1002/j.1556-6676.1996.tb01886.x

Piechowski, M. M. (2014). *"Mellow out," they say. If I only could.* Unionville, NY: Royal Fireworks Press.

Speirs Neumeister, K. L. (2007). Perfectionism in gifted students: An overview of current research. *Gifted Education International, 23,* 254–263.

Webb, J. T., Amend, E. R., Beljan, P., Webb, N. E., Kuzukanakis, M., Olenchak, F. R., & Goerss, J. (2016). *Misdiagnosis and dual diagnoses of gifted children and adults* (2nd ed.). Tuscon, AZ: Great Potential Press.

Book Chapters

Mendaglio, S. (2007). Affective-cognitive therapy for counseling gifted individuals. In S. Mendaglio & J. S. Peterson (Eds.), *Models of counseling gifted children, adolescents, and young adults* (pp. 35–68). Waco, TX: Prufrock Press.

Olszewski-Kubilius, P. (2010). Gifted adolescents. In F. A. Karnes & K. R. Stephens (Eds.), *The practical strategies series in gifted education.* Waco, TX: Prufrock Press.

Piechowski, M. M. (1999). Overexcitabilities. In M. A. Runco & S. R. Pritzker (Eds.), *Encyclopedia of creativity* (Vol. 2, pp. 325–334). San Diego, CA: Academic Press.

Probst, B., & Piechowski, M. (2012). Overexcitabilities and temperament. In T. L. Cross & J. R. Cross (Eds.), *Handbook for counselors serving students with gifts and talents* (pp. 53–73). Waco, TX: Prufrock Press.

Silverman, L. K. (2013). Asynchronous development: Theoretical bases and current applications. In C. S. Neville, M. M. Piechowski, & S. S. Tolan (Eds.), *Off the charts: Asynchrony and the gifted child* (pp. 18–47). Unionville, NY: Royal Fireworks Press.

Speirs Neumeister, K. L. (2009). Perfectionism. In B. Kerr (Ed.). *Encyclopedia of giftedness, creativity, and talent* (Vol. 2, 675–677). Thousand Oaks, CA: Sage.

Books

Daniels, S., & Piechowski, M. (Eds.). (2008). *Living with intensity: Understanding the sensitivity, excitability, and the emotional development of gifted children, adolescents, and adults.* Scottsdale, AZ: Great Potential Press.

Galbraith, J., & Delisle, J. (2015). *When gifted kids don't have all the answers: How to meet their social and emotional needs.* Minneapolis, MN: Free Spirit.

Greenspon, T. (2007). *What to do when good enough isn't good enough: The real deal on perfectionism*. Minneapolis, MN: Free Spirit.

Hollingworth, L. S. (1926). *Gifted children: Their nature and nurture*. New York, NY: Macmillan.

VanTassel-Baska, J., Cross, T. L., & Olenchak, R. (Eds.). (2009). *Social–emotional curriculum with gifted and talented students*. Waco, TX: Prufrock Press.

Webb, J. R. (2013). *Searching for meaning: Idealism, bright minds, disillusionment, and hope*. Tucson, AZ: Great Potential Press.

Webb, J. T., Amend, E. R., Beljan, P., Webb, N. E., Kuzukanakis, M., Olenchak, F. R., & Goerss, J. (2016). *Misdiagnosis and dual diagnoses of gifted children and adults* (2nd ed.). Tuscon, AZ: Great Potential Press.

Websites

Supporting the Emotional Needs of Gifted. Retrieved from http://sengifted.org/resources

● ● ●

CHAPTER 4 DIVERSE GIFTED STUDENTS: INTERSECTIONALITY OF CULTURES

Articles

Connor, D. (2006). Michael's story: "I get into so much trouble just by walking": Narrative knowing and life at the intersections of learning disability, race, and class. *Equity & Excellence in Education, 39*, 154–165.

Foley-Nicpon, M., & Assouline, S. G. (2015). Counseling considerations for the twice-exceptional client. *Journal of Counseling & Development, 93*(2), 202–211. doi:10.1002/j.1556-6676.2015.00196.x

Ford, D. Y., & Moore, J. L., III. (2013). Understanding and reversing underachievement, low achievement, and achievement gaps among high-ability African American males in urban school contexts. *Urban Review, 45*(4), 399–415.

Ford, D. Y., Trotman Scott, M., Moore, J. L., III, & Amos, S. O. (2013). Gifted education and culturally different students: Examining prejudice and discrimination via microaggressions. *Gifted Child Today, 36*, 205–208.

Gentry, M., & Fugate, C. M. (2012). Gifted native American students: Underperforming, under identified and overlooked. *Psychology in the Schools, 49*(7), 631–646. doi:10.1002/pits.21624

Gentry, M., Fugate, C. M., Wu, J., & Castellano, J. A. (2013). Gifted native American students: Literature, lessons, and future directions. *Gifted Child Quarterly, 58*(2), 98–110.

Gillborn, D. (2015). Intersectionality, critical race theory, and the primacy of racism: Race, class, gender, and disability in education. *Qualitative Inquiry, 21*, 277–287.

Harris, P. C., Mayes, R. D., Vega, D., & Hines, E. M. (2016). Reaching higher: College and career readiness for African American males with learning disabilities. *Journal of African American Males in Education, 7*(1) 52–69.

Kao, C., & Hébert, T. P. (2006). Gifted Asian American adolescent males: Portraits of cultural dilemmas. *Journal for the Education of the Gifted, 30*(1), 88–117.

Lovett, B. J., & Sparks, R. L. (2011). The identification and performance of gifted students with learning disability diagnoses: A quantitative synthesis. *Journal of Learning Disabilities, 46*, 304–316.

Mayes, R. D., & Moore, J. L., III. (2016). Adversity and pitfalls of twice exceptional urban learners. *Journal of Advanced Academics, 27*(3), 167–189.

Mayes, R. D., & Moore, J. L., III. (2016). The intersection of race, disability, and gifted-ness: Understanding the education needs of twice-exceptional, African American students. *Gifted Child Today, 39*(2), 98–104.

Owens, C. M., Ford, D. Y., Lisbon, A. J., & Owens, M. T. (2016). Shifting paradigms to better serve twice-exceptional African-American learners. *Behavioral Disorders, 41*(4), 196–208.

Robinson, S. A. (2016). Triple identity theory: A theoretical framework for under-standing gifted Black males with dyslexia. *Urban Education Research and Policy Annuals* (1), 147–158. Retrieved from https://journals.uncc.edu/urbaned/article/view/415/502

Stambaugh, T., & Ford, D. Y. (2015). Microaggressions, multiculturalism, and gifted individuals who are Black, Hispanic, or low income. *Journal of Counseling & Development, 93*, 192–201.

Toldson, I. A. (2011). How Black boys with disabilities end up in honors classes while others without disabilities end up in special education. *Journal of Negro Education, 80*, 439–443.

Wang, C. W., & Neihart, M. (2015). Academic self-concept and academic self-efficacy: Self-beliefs enable academic achievement of twice-exceptional students. *Roeper Review, 37*, 63–73.

Willard-Holt, C., Weber, J., Morrison, K. L., & Horgan, J. (2013). Twice-exceptional learners' perspectives on effective learning strategies. *Gifted Child Quarterly, 57*(4), 247–262. doi:10.1177/0016986213501076

Wood, E. L., & Davis, J. L. (2016). Family engagement and advocacy for culturally diverse 2E learners. *Wisconsin English Journal, 58*, 189–192.

Yoon, S. Y., & Gentry, M. (2009). Racial and ethnic representation in gifted programs: Current status of and implications for gifted Asian American students. *Gifted Child Quarterly, 53*(2), 121–136. doi:10.1177/0016986208330564

Book Chapters

Ford, D. (2015). Like finding a needle in a haystack: Gifted Black and Hispanic students in rural settings. In T. Stambaugh & S. Wood (Eds.), *Serving gifted students in rural settings: A framework for bridging gifted education in rural classrooms* (pp. 71–90). Waco, TX: Prufrock Press.

Mayes, R. D., Harris, P. C., & Hines, E. M. (2016). Meeting the academic and socio-emotional needs of twice exceptional African American students through group counseling. In J. L. Davis & J. L. Moore III (Eds.), *Gifted children of color around the world* (pp. 53–69). Charlotte, NC: Information Age Publishing.

Books

Baum, S., & Schader, R. (2017). *To be gifted and learning disabled: Strength-based strategies for helping twice-exceptional students with LD, ADHD, and other disorders* (3rd ed.). Waco, TX: Prufrock Press.

Castellano, J., & Frazier, A.D. (2010). *Special populations in gifted education: Understanding our most able students from diverse backgrounds.* Waco, TX: Prufrock Press.

Davis, J. L. (2010). *Bright, talented and black: A guide for families of African American gifted learners.* Scottsdale, AZ: Great Potential Press.

Ford, D. Y. (2013). *Recruiting and retaining culturally different students in gifted education.* Waco, TX: Prufrock Press.

Ford, D. Y., Davis, J. L., & Grantham, T. C. (2017). *Changing the narrative: Profiles of young, black gifted scholars.* Waco, TX: Prufrock Press.

Grantham, T. C., Ford, D. Y., Henfield, M. S., Scott, M. T., Harmon, D. A., Porcher, S., & Price, C. (Eds.). (2011). *Gifted and advanced black students in schools.* Waco, TX: Prufrock Press.

Lewis, J. (2009) The challenges of educating the gifted in rural areas. In F. A. Karnes & K. R. Stephens (Eds.), *The practical strategies series in gifted education.* Waco, TX: Prufrock Press.

Roberts, J. L., & Jolly, J. (2012). *A teacher's guide to working with children and families from diverse backgrounds.* Waco, TX: Prufrock Press.

Stambaugh, T., & Wood, S. (Eds.). (2015). *Serving gifted students in rural settings: A framework for bridging gifted education in rural classrooms.* Waco, TX: Prufrock Press.

Trail, B. A. (2011). *Twice-exceptional gifted children: Understanding, teaching, and counseling gifted students.* Waco, TX: Prufrock Press.

VanTassel-Baska, J. (2010). *Patterns and profiles of promising learners from poverty.* Waco, TX: Prufrock Press.

Websites

Assouline, S., Foley, M., Colangelo, N., & O'Brien, M. (2008). *The paradox of twice-exceptionality: Packet of information for professionals* (PIP-2; 2nd ed.). Iowa City: Connie Belin & Jacqueline N. Blank International Center for Gifted Education and Talent Development, College of Education, University of Iowa. Retrieved from://www2.education.uiowa.edu/belinblank/clinic/pdfs/pip2.pdf

Montgomery County Public Schools. (2014). Twice exceptional students: A staff guidebook for supporting the achievement of gifted students with disabilities. Retrieved from http://www.montgomeryschoolsmd.org/uploadedFiles/curriculum/enriched/ programs/gtld/0470.15_TwiceExceptionalStudents_Handbook_Web.pdf

National Association of Gifted Children. (2009). Twice-exceptionality [White paper]. Retrieved from https://www.nagc.org/sites/default/files/Position%20Statement/ twice%20exceptional.pdf

National Association for Gifted Children. (2011). Position statement: Identifying and serving culturally and linguistically diverse gifted students. Retrieved from https://www.nagc.org/sites/default/files/Position%20Statement/Identifying%20 and%20Serving%20Culturally%20and%20Linguistically.pdf

National Association for Gifted Children. (2013). Ensuring gifted children with disabilities receive appropriate services: Call for comprehensive assessment [Position statement]. Retrieved from https://www.nagc.org/sites/default/files/Position%20 Statement/Ensuring%20Gifted%20Children%20with%20Disabilities%20 Receive%20Appropriate%20Services.pdf

• • •

CHAPTER 5 THEORIES THAT SUPPORT PROGRAMS AND SERVICES IN SCHOOLS

Articles

Tieso, C. L. (2007). Patterns of overexcitabilities in identified gifted students and their parents: A hierarchical model. *Gifted Child Quarterly, 51*, 11–22.

Book Chapters

Cross, T. L., & Coleman, L. J. (2005). School-based conception of giftedness. In R. J. Sternberg & J. E. Davidson (Eds.), *Conceptions of giftedness* (2nd ed., pp. 52–63). Cambridge, UK: Cambridge University Press.

Mendaglio, S. (2008). Dabrowski's theory of positive disintegration: A personality theory for the 21st century. In S. Mendaglio (Ed.), *Dabrowski's theory of positive disintegration* (pp. 13–40). Scottsdale, AZ: Great Potential Press.

Books

Bets, G., & Kapushion, B. (2016). *Autonomous learner model resource book*. Waco, TX: Prufrock Press.

Dabrowski, K., & Piechowski, M. M. (1977). *Theory of levels of emotional development: Multilevelness and positive disintegration* (Vol. 1). Oceanside, NY: Dabor Science Publications.

Daniels, S., & Piechowski, M. M. (Eds.). (2009). *Living with intensity: Understanding the sensitivity, excitability, and emotional development of gifted children, adolescents, and adults*. Scottsdale, AZ: Great Potential Press.

Gentry, M., & Mann, R. L. (2009). *Total school cluster grouping and differentiation: A comprehensive, research-based plan for raising student achievement and improving teacher practices.* Waco, TX: Prufrock Press.

Mendaglio, S. (Ed.). (2008). *Dabrowski's theory of positive disintegration.* Scottsdale, AZ: Great Potential Press.

Neville, C. S., Piechowski, M. M., & Tolan, S. S. (Eds.). (2013). *Off the charts: Asynchrony and the gifted child* (pp. 9–17). Unionville, NY: Royal Fireworks Press.

Peters, S. J., Matthews, M. S., McBee, M. T., & McCoach, D. B. (2014). *Beyond gifted education: Designing and implementing advanced academic programs.* Waco, TX: Prufrock Press.

Peterson, J. S. (2008). *The essential guide or talking with gifted teens. Ready-to-use discussions about identity, stress, relationships, and more.* Minneapolis, MN: Free Spirit.

Silverman, L. K. (Ed.). (1993). *Counseling the gifted and talented.* Denver, CO: Love.

VanTassel-Baska, J., Cross, T. L., & Olenchak, R. (Eds.). (2009). *The critical issues in equity and excellence in gifted education: Social–emotional curriculum with gifted and talented students.* Waco, TX: Prufrock Press.

Webb, J. R. (2013). *Searching for meaning: Idealism, bright minds, disillusionment, and hope.* Tucson, AZ: Great Potential Press.

Webb, J. T., Amend, E. R., Beljan, P., Webb, N. E., Kuzukanakis, M., Olenchak, F. R., & Goerss, J. (2016). *Misdiagnosis and dual diagnoses of gifted children and adults* (2nd ed.). Tuscon, AZ: Great Potential Press.

Webb, J. T., Gore, J. L., Amend, E. R., & DeVries, A. R. (2007). *A parent's guide to gifted children.* Tucson, AZ: Great Potential Press.

• • •

CHAPTER 6 IDENTIFYING GIFT AND TALENTED LEARNERS IN SCHOOLS: COMMON PRACTICES AND BEST PRACTICES

Articles

Horn, C. V. (2015). Young scholars: A talent development model for finding and nurturing potential in underserved populations. *Gifted Child Today, 38,* 19–31.

Olszewski-Kubilius, P., & Thomson, D. (2010). Gifted programming for poor or minority urban students: Issues and lessons learned. *Gifted Child Today, 33*(4), 58–64.

Peterson, J. S. (1999). Gifted—through whose cultural lens? An application of the postpositivistic mode of inquiry. *Journal for the Education of the Gifted, 22,* 354–383.

Pfeiffer, S. I. (2002). Identifying gifted and talented students: Recurring issues and promising solutions. *Journal of Applied School Psychology, 1,* 31–50.

Subotnik, R., F., Olszewski-Kubilius, P., & Worrell, F. C. (2011). Rethinking giftedness and gifted education: A proposed direction forward based on psychological science. *Psychological Science in the Public Interest, 12*(1), 3–54

Books

Johnson, S. (2011) *Identifying gifted students: A practical guide* (2nd ed.). Waco, TX: Prufrock Press.

Olszewski-Kublius, P., & Clarenbach, J. (2012). *Unlocking emergent talent: Supporting high achievement of low-incoming, high-ability students.* Washington, DC: National Association for Gifted Children. Retrieved from http://www.jkcf.org/assets/1/7/Unlocking_Emergent_Talent.pdf

Silverman, L. (2013). *Giftedness 101.* New York, NY: Springer.

VanTassel-Baska, J. (2008). *Alternative assessments with gifted and talented students.* Waco, TX: Prufrock Press.

Webb, J. T., Amend, E. R., Beljan, P., Webb, N. E., Kuzukanakis, M., Olenchak, F. R., & Goerss, J. (2016). *Misdiagnosis and dual diagnoses of gifted children and adults* (2nd ed.). Tuscon, AZ: Great Potential Press.

Websites

Jack Kent Cooke Foundation. (n.d.). Young scholars program. Retrieved from http://www.jkcf.org/scholarship-programs/young-scholars

National Association for Gifted Children. (n.d.). Identification. Retrieved from https://www.nagc.org/resources-publications/gifted-education-practices/identification

National Association for Gifted Children. (n.d.). Identifying gifted children from diverse populations. Retrieved from https://www.nagc.org/resources-publications/resources/timely-topics/ensuring-diverse-learner-participation-gifted-0

National Association for Gifted Children. (2008). Position statement: The role of assessments in the identification of gifted students. Retrieved from https://www.nagc.org/sites/default/files/Position%20Statement/Assessment%20Position%20Statement.pdf

National Association for Gifted Children. (2011). Position statement: Identifying and serving culturally and linguistically diverse gifted students. Retrieved from http://www.nagc.org/sites/default/files/Position%20Statement/Identifying%20and%20Serving%20Culturally%20and%20Linguistically.pdf

Purdue University. (n.d.). Diversity initiatives for gifted students (DIGS). Retrieved from https://www.education.purdue.edu/geri/youth-programs/diversity-initiatives

Vanderbilt University's Programs for Talented Youth. Retrieved from https://pty.vanderbilt.edu

• • •

CHAPTER 7 WORKING WITH CLASSROOMS AND SMALL GROUPS

Articles

Hébert, T. P. (2000). Helping high ability students overcome math anxiety through bibliotherapy. *Journal of Secondary Gifted Education, 8,* 164–178.

Hébert, T. P., & Hammond, D. R. (2006). Guided viewing of film with gifted students: Resources for educators and counselors. *Gifted Child Today, 29*, 14–27.

Peterson, J. S. (2013). School counselors' experiences with children from low-income families and other gifted children in a summer program. *Professional School Counseling, 16*, 194–204.

Peterson, J. S., & Lorimer, M. R. (2011). Student response to a small-group affective curriculum in a school for gifted children. *Gifted Child Quarterly, 55*, 167–180.

Peterson, J. S., & Lorimer, M. R. (2012). Small-group affective curriculum for gifted students: A longitudinal study of teacher-facilitators. *Roeper Review, 34*, 158–169.

Book Chapters

Hébert, T. P., Long, L., & Speirs Neumeister, K. L. (2005). Using biography to counsel gifted young women. In S. Johnsen & J. Kendrick (Eds.), *Teaching and counseling gifted girls* (pp. 89–118). Waco, TX: Prufrock Press.

Peterson, J. S. (2012). Differentiating counseling approaches for gifted children and teens: Needs and strategies. In T. L. Cross & J. R. Cross (Eds.), *Handbook for counselors serving students with gifts and talents: Development, relationships, school issues, and counseling needs/interventions* (pp. 681–698). Waco, TX: Prufrock Press.

Peterson, J. S. (2012). The counseling relationship. In T. L. Cross & J. R. Cross (Eds.), *Handbook for counselors serving students with gifts and talents: Development, relationships, school issues, and counseling needs/interventions* (pp. 443–459). Waco, TX: Prufrock Press.

Peterson, J. S. (2016). Affective curriculum: Proactively addressing the challenges of growing up. In K. R. Stephens & F. A. Karnes (Eds.), *Best practices for curriculum design in gifted education* (pp. 307–330). Waco, TX: Prufrock Press.

Peterson, J. S., Betts, G., & Bradley, T. (2009). Discussion groups as a component of affective curriculum for gifted students. In J. VanTassel-Baska, T. L. Cross, & R. Olenchak (Eds.), *Social–emotional curriculum with gifted and talented students* (pp. 289–320). Waco, TX: National Association for Gifted Children/Prufrock Press.

Peterson, J. S., & Servaty-Seib, H. (2008). Focused, but flexible: A developmental approach to small-group work in schools. In H. L. K. Coleman & C. Yeh (Eds.), *Handbook of school counseling* (pp. 409–429). Mahwah, NJ: Lawrence Erlbaum.

Wood, S. M., & Lane, E. M. D. (2017). Using the integrated curriculum model to address social, emotional, and career needs of advanced learners. In J. VanTassel-Baska & C. W. Little (Eds.), *Content-based curriculum for high-ability learners* (3rd ed., pp. 523–542). Waco, TX: Prufrock Press.

Books

Karnes, F. A., Stephens, K. R., Ferguson, S. K., & Nugent, S. A. (Eds.). (2005). *Social and emotional teaching strategies.* Waco, TX: Prufrock Press.

Peterson, J. S. (2008). *The essential guide to talking with gifted teens: Ready-to-use discussions about identity, stress, relationships, and more.* Minneapolis, MN: Free Spirit.

VanTassel-Baska, J., Cross, T. L., & Olenchak, F. R. (Eds.). (2009). *Social–emotional curriculum with gifted and talented students*. Waco, TX: National Association for Gifted Children/Prufrock Press.

Websites

College of William & Mary, School of Education, Center for Gifted Education. Retrieved from http://education.wm.edu/centers/cfge/index.php

Renzulli, J. S., & Reis, S. M. (2016). The schoolwide enrichment model executive summary. Retrieved from http://www.gifted.uconn.edu/schoolwide -enrichment-model/semexec

• • •

CHAPTER 8 ACADEMIC ADVISING AND CAREER PLANNING FOR GIFTED AND TALENTED STUDENTS

Articles

Jung, J. Y. (2012). Giftedness as a developmental construct that leads to eminence as adults: Ideas and implications from an occupational/career decision-making perspective. *Gifted Child Quarterly, 56*, 189–193. doi:10.1177/0016986212456072

Kerr, B., & Kurpius, S. E. (2004). Encouraging talented girls in math and science: Effects of a guidance intervention. *High Ability Studies, 15*, 85–102. doi:10.1080/1359813042000225357

Muratori, M. C., & Smith, C. K. (2015). Guiding the talent and career development of the gifted individual. *Journal of Counseling & Development, 93*(2), 173–182. doi:10.1002/j.1556-6676.2015.00193.x

Watters, J. J. (2010). Career decision making among gifted students: The mediation of teachers. *Gifted Child Quarterly, 54*, 222–238. doi:10.1177/0016986210369255

Wood., S., Portman, T. A. A., Cigrand, D., & Colangelo, N. (2010). School counselors' perceptions and experience with acceleration as a program option for gifted and talented students. *Gifted Child Quarterly, 54*(3) 168–178. doi:10.1177/0016986210367940

Book Chapters

Hébert, T., & Kelly, K. (2006). Identity and career development in gifted students. In F. A. Dixon & S. M. Moon (Eds.), *Handbook of secondary gifted education* (pp. 35–63). Waco, TX: Prufrock Press.

Peterson, J. S. (2018). Counseling gifted children and teens. In S. I. Pfeiffer, E. Shaunessy-Dedrick, & M. Foley-Nicpon (Eds.), *APA handbook of giftedness and talent* (pp. 511–527). Washington, DC: American Psychological Association.

Sampson, J. P., & Chason, A. K. (2008). Helping gifted and talented adolescents and young adults make informed and careful career choices. In S. I. Pfeiffer (Ed.), *Handbook of giftedness in children: Psychoeducational theory, research, and best practices* (pp. 327–346). New York, NY: Springer-Verlag.

Books

Assouline, S. G., Colangelo, N., & VanTassel-Baska, J. (2015). *A nation empowered: Evidence trumps the excuses holding back America's brightest students* (Vol. 1). Iowa City, IA: Connie Belin & Jacqueline N. Blank International Center for Gifted Education and Talent Development.
Colangelo, N., Assouline, S., & Gross, M. (Eds.). (2004). *A nation deceived: How schools hold back America's brightest students* (Vol. 1). Iowa City, IA: Connie Belin & Jacqueline N. Blank International Center for Gifted Education and Talent Development.
Institute for Research and Policy on Acceleration, National Association for Gifted Children, & Council for the State Directors of Programs for the Gifted. (2009). *Guidelines for developing an academic acceleration policy.* Iowa City, IA: Institute for Research and Policy on Acceleration. Retrieved from http://www.nagc.org/sites/default/files/Advocacy/Acceleration%20Policy%20Guidelines.pdf

Websites

Acceleration Institute. Retrieved from http://accelerationinstitute.org
American School Counselor Association. (2014). *Mindsets & behaviors for student success: K-12 college- and career-readiness standards for every student.* Alexandria, VA: Author. Retrieved from https://schoolcounselor.org/asca/media/asca/home/MindsetsBehaviors.pdf
Bucksbaum Early Entrance Program. Retrieved from https://www2.education.uiowa.edu/belinblank/students/academy
Imagine. Big ideas for bright minds. Retrieved from http://cty.jhu.edu/imagine
The Iowa Acceleration Scale (3rd ed.). Retrieved from http://www2.education.uiowa.edu/belinblank
National Association for Gifted Children. Acceleration. Retrieved from https://www.nagc.org/resources-publications/gifted-education-practices/acceleration

● ● ●

CHAPTER 9 PERSONAL/SOCIAL COUNSELING AND MENTAL HEALTH CONCERNS

Articles

Peterson, J. S. (1997). Bright, troubled, and resilient, and not in a gifted program. *Journal of Secondary Gifted Education, 8,* 121–136.

Peterson, J. S. (2014). Giftedness, trauma, and development: A longitudinal case study. *Journal for the Education of the Gifted, 37*, 295–318.

Roberts, S. M., & Lovett, S. B. (1994). Examining the "F" in gifted: Academically gifted adolescents' psychological and affective responses to scholastic failure. *Journal for the Education of the Gifted, 17*, 241–259.

Wood, S. M., & Craigen, L. M. (2011). Self-injurious behavior in gifted and talented youth: What every educator should know. *Journal for the Education of the Gifted, 34*, 839–859.

Book Chapters

Mendaglio, S. (2007). Affective-cognitive therapy for counseling gifted individuals. In S. Mendaglio & J. S. Peterson (Eds.), *Models of counseling gifted children, adolescents, and young adults* (pp. 35–68). Waco, TX: Prufrock Press.

Peterson, J. S. (2011). The counseling relationship. In T. L. Cross & J. R. Cross (Eds.), *Handbook for counselors serving students with gifts and talents: Development, relationships, school issues, and counseling needs/interventions* (pp. 443–459). Waco, TX: Prufrock Press.

Books

Cross, T. L., & Cross, J. R. (2012). *Handbook for counselors serving students with gifts and talents: Development, relationships, school issues, and counseling needs/interventions.* Waco, TX: Prufrock Press.

Daniels, S., & Piechowski, M. M. (2009). *Living with intensity: Understanding the sensitivity, excitability and emotional development of gifted children, adolescents and adults.* Scottsdale, AZ: Great Potential Press.

Gross, M. U. M. (2004). *Exceptionally gifted children* (2nd ed.). London, UK: Routledge Falmer.

Mendaglio, S., & Peterson, J. S. (Eds.). (2007). *Models of counseling: Gifted children, adolescents, and young adults.* Waco, TX: Prufrock Press.

Neihart, M., Pfieffer S., & Corss, T.L. (Eds.). (2016). *The social and emotional development of gifted children: What do we know?* (2nd ed.). Waco, TX: Prufrock Press.

Neville, C. S., Piechowski, M. M., & Tolan, S. S. (Eds.). (2013). *Off the charts: Asynchrony and the gifted child* (pp. 9–17). Unionville, NY: Royal Fireworks Press.

Pfeiffer, S. I. (2013). *Serving the gifted: Evidence-based clinical and psychoeducational practice.* New York, NY: Routledge.

Websites

Amy Yermish's DaVinci Learning. Retrieved from http://www.davincilearning.org/index.html

Hoagie's Gifted Education Page. Retrieved from http://www.hoagiesgifted.org/counseling.htm

Supporting Emotional Needs of Gifted. Mental health professionals. Retrieved from http://sengifted.org/resources/recognized-professionals

• • •

CHAPTER 10 COLLABORATION, CONSULTATION, AND SYSTEMIC CHANGE: CREATING A SUPPORTIVE SCHOOL CLIMATE FOR GIFTED STUDENTS

Articles

Hernandez, T. J., & Seem, S. R. (2004). A safe school climate: A systemic approach and the school counselor. *Professional School Counseling, 7*(4), 256–262.

Lee, S-Y., Olszewski-Kubilius, P., & Thomson, D. T. (2012). Academically gifted students' perceived interpersonal competence and peer relationship. *Gifted Child Quarterly, 56*(2), 90–104. doi:10.1177/0016986212442568

Matthews, D., Foster, J., Gladstone, D., Schieck, J., & Meiners, J. (2007). Supporting professionalism, diversity, and context within a collaborative approach to gifted education. *Journal of Educational and Psychological Consultation, 17*(4), 315–345. doi:10.1080/10474410701634161

Matthews, D., & Kitchen, J. (2007). School-within-a-school gifted programs: Perceptions of students and teachers in public secondary schools. *Gifted Child Quarterly, 51*(3), 256–271.

Peterson, J. S. (2007). Consultation related to giftedness: A school counseling perspective. *Journal of Educational and Psychological Consultation, 17*(4), 273–296. doi:10.1080/10474410701634096

Peterson, J. S., & Ray, K. E. (2006). Bullying among the gifted: The subjective experience. *Gifted Child Quarterly, 50*, 252–269.

Peterson, J. S., & Ray, K. E. (2006). Bullying and the gifted: Victims, perpetrators, prevalence, and effects. *Gifted Child Quarterly, 50*, 148–168.

Gruenert, S. (2008, March/April). School culture, school climate: They are not the same thing. *Principal*, 56–59.

Book Chapters

Chandler, K. (2012). The role of central office and building administration in serving gifted students. In T. L. Cross & J. R. Cross (Eds.), *Handbook for counselors serving students with gifts and talents: Development, relationships, school issues, and counseling needs/interventions* (pp. 555–567). Waco, TX: Prufrock Press.

Coleman, L. J. (2012). Lived experience, mixed messages, and stigma. In T. L. Cross & J. R. Cross (Eds.), *Handbook for counselors serving students with gifts and talents: Development, relationships, school issues, and counseling needs/interventions* (pp. 371–392). Waco, TX: Prufrock Press.

Lee, S. (2016). Supportive environments for developing talent. In M. Neihart, S. I. Pfeiffer, & T. L. Cross (Eds.), *The social and emotional development and gifted children: What do we know?* (pp. 191–204). Waco, TX: Prufrock Press.

Rimm, S. (2002). Peer pressures and social acceptance of gifted students. In M. Neihart, S. M. Reis, N. M. Robinson, & S. M. Moon (Eds.), *The social and emotional development of gifted children: What do we know?* (pp. 13–18). Waco, TX: Prufrock Press.

Robinson, A., & Bryant, L. (2012). Gifted students and their teachers: Relationships that foster talent development. In T. L. Cross & J. R. Cross (Eds.), *Handbook for counselors serving students with gifts and talents: Development, relationships, school issues, and counseling needs/interventions* (pp. 427–442). Waco, TX: Prufrock Press.

Swiatek, M. A. (2012). Social coping. In T. L. Cross & J. R. Cross (Eds.), *Handbook for counselors serving students with gifts and talents: Development, relationships, school issues, and counseling needs/interventions* (pp. 665–680). Waco, TX: Prufrock Press.

Wood, S. M., & Peterson, J. S. (2014). Superintendents, principals, and counselors: Facilitating secondary gifted education. In S. Moon & F. A. Dixon (Eds.), *The handbook of secondary gifted education* (pp. 627–649). Waco, TX: Prufrock Press.

Book

Cowan, K. C., Vailancourt, K., Rossen, E., & Politt, K. (2013). *A framework for safe and successful schools* [Brief]. Bethesda, MD: National Association of School Psychologists.

Websites

Alliance for the Study of School Climate. Retrieved from http://web.calstatela.edu/centers/schoolclimate

Association for Supervision and Curriculum Development. Retrieved from http://www.ascd.org

GLSEN 2015 National School Climate Survey. Retrieved from https://www.glsen.org/article/2015-national-school-climate-survey

National Association for Gifted Children, & Council for Exceptional Children. (2013). NAGC–CEC teacher preparation standards in gifted and talented education. Retrieved from http://www.nagc.org/sites/default/files/standards/NAGC-%20CEC%20CAEP%20standards%20%282013%20final%29.pdf

National School Climate Center. Retrieved from http://www.schoolclimate.org

Survey instruments to help you in your investigations of schools by Dr. Megan Tschannen-Moran at the College of William and Mary School of Education. Retrieved from http://wmpeople.wm.edu/site/page/mxtsch/researchtools

● ● ●

CHAPTER 11 EMPOWERING PARENTS OF GIFTED STUDENTS

Articles

Bordeau, B., & Thomas, V. (2003). Counseling gifted clients and their families: Comparing clients' and counselors' perspectives. *Journal of Secondary Gifted Education, 14,* 114–126.

Colangelo, N., & Dettman, D. F. (1983). A conceptual model of four types of parent–school interactions. *Journal for the Education of the Gifted, 5,* 120–126.

Cornell, D. G. (1983). Gifted children: The impact of positive labeling on the family system. *American Orthopsychiatric Association, 53*(2), 322–335.

Griffin, D., & Steen, S. (2010). School–family–community partnerships: Applying Epstein's theory of the six types of involvement to school counselor practice. *Professional School Counseling, 13,* 218–226.

Moon, S., & Hall, A. S. (1998). Family therapy with intellectually and creatively gifted children. *Journal of Marital and Family Therapy, 24*(1), 59–80.

Moon, S., & Thomas, V. (2003). Family therapy with gifted and talented adolescents. *Journal of Secondary Gifted Education, 14*(2), 107–113.

Book Chapters

Hertzog, N. B. (2012). Counseling for young gifted children. In T. L. Cross & J. R. Cross (Eds.), *Handbook for counselors serving students with gifts and talents* (pp. 195–208). Waco, TX: Prufrock Press.

Robinson, A., Shore, B., & Enerson, D. (2007). Parent involvement. In A. Robinson, B. Shore, & D. Enerson (Eds.), *Best practices in gifted education: An evidence-based guide* (pp. 7–14). Waco, TX: Prufrock Press.

Schader, R. M. (2008). Parenting. In J. A. Plucker & C. M. Callahan (Eds.), *Critical issues and practice in gifted education* (pp. 479–492). Waco, TX: Prufrock Press.

Silverman, L. K. (2012). Asynchronous development: A key to counseling the gifted. In T. L. Cross & J. R. Cross (Eds.), *Handbook for counselors serving students with gifts and talents* (pp. 261–280). Waco, TX: Prufrock Press.

Silverman, L. K., & Golon, A. S. (2008). Clinical practice with gifted families. In S. Pfeiffer (Ed.), *Handbook of giftedness in children: Psychoeducational theory, research, and best practices* (pp. 223–246). New York, NY: Springer.

Books

Delisle, J. (2006). *Parenting gifted kids: Tips for raising happy and successful gifted children.* Waco, TX: Prufrock Press.

Treffinger, D., & Inman, T. (2010). *Parenting gifted children: The authoritative guide from the National Association for Gifted Children.* Waco, TX: Prufrock Press.

Webb, J. T., & Gore, J. L. (2007). *A parent's guide to gifted children.* Scottsdale, AZ: Great Potential Press.

Websites

Gifted challenges by Gail Post. Top blogs about gifted children, gifted education, and parenting. Retrieved from http://giftedchallenges.blogspot.com/2013/08/top-blogs-about-gifted-children-gifted.html

National Association for Gifted Children. Resources for parents. Retrieved from http://www.nagc.org/resources-publications/resources-parents

Supporting Emotional Needs of Gifted. Retrieved from sengifted.org

● ● ●

CHAPTER 12 SCHOOL COUNSELORS AS LEADERS AND ADVOCATES FOR
GIFTED STUDENTS

Articles

Dollarhide, C., Gibson, D., & Saginak, K. (2008). New counselors' leadership efforts in
school counseling: Themes from a year-long qualitative study. *Professional School
Counseling, 11*(4), 262–271. doi:10.5330/PSC.n.2010-11.262

Grantham, T. C., Frasier, M. M., Roberts, A. C., & Bridges, E. M. (2005). Parent advocacy for culturally diverse gifted students. *Theory Into Practice, 44*(2), 138–147.
doi:10.1207/s15430421tip4402_8

Griffin, D., & Farris, A. (2010). School counselors and collaboration: Finding resources
through community asset mapping. *Professional School Counseling, 13*(5), 248–256.

Mason, E. C., & McMahon, H. G. (2009). Leadership practices of school counselors.
Professional School Counseling, 13, 107–115. doi:10.5330/PSC.n.2010-13.107

McMahan, E. H., Singh, A. A., Urbano, A., & Haston, M. (2010). The personal is political: School counselors' use of self in social justice advocacy work. *Journal of School
Counseling, 8*(18), 1–29. Retrieved from http://jsc.montana.edu/articles/v8n18.pdf

Ratts, M. J., & Hutchins, A. M. (2009). ACA advocacy competencies: Social justice
advocacy at the client/student level. *Journal of Counseling & Development, 87*(3),
269–275. doi:10.1002/j.1556-6678.2009.tb00106.x

Ratts, M. J., DeKruyf, L., & Chen-Hayes, S. F. (2007). The ACA advocacy competencies: A social justice advocacy framework for school counselors. *Professional School
Counseling, 11*(2), 90–97. doi:10.5330/PSC.n.2010-11.90

Shillingford, M., & Lambie, G. (2010). Contribution of professional school counselors'
values and leadership practices to their programmatic service delivery. *Professional
School Counseling, 13*(4), 208–217. doi:10.5330/PSC.n.2010-13.208

Singh, A. A., Urbano, A., Haston, M., & McMahan, E. (2010). School counselors' strategies for social justice change: A grounded theory of what works in the real world.
Professional School Counseling, 13(3), 135–145. doi:10.5330/PSC.n.2010-13.135

Young, A., Dollarhide, C. T., & Baughman, A. (2015). The voices of school counselors:
Essential characteristics of school counselor leaders. *Professional School Counseling,
19*(1), 36–45. doi:10.5330/1096-2409-19.1.36

Websites

American School Counselor Association. (2013). *The school counselor and gifted and talented
programs*. Alexandria, VA: Author. Retrieved from https://www. schoolcounselor
.org/asca/media/asca/PositionStatements/PS_Gifted.pdf

American School Counselor Association. (2016). *Ethical standards for school counselors*.
Alexandria, VA: Author. Retrieved from: https://www.schoolcounselor.org/asca/
media/asca/Ethics/EthicalStandards2016.pdf

Lewis, J. A., Arnold, M. S., House, R., & Toporek, R. L. (2002). ACA advocacy competencies. Retrieved from https://www.counseling.org/Resources/Competencies/Advocacy_Competencies.pdf

National Association of Gifted Children. (n.d.). Myths about gifted children. Retrieved from http://www.nagc.org/resources-publications/resources/myths-about-gifted-students

National Association of Gifted Children. (2015). Questions and answers about the Every Student Succeeds Act. Retrieved from http://www.nagc.org/sites/default/files/Advocacy/ESSA%20Q%20%2B%20A.pdf

NOSCA's School Counselor Strategic Planning Tool. Retrieved from https://secure-media.collegeboard.org/digitalServices/pdf/nosca/11b_4393_counseling_page_WEB_111107.pdf

Shea, M. Gain school board support [Video]. Retrieved from https://www.youtube.com/watch?v=oXPXuLj2Sa0&feature=youtu.be

Index

academic advising
  career development, 122
  interventions, 125
  microaggressions, 125
  overchoice syndrome/
    multipotentiality, 123
  personality traits, 123
acceleration, 128–129
achievement
  assumptions about achievement,
    142–143
  high achievers, 36–37, 78–79, 142–143
  underachievers, 37, 142–143, 144–146
ACT, 84, 127
ADHD. *See* attention deficit
    hyperactivity disorder
advocacy, leadership and. *See* leadership
    and advocacy
advocacy, role of school counselors, 56–59
ALM. *See* Autonomous Learner Model
American School Counseling Association
    (ASCA), 52, 84, 128, 192, 194
  Ethical Standards for School
    Counselors, 23, 24, 191
  National Model, 9, 10, 16, 20,
    104–105, 191
    accountability, 27–28
    beliefs and vision, 21
    foundation component, 20–21
    management systems, 25–26
    professional competencies, 23–24
    service delivery, 24–25
    skills and dispositions, 28
    student competencies, 23

anxiety, 34–35
ASCA. *See* American School Counseling
    Association (ASCA)
asset-burden paradox, of giftedness, 5
asynchronous development, 34
attention deficit hyperactivity disorder
    (ADHD), 60
Autonomous Learner Model (ALM), 74–75

Betts, George T., 74–75

CACREP. *See* Council for Accreditation
    of Counseling and Related
    Educational Programs
career counseling, 126–134
change-loss-grief framework, 43
classroom guidance, 104–105
Colangelo, Nicholas, 76–77
collaboration, 164, 165
  with building administrators, 167
  with classroom teachers, 165–166
  empowering parents, of gifted
    students, 174
collaborator, 55–56
Columbus Group (1991), 70
consultant, 55
consultation, 164, 165
coordinator, 56
Council for Accreditation of
    Counseling and Related
    Educational Programs
    (CACREP), 83–84, 96, 141

Council for Exceptional Children, 159
counseling relationship
  nonjudgment, compassion, curiosity,
    and respect, 150–151
  self-monitoring for bias, 151
cultural values
  minority-culture communities, 68–69
  missed students, 69
  teachers' language, 67–68

Dabrowski, Kazimierz, 75–76
development of students, 41–42, 72–73
Differentiated Model of Giftedness
    and Talent (DMGT)
    (Gagné), 71–72

educator perceptions, of gifted
    students, 160–161
empowering families, of gifted students
  advocacy, 187
  building relationships, 186
  characteristics associated with
    giftedness, 175–176
  collaborative process, 174
  cultural competence, 186
  families characteristics and needs,
    174–175
  gifted label, 176–179
  interactions with schools, 181–184
  "otherness" of, 179–181
  research-based information and
    resources, 185
  talent identification, 175
ethical standards, 6
Every Student Succeeds Act, 86
Exploring Beliefs About Gifted
    Students, 21
existential depression, 35–36
family-school interaction, 181–184

Gagné, Françoys 71–72
gay, lesbian, bisexual, and transgender
    (GLBT), 39, 40

Gifted Program Advocacy Model
    (G-PAM), 57–59
GLBT. *See* gay, lesbian, bisexual, and
    transgender
Gottfredson's career theory
  optimizing experience, 130–131
  optimizing learning, 126–130
  optimizing self-insight, 132–133
  optimizing self-investment,
    133–134
GPA. *See* grade point average
G-PAM. *See* Gifted Program Advocacy
    Model
grade-point average (GPA), 27

Identifying and Serving Culturally and
    Linguistically Diverse Gifted
    Students, 53
identifying gifted students, 85–87
  context and demographics, 91–92
  encourage early-access, 91
  extracurricular activities, 93–94
  misconceptions and guiding
    principles for, 87
  multiple measures and qualified
    teams, 88–89
  populations and scoring profile
    characteristics, 92–93
  talent area and services, 94
  valid and reliable assessments, 90
  whole-grade screening, 89
identities, intersectionality of
  ability status, 49–50
  culture matters, 50–51
  gender, 51
  geographical context, 51–52
  GPAM. *See* Gifted Program Advocacy
    Model
  group counseling, 54–55
  individual counseling, 53–54
  role of, 53
  twice-exceptional students, 60–61
individual educational plan (IEP)
    process, 54

Integrated Curriculum Model (ICM)
(VanTassel-Baska), 105
intensity, 33
Iowa Acceleration Scale, 127, 129

Jacob Javits Gifted and Talented
Students Education Act, 86

leadership and advocacy
assistance, 202–203
definitions and concepts, 192
follow-up and evaluation, 203
nurturing dispositions, 193
plan creation, 200–201
relationship development, 194
resources, potential barriers and
allies, 195
self-efficacy, 202
stakeholder's perspective, issues from, 195
understanding school culture, 193–194

mental health concerns
conceptualization, 149–150
hidden, denied and controlled
emotions, 38–39
substance use, 149
minority-culture communities, 68–69
misdiagnosis, 41
models and theories
emphasizing achievement, 70–72
emphasizing affective development,
75–77
Moon's model, talent-development
model, 73–74
multipotentiality, concept of, 38

National Association for Gifted Children
(NAGC), 6, 8, 48, 128, 159
*Nation Deceived: How Schools Hold Back
America's Brightest Students,
A* (Colangelo, Assouline &
Gross), 128

"Natural Development," 180
No Child Left Behind Act, 85

overexcitabilities (OEs), 33–34, 41, 75,
147–148

perfectionism, 34–35
personal/social counseling
assumptions about achievement, 142–143
circumstances and needs, 140–141
social and emotional concerns, 141
Peterson, Jean Sunde, 77
Prevention-oriented groups, 111
Proactive Developmental Attention
(PPDA) model, 77, 105, 107

reframing, 42–43
Renzulli, Joseph, 74

SAT, 84, 129
school climate
assumptions, 159
connection with teachers, 159–160
definition of, 157
educator perceptions of students,
160–161
need for safe environment, 161–164
school-family-community
partnerships, 56, 60
Schoolwide Enrichment Model
(SEM), 74
sensitivity, 32–33
SGP. *See* stigma of giftedness paradigm
Silverman, Linda K., 76
small group counseling, 104
affective component, 106
code of ethics, 116
content from students, 113–114
counseling tenets, 115–116
determining group membership,
109–110
developmental aspect, 106–107

small group counseling (*continued*)
  extend group topics into classrooms,
    114–115
  logistics, 110
  proactive aspect, 106
  rationale, 110–111
  teachers' adjustments, 116–117
stigma of giftedness paradigm
    (SGP), 161, 162
strenghs based developmental
    approach, 76–77

talent-development model,
    73–74
talented students
  age peers, 7
  cultural paradigm, 3
  differentiated counseling approach, 7
  ethical standards, 6
  foundational knowledge, 8
  mental health issues, 4, 147–149

myths and stereotypes, 3
  role and function, 6
  service delivery, 9
  special population, 7
talent identification, empowering
    parents, 175
Teacher Knowledge and Skills
    Standards, 159
theory of positive disintegration (TPD)
    (Dabrowski), 33, 75–76
three-ring conception of giftedness, 74
Total School Cluster Grouping
    (TSCG), 74–75
TPD. *See* theory of positive
    disintegration
TSCG. *See* Total School Cluster
    Grouping
twice-exceptional students, 50, 60–61

Webb, James T., 77
whole-grade screening protocol, 89

Made in the USA
Monee, IL
28 June 2021